T0419166

Reel Freedom

In the series *Urban Life, Landscape, and Policy*, edited by David Stradling, Larry Bennett, and Davarian Baldwin. Founding editor, Zane L. Miller.

ALSO IN THIS SERIES:

A list of additional titles in this series appears at the back of this book.

Alyssa Lopez

Reel Freedom

*Black Film Culture in Early
Twentieth-Century New York City*

TEMPLE UNIVERSITY PRESS
Philadelphia • *Rome* • *Tokyo*

TEMPLE UNIVERSITY PRESS
Philadelphia, Pennsylvania 19122
tupress.temple.edu

Library of Congress Cataloging-in-Publication Data

Names: Lopez, Alyssa, 1993– author.
Title: Reel freedom : Black film culture in early twentieth-century New
York City / Alyssa Lopez.
Other titles: Urban life, landscape, and policy.
Description: Philadelphia : Temple University Press, 2025. | Series: Urban
life, landscape, and policy | Includes bibliographical references and
index. | Summary: "Traces the origins of Black New Yorkers' interactions
with cinema in the city, arguing that moviegoing was intimately tied to
larger struggles for equality, inclusion, and modernity"— Provided by
publisher.
Identifiers: LCCN 2024039600 (print) | LCCN 2024039601 (ebook) | ISBN
9781439924129 (cloth) | ISBN 9781439924136 (paperback) | ISBN
9781439924143 (pdf)
Subjects: LCSH: Black people in the motion picture industry—New York
(State)—New York—History—20th century. | Motion picture
audiences—New York (State)—New York—History—20th century. | Motion
picture theaters—New York (State)—New York—History—20th century. |
Black people—Civil rights—New York (State)—New York—History—20th
century. | Harlem (New York, N.Y.)—Race relations—History—20th
century. | Harlem (New York, N.Y.)—Social conditions—20th century.
Classification: LCC PN1995.9.B585 L67 2025 (print) | LCC PN1995.9.B585
(ebook) | DDC 302.23/430899607307471—dc23/eng/20250101
LC record available at https://lccn.loc.gov/2024039600
LC ebook record available at https://lccn.loc.gov/2024039601

The manufacturer's authorized representative in the EU for product safety is
Temple University Rome, Via di San Sebastianello, 16, 00187 Rome RM, Italy
(https://rome.temple.edu/).
tempress@temple.edu

Printed in the United States of America

9 8 7 6 5 4 3 2 1

Contents

Acknowledgments

It took about ten years and a lot of help to get *Reel Freedom* to this point. I have many people to thank for that.

First, I want to express unceasing gratitude for the guidance and support of Pero Dagbovie. I have said and written this in many places by now, but it is worth repeating: without his affirming guidance, I would not be where I am today. Thank you for believing in me and my work from the start and through the many moments of doubt and fear. LaShawn Harris, Joshua Yumibe, Michael Stamm, and Shannon King all offered critical feedback at the project's earliest stages and shepherded me through the graduate school process. The initial spark that lit the fire for my love of Black film history happened in Peter Connelly-Smith's film history class at Queens College. Others there, including Ross Wheeler, Francois Pierre-Louis, Ellen Scott, and Deirdre Cooper-Owens, pushed me in ways that made me a better scholar and person.

When I became a Mellon Mays fellow, it felt like my world had only just begun to open up. Mary Pena, Cherkira Lashley, Christian Hosam, Kelsey Henry, Adjua Pryor, and Uriel Medina-Espino were all part of that and the first baby steps of this project. Feedback at conferences over the years, especially at the Association for the Study of African American Life and History, the Society for Cinema and Media Studies, and the Urban History Association, has made this work much stronger. I am thankful, too, for the many writing group friends who have kept me accountable: Ashley Smith-Purviance, Eva Wheeler, Osama Siddiqui, SaraEllen Strongman, Brittney Edmonds, Ángela Pérez-Villa, Jorge Leal, Aida Villanueva Montalvo, and Evelyn Sotos.

I have been lucky enough to have colleagues at Providence College who have helped sustain this work (and me!) as it moved from dissertation to book, including Justin Brophy, Sharon Murphy, Steve Smith, Osama Siddiqui, Virginia Thomas, Bruno Shah, and Meredith Haluga. From reading drafts to listening to me vent or getting drinks at the Abbey, somehow you knew exactly what I needed in those moments. I appreciate you. Thanks also to Peter Rogers, who crafted the maps within *Reel Freedom*.

This project received critical funding from Providence College in the form of a Committee to Aid Faculty Research Grant and a SPaRC Research Dissemination Grant. Thanks to Provost Sean Reid for the opportunity to take a yearlong research leave so that I could finally complete the book. Funding for this project also came from a Mellon Mays Undergraduate Fellows Research and Travel Grant, a Gilder Lehrman Scholarly Fellowship, and a Career Enhancement Fellowship. I am grateful for the help of archivists at the Schomburg Center for Research in Black Culture, the New York Public Library, the Municipal Archives of New York City (especially Ken Cobb and Eirini Melena Karoutsos), and the New York State Archives (especially Maggi Gonsalves and Bill Gorman). Remote research assistance came at critical moments from the kind archivists at the Black Film Center/Archive, the Tamiment Library and Robert F. Wagner Archive, and the Walter P. Reuther Library.

I owe much to Davarian Baldwin and Aaron Javsicas for their interest in my project and their crucial help in getting it where it needed to be. The anonymous reviewers at Temple University Press were so diligent in their feedback; the book is the better for it. The mentorship of Cara Caddoo and Paula Massood in the book's last stages was crucial in finalizing the manuscript. Their insights and detailed notes greatly improved my writing.

While support for my scholarship made the book happen, my friends made sure that I stayed sane during the long journey. Unending gratitude to Jasmin Howard and especially Shelby Pumphrey for grounding me constantly. Shelby, I did not know there was so much good television in the world, but I am so grateful I get to watch it with you. Justin, Caitlin and Jesse, Taylor, Ethan and Ty, and Elise reminded me to be human every once in a while. The Galluscios, especially Ariana and Arielle, ensured that my trips to Charleston were about play, not work.

My family has not only sustained me but also housed me in my many research trips to New York City. My parents, Dave and Angela, kept my cabinets stocked and the care packages coming from the moment I went to graduate school to this day. Americus and Billy offered me moments of laughter, rest, and joy. Piper and Andre never let me skip a meal or leave my desk earlier than I wanted to. My partner, Sam, has been my rock in the stormy weather that defines an academic life. For him, I can never be thankful enough.

Reel Freedom

Introduction

In October 1924, Walter White was troubled. The assistant secretary of the National Association for the Advancement of Colored People (NAACP) had been receiving an influx of complaints from Black New Yorkers about discrimination in the city's theaters, where they were relegated to balcony seating. Concerned that neither he nor the NAACP as an organization could "handle all of these civil rights cases," White reached out to local Black newspapers to request help and spread awareness. He warned the city's top Black editors that "there is a definite campaign being carried out in New York City to limit the civil rights of colored people," with most of it taking place right on 125th Street, a main thoroughfare running through Harlem.[1]

While restricting Black theatergoers to segregated seating remained a somewhat regular practice in the city throughout the early twentieth century, White's concern about theaters on 125th Street reflected growing tensions around the expansion of the Black community in that area. For almost twenty years Black New Yorkers (from natives to migrants and immigrants) had made their way to Harlem, but as the community grew, the artificial, but quite material, boundaries placed on them began to expand by necessity. What is now considered a main artery through the Black Mecca was at this moment a deeply segregated space with borders aggressively policed by white residents, police officers, and business owners.

The Loew's Victoria Theatre, located just steps from the famed Apollo Theatre between Seventh and Eighth Avenues on 125th Street, was in a contentious area for Black and white residents of the neighborhood, resting as it did in a porous space where Black New Yorkers were sometimes forced to test invisible racial boundaries. By the mid-1920s, the theater had earned itself a reputation as particularly hostile to its Black patrons. While some, like Walter White and Black journalists, chose to utilize the press to protest racism in the city's theaters, some patrons quite literally took their rights into and with their own hands.

On April 27, 1926, Robert Thomas, a Black college student, accompanied his friend to an evening showing at the Loew's Victoria.[2] When he went to take the floor seat he had purchased, a white female usher attempted to direct him to the balcony. Brushing her off, he proceeded to the orchestra only to be stopped again. When a male usher grabbed his coat, Thomas "hit [him] as he tried to force [Thomas] out of the theatre."[3] The theater's white manager also felt Thomas's "physical accomplishment" when Thomas "struck [him] a severe blow in his right eye" as the manager lunged at him.[4] The violence did not deter Thomas or his friend. By the time that six riot police officers arrived on the scene, the two were enjoying the show in their orchestra seats, "to which," the *New York Age* insisted, "they were entitled."[5]

According to the *Age*, when Thomas was escorted out of the theater, an officer reportedly made reference to recent riots in Carteret, New Jersey, saying "that Thomas ought to be treated as the Carteret Negroes were."[6] Just days before the excitement at the Loew's Victoria, tensions between Black strikebreakers and white laborers erupted into an assault on Carteret's Black residents, resulting in $3,000 worth of damage and the forced removal of all "colored families from their homes, driving them out of town, and beating and assaulting individual Negroes wherever they were found."[7] The officer, by referring to Carteret, was making it clear to Thomas that his decision to exercise his rights at this movie theater was deserving of violence, brutality, and a decisive exile. The *Age* forcefully illustrated the links between Thomas and Carteret by positioning articles about each close to one another; the intentional spatial proximity of the articles on the front page undeniably connected unequal access to the city's theaters to more insidious forms of racism elsewhere. Indeed, Gertrude Daly, the white female usher who pressed charges against Thomas, alleged that he had tried to choke her in his desire for orchestra seats. Not only was racism in New York's theaters on par with New Jersey's vicious race riots but the *Age*'s reporting implicitly tied it to unfounded fears of supposedly violent Black masculine aggression toward white women, typically associated with southern racism.

Continuing to push these parallels, another article scornfully remarked that though the white ushers, managers, and officers, who were Jewish and Irish, could not join the Ku Klux Klan, "they were actively practising the racial intolerance the klan preaches." Even worse, "all of this happened in Harlem," the article noted, "where the Negro has established a city within a city."[8] In other words, even somewhere like Harlem, which "epitomized a kind of freedom that" many Black Americans "did not know," was hardly safe from the racism and prejudice that most believed were absent in the North.[9] It was certainly ironic that Thomas, who lived less than five blocks away from the theater, was manhandled and directed to a segregated balcony in his own neighborhood, while Daly, the white female usher, did not even live in or within walking distance of the Loew's Victoria or Harlem.[10]

Thomas's experiences at the Loew's Victoria and the white response to his presence are a fitting start to *Reel Freedom*, intimately capturing the relationship between Black film culture and city space. Occurring in the midst of disputes over the racial future of New York City, and especially Harlem, Thomas's story reminds us that interactions in and around theaters were connected to Black New Yorkers' demands for equality and claims to city space. Critical to this are actions, events, and scenes that took place beyond the screen and that were inflected with a concern for the local. Black film culture, as demonstrated in part by Thomas's fight at the Loew's Victoria, is a manifestation of Black placemaking efforts in the city. As such, it encompasses both Black New Yorkers' desire to make a home out of the city and claim it as their own and distinct efforts to make that home more hospitable.

Reel Freedom traces Black film culture in New York City from its origins in the early twentieth century to its firm establishment in the 1930s. As I define it, Black film culture is composed of Black New Yorkers' *interactions* with cinema and surrounding institutions, not necessarily the cinematic output itself. It is marked by community, struggles over public space, and assertations of equality and access. *Reel Freedom* moves beyond a singular focus on the moving image. Here, Black film culture encompasses the very people sitting in the theater seats, who sometimes forced their way in, and the director who fought censorship to provide his New York City audiences with an unfiltered look at race relations. It also includes the motion picture operators responsible for a good show who demanded fair pay and the journalists who reported on it all, working to link film to Black life in New York City.

This book takes as an important premise that Black film culture is locally grounded and place-based, actively forged, and used by Black New Yorkers to enjoy city living to its fullest. It is a representation of Black New Yorkers' "dogged commitment to make freedom real in the big city," to borrow from Shannon King, that started in the nickelodeon period and stretched into the 1930s, running parallel to and sometimes aligned with larger contemporary social and cultural currents.[11] By putting the local in conversation with

Figure I.1 Loew's Victoria Theatre. *(Courtesy Municipal Archives, City of New York)*

the cultural, *Reel Freedom* argues that Black film culture was an important avenue of both entertainment and resistance for Black New Yorkers: a critical site of interaction with the cultural phenomenon and a battleground to stridently fight for their right to belong in the city.

For all the attention afforded New York City in film history, few scholars have engaged in a nuanced exploration of Black moviegoing in the city. In their rigorous debate on the ethnic and class makeup of nickelodeons in the city, film scholars Ben Singer and Robert C. Allen do not pay much attention at all to Black New Yorkers, neither in Harlem nor in Midtown.[12] Others have defined Black moviegoing solely through the lens of segregation and exclusion. As historian David Nasaw writes about the nickelodeon period, "Mixing blacks and whites in the cramped, darkened storefronts was beyond the bounds of possibility," even in places like New York City, where convictions for violating antidiscrimination laws "did not result in changed admission policies."[13] Black moviegoers in these works are primarily understood as a void, one determined through absence or negation.[14] In these cases, the Black moviegoing experience is one of only exclusion or discrimination. This perspective ignores the agency of Black New Yorkers, who, from film's arrival in the city, were engaging with and shaping cinema and its surrounding institutions. It also discounts their interests and activism while privileging the power of white institutions.

Some have given more acute attention to Black experiences in New York beyond the discriminatory, exploring Black film criticism and filmmaking efforts. For example, in their pioneering discussion of Black moviegoers in Harlem, Alison Griffiths and James Latham chart the growth of the neighborhood as a moviegoing enclave for Black New Yorkers during the nickelodeon period.[15] Meanwhile, Paula Massood and Richard Koszarski provide rich histories of Black filmmaking efforts in Harlem and the city at large. Massood demonstrates that filmic representations of Harlem, particularly in post–World War II crime films, "document and dialogue with the tropes of citizenship and progress that have been central to African American life," convincingly tying Harlem's ever-shifting imagery to the African American experience.[16] Koszarski adeptly traces race filmmaker Oscar Micheaux's production efforts in the city, tracking the various locations throughout the state and region where he filmed much of his work post-1921.[17] More recently, Agata Frymus has explored Black reception of Hollywood vehicles and reconsidered what theaters were potentially available to Black moviegoers during the silent period.[18] These works offer valuable starting points for understanding Black New Yorkers' interactions with cinema, but they are not enough to get at the fullness of Black film culture in the city.

Pioneering work conducted by Jacqueline Stewart, Davarian Baldwin, Cara Caddoo, Anna Everett, and Charlene Regester has excavated a rich history of Black interactions with cinema, involving spectatorship, film criticism, exhibition, theater ownership, and other experiences.[19] These scholars tend to agree that Black film culture constitutes a series of "overlapping public spheres" that includes other Black social and cultural institutions with a social justice orientation, like the church and press. Still, attention to Chicago and the U.S. South continues to dominate explorations of Black film history on the ground level.[20] Further, few studies relate Black film culture's expansiveness to its ubiquity in the lives of urbanites. *Reel Freedom* demonstrates that not only is Black film culture tied to community building, labor struggles, and efforts at belonging—ways that Black New Yorkers tried to make New York City a more hospitable home for themselves and their families—but that New York is still a location ripe for exploration.

The turn to the local in film history came at the expense of New York City and also Black New Yorkers. Kathryn Fuller, for example, has stressed that "the movies were never an urban experience," while Robert C. Allen cites an "evidentiary pull" that leads to an overemphasis on Manhattan. This conflation between local and nonurban has reasonably been questioned. As Nathaniel Brennan argues, "Was the modern metropolis any less local to those who lived in the East Village, Harlem, or Yorkville?"[21] *Reel Freedom* makes it clear that there are a whole host of decidedly urban and locally specific developments in Black film culture in New York City that have been ignored.[22] As film scholar Jacqueline Stewart put it so convincingly, "Local Black uses of cinema suggest that from very early on African Americans approached the cinema as they approached so many other elements of public life—with a range of individual and collective strategies to incorporate, reject, and/or reconstruct the institutions and practices shaping their daily lives."[23] With this in mind, *Reel Freedom* presupposes that the most effective way to uncover Black film culture in New York City is by utilizing what Gregory Waller describes as a "concrete, sociohistorical, local perspective" that does not rely on the film text alone.[24] In her rejection of extant film as "the reified object" in *Uplift Cinema*, Allyson Nadia Field cogently proves the possibility and importance of doing such film scholarship.[25]

In conversation with this, *Reel Freedom* insists that Black film culture is more expansive than the screen or even the theater itself and that it is explicitly tied to larger placemaking efforts in New York. Here, filmmakers' responses to legal censorship, journalists' engagement with film criticism, young girls' defiance of familial restrictions when moviegoing, and projectionists' demands for unionization are all part of how Black New Yorkers endeavored to make the city much less hostile to their existence. Thus, Black film culture is about how cinema and its surrounding institutions were leveraged by Black New Yorkers to make the city their own, as Robert Thomas's public demonstration shows us. They fought publicly over theater seats, argued for neighborhood rights as Black workers in Harlem, went to the movies to free themselves of the weight of state and familial surveillance, and held that cinema had a direct link to how they were treated in the streets. The sources availed upon here—including court dockets, Harlem Renaissance literature, state prison records, and censorship documents—suggest the depth with which film culture worked itself into the daily lives of Black New Yorkers. Or rather, more directly, how Black New Yorkers made film culture part and parcel with their survival in the city. By patchworking archival remnants and other extant sources, *Reel Freedom* reveals the wide-ranging and remarkable pervasiveness of Black film culture in New York City.

It is at once inconceivable to tell a film history of New York City without Black experiences and impossible to explore Black culture in the city without film. Thus, *Reel Freedom* also reframes how we understand Black New York in this period, generally viewed through the lens of the Harlem Renaissance. Countering racism through "high art," historian David Levering Lewis asserts, "seemed to be the sole battle plan that afforded both high visibility and low vulnerability."[26] With this mindset, film was excluded from "the prevalent thought of the day, which denied any recognition of [its] intellectual potential."[27] Recent scholarship has worked to more concretely place the Renaissance within the larger New Negro movement, expanding its geographical, temporal, and constitutive boundaries.[28] *Reel Freedom* continues this discourse of expansion by placing one of the most important forms of mass leisure at the center of the cultural transformation typically associated with the Harlem Renaissance. So much is lost, especially the very people living in the city, when the Harlem Renaissance is discussed separately from the fervor that took hold of New York City's Black life in a range of arenas from grassroots politics to popular culture. In this reconsideration of time and place, Black film culture stands central.[29]

In line with Jacob S. Dorman's rejection of "the abstracted Harlem" that Renaissance discourse tends to rely on, this book also positions the people responsible for the creation, consumption, and exhibition of film, like Robert Thomas, as real agents of progress. In *Reel Freedom*, these Black New Yorkers and the streets and theaters they stake claim to take center stage. For a place considered the "Black Mecca" or "the cultural capital" of Black America, so very little has been written on how Black New Yorkers interacted with the medium and its surrounding institutions.[30] *Reel Freedom* remedies this, offering the first book-length treatment that considers how ordinary people, such as young girls and women, migrants, labor activists, theater manager and owners, and local journalists, shaped Black film culture in early twentieth century New York.

This book is also, therefore, a cultural history of city dwellers who understood that living life to the fullest in urban America meant unfettered admission to the area's amusement options. Historian Victoria W. Wolcott has asserted that struggles for access to these types of spaces can be viewed "as part of a broader struggle for control of and access to urban space."[31] Just like access to fair housing, transportation, and job opportunities, the ability to engage in the city's entertainment landscape was a key part of what constituted living a full life, especially for some migrants and immigrants who relocated with visions of a brighter, more free future. *Reel Freedom* argues that Black film culture is one lens through which to see the intimate ways something as seemingly inconsequential as amusement is tied to labor, civil rights, artistic expression, and placemaking.

Reel Freedom bridges these discourses—on New York City's film history, Black film history, and Black urban and cultural history—to reveal a Black film culture that grew to be integral to Black New Yorkers' lives in early twentieth-century New York City. Rather than solely emphasizing "the bigoted constrictions imposed on people of color" as some works on Black New Yorkers and cinema continue to do, this book stresses that Black New Yorkers endeavored to constitute a film culture of belonging, community, and, occasionally, active and outright resistance.[32] This is where understanding Black film culture as placemaking becomes crucially important. Black New Yorkers were not simply reactionary, bound by fights against racism in the city's theaters. Instead, they lived in ordinary ways, such as deciding to go to a movie or striking up a conversation with a stranger in a theater, that constituted an effort to simply exist without constantly living life through the lens of racism.

While politics, picket lines, and even dance halls and saloons have all been explored extensively, Black film culture has been conspicuously ignored as a viable path toward placemaking for Black New Yorkers. Placemaking has long been a part of how Black people existed, survived, and thrived in New York City. Dating back to the African Burial Ground, the founding of Seneca Village, and the creation of Black Bohemia, these efforts at community cultivation and physical belonging have allowed for a "cultural landscape of resistance and self-definition for the race."[33] Black film culture offers another look at how Black New Yorkers continued to do this throughout the twentieth century, adapting this strategy to one of the most popular forms of entertainment in the early twentieth century.[34] Abolitionist scholar Ruth Wilson Gilmore has persuasively argued that "a geographical imperative lies at the heart of every struggle for social justice; if justice is embodied, it is then therefore always spatial, which is to say, part of a process of making a place."[35] Despite a desire from some scholars to "escape from New York," *Reel Freedom* definitively links culture, physical space, and the struggle for place in the city by foregrounding Black film culture.[36]

Reel Freedom unfolds thematically as it uncovers Black film culture's development from the early twentieth century to the 1930s. Each chapter lays

Figure I.2 Lafayette Theatre, shown here advertising their weekly Elks night, which started years earlier under Lester Walton. *(Public domain)*

out a particular stakeholder, addressing what they wanted out of cinema and how they used film culture in their own lives. From theater owners and managers, Black girls and women, and filmmakers to Harlem's projectionists and film critics, all took a varied approach and orientation to film culture. Each, though, helped forge it, leading to the same outcome: a claim to belonging in the city grounded in film and its surrounding institutions.

Chapter 1 addresses the glaring absence of Black New Yorkers from the city's earliest film (hi)stories. Starting with the 1896 Vitascope display, the very first film exhibition in the city, I ask, Why has Black moviegoing, especially before the 1920s, been so consistently sidelined? What did Black moviegoing look like, if its elements can be traced and teased out, in a place committed to de facto Jim Crow? If not in Midtown theaters, where were Black audiences? I find the first iterations of Black moviegoing in churches and parks, where film exhibition was purposefully tied to community and race pride. Turning to the opening of the first Black-oriented theaters in the city, I consider how some theaters worked to ingratiate themselves within the Black community, holding fundraising events, offering special shows for children, and occasionally responding to critical feedback from journalists. Here, in these early moments of interaction and consumption, Black film culture finds its defining characteristics: decidedly community oriented with an emphasis on place and access.

Chapter 2 focuses on the multiple lives of movie theaters. It starts with an analysis of how theaters were used as public spaces to be reclaimed by Black New Yorkers for thrills other than watching the movies, including criminal activity. Keeping in mind this atmosphere of potential criminality and liberation, I then move to explore how Black girls and women used going to the movies as a symbol of freedom, independence, and control over their lives. Yet constricting Black girls' and women's movement, especially that of over-policed migrants, was considered "a matter of public safety" for some onlookers, sometimes resulting in criminalization.[37] As one contemporary believed, "The only chance for salvage to society and the prevention of further spread of the trouble in these cases [of young Black girls in need] lies in commitment."[38] State and city carceral records reveal the complicated relationship Black girls and women held with moviegoing and their ability to claim city space.[39] Yet focusing on them and their choices allows us, as Paula C. Austin puts it, "to reimagine black communities in early twentieth-century urban enclaves" in ways that center Black film culture and the local.[40]

I discuss race filmmaker Oscar Micheaux's negotiated resistance with the New York State Motion Picture Commission in Chapter 3. Micheaux, at the forefront of a cadre of Black filmmakers in New York City who also came before the commission, regularly fought with the state censors over material cut from his movies. His exchanges were not simply about an abstract desire for a perfect image. To him, getting his films shown to New York City's Black audiences in their original form was tantamount to New Negroes demanding an end to white supremacy. He aimed to center his audiences, who he felt deserved his full, uncensored, and often resistive films. The pieces of the film cut and the demands and concessions that Micheaux made to the censors are just as important as the final product itself.[41] Resisting what film studies scholar Ellen Scott terms the "system of vetting" that resulted in problematic images of Blackness, Micheaux's defiant letters to the commission are an aspect of Black film culture that may seem less obvious than moviegoing or film criticism.[42] And yet this chapter demonstrates that they constitute a formative aspect of how Black New Yorkers (which Micheaux, perhaps, became in 1921 when he shifted his business offices there) moved to command respect and assert a say in what images of Blackness proliferated in the city.

Chapter 4 moves into the projectionist booth to explore labor's role in Black film culture. I look at two strikes—one in 1926 and another in 1930—

where Harlem's Black projectionists relentlessly called out theaters in the area that failed to hold true to their promises of community support forged decades earlier. With a know-how of electric currents and mechanics and after years of apprenticeship and a formal exam, "the safety of human lives depend[ed] on his [the projectionist's] knowledge," competence, and focus.[43] However, Harlem's Black projectionists did not feel they received proper recognition for their work, which resulted in the formation of the United Association of Colored Motion Picture Operators (UACMPO) and their eventual unionization. The core of their argument—that the theaters in the neighborhood catered almost exclusively to Black patrons and should, therefore, hire Black projectionists and pay them fairly—is a prime example of the relationship between Black film culture and place. In purposefully linking place (and their belonging there) and their labor on the cultural front, they elucidate how Black film culture was wielded by Black New Yorkers to demand equality and claim the city for themselves.

Throughout this entire process—the development and strengthening of Black film culture and its use as a tool to fashion equity, access, and community—Black journalists kept their readers abreast of major developments in the medium and its specific relationship to race relations in the city. In doing so, they were actively connecting the modern phenomenon to Black life in New York. In Chapter 5, I position the *Age* as a vital source of this information, offering a focus on the local press that opens up new perspectives on Black film criticism. The writings that came out of the paper—namely, from Lester Walton and Vere E. Johns—made it evident that cinema was not simply a mode of entertainment; theaters were "a sphere for struggle" for civil rights, and the Black press made that clear to its readers.[44] Starting in 1909, as the very first movie theaters opened their doors to Black New Yorkers, the *Age* began a legacy of film criticism that sought to call out racism in the industry as it occurred on the city's screens. While scholars have detailed the ins and outs of Black film criticism more generally, focusing on film criticism in the *Age* elucidates the intimate relationships between Black film culture and place. Deemed members of "a fighting press," the city's journalists critically assessed the way Blackness was represented onscreen and the implications of those representations on Black life in the city.[45]

Black film culture is composed of the moviegoers who sat captivated in theater seats and the transient groups who used those same seats for pleasure or crime. It is the journalists who reported on the seats denied and those who, in turn, refused to be treated as less than. The laborers inside small booths who screened imaginary worlds on large canvas and the filmmakers who made their labor necessary are also a part of Black film culture. When viewed individually, these various groups of people made their own indelible contributions to how cinema was adopted in the range of amusement options for Black New Yorkers. But when considered together, they reveal the very means through which Black film culture was forged in Manhattan and the unmistakable ways that it was founded on desires for access, equality, and belonging. Each used film culture in their own ways, but they are all part of a larger placemaking process in the city. In what follows, *Reel Freedom* traces this history, bringing to light the vibrant Black film culture that thrived in New York City—one bursting with stories much bigger than what the screen alone can offer.

Black Moviegoing in Manhattan

The absence of Black New Yorkers from New York City's film history begins at the start: with the very first exhibition of the medium at Koster and Bial's Music Hall. As the story goes, on April 23, 1896, audiences were held captive by "Edison's latest triumph." Written about contemporarily by local papers like the *New York Times* and understood as a key aspect of "the story of the film industry," the tale has been retold countless times by historians and laypeople alike. The general contours of each version usually remain the same: In the center of the theater's middle balcony sat a machine. It was positioned toward the stage, which on that momentous evening was adorned with a large, framed canvas. As the lights dimmed, the machine's curious silence gave way to "a buzzing and a roaring" that resulted in "an unusually bright light" across the canvas.[1] Suddenly, audiences were fascinated, eyes fixated on the screen and little else. They watched as "the bare canvas" became "instantly a stage upon which living beings move[d] about."[2] The most consistent feature of the event's narrative in each subsequent version remains the audience's shock and awe at the technology. In every retelling, too, there is an enduring presumption of whiteness; the event's various onlookers just do not mention race so much as the theatergoer's sheer amazement.

An advertisement for the Vitascope, titled "Edison's Greatest Marvel," most likely created after the Koster and Bial's demonstration, offers a view of the audience that night (whether real or imagined). The entire bottom third of the work is composed of moviegoers facing the brightly lit canvas. The men and women, all undeniably white, are fashionably clothed: the men in fine suits

Figure 1.1 "Edison's greatest marvel—The Vitascope," ca. 1896. *(New York: Metropolitan Print Company. Original held at the Library of Congress)*

and the women in colorful dresses and feathered hats. Almost every single eye is on the stage; some stare in blatant awe at the girls on the screen dancing around, twirling their dresses. A few women are smiling just slightly; one tilts her head back on an angle to get a full view of the canvas; a couple whispers to each other in the back rows. Without further exploration, the advertisement and countless stories of the medium's debut could easily serve as an excuse to discount Black interest in the medium. They could also demonstrate an overpowering racism built into the industry that limited Black engagement. Following this line of thinking, if Black New Yorkers did not share in this momentous event, or if the imagined audience is inherently and totally white, then why should they be interested in cinema?

It is true that this moment proves difficult for tracing the city's Black film history. There is no consistent reporting on film in the local Black press until 1909, for example. And, though there was a cadre of elite Black New Yorkers capable of paying the relatively high price of $1.50 for orchestra tickets and an even larger group who could spare the $0.25 for the gallery at the Vitascope demonstration, the city's antidiscrimination laws were regularly ignored. Black audiences very well may have chosen to stay away from Koster and Bial's, despite the draw of a technological marvel. Even six months later, when the

Figure 1.2 John Sloan, *Movies, Five Cents*, 1907. *(Public domain)*

famed Black vaudevillians Bert Williams and George Walker began their successful introduction to the city's entertainment scene and performed on the same bill as American Biograph shorts throughout the city, it is unclear if Black New Yorkers were in these early audiences to share in the novelty of these performances.

Instead of representing an impenetrable wall, the glaring nonexistence of Black New Yorkers in the city's earliest film stories raises a series of questions: If not at Koster and Bial's or any of the nearby theaters that quickly added motion pictures to their bills, such as Proctor's 23rd Street or Keith's New Union Square, where were they during cinema's earliest years in the city? Were they a part of the next phase of motion picture entertainment, known as the nickelodeon period, crowded into storefront neighborhood theaters, sitting in legitimate vaudeville houses? Or were they elsewhere watching one of the most important developments of the early twentieth century do its work?

Another piece of artwork that centers the city's movie audiences answers some questions but raises others about the potential of Black moviegoing in this early period. About ten years later, in 1907, New York–based artist John Sloan painted *Movies, Five Cents*. Known for their "candid urban realism," Sloan's works, art historian Rebecca Zurier explains, encourage viewers to "engage . . . the humdrum but startling human interactions to be seen each day on a New York Street."[3] In *Movies, Five Cents*, the setting is an interior city space: a small, somewhat crowded movie theater. As in the Vitascope advertisement, the audience commands the viewer's attention. Some patrons stare directly at the screen, engrossed in the show; one man sleeps; another woman is turned away, glancing, as if knowingly, at the viewer. Or is she looking at someone else? Just two rows back from the disengaged woman, in the cramped and dark space, is a Black woman. Alone in this sea of white faces, she is smiling, facing forward toward the embracing couple on the screen. She sits in the rear of the theater, though not entirely in the back row. She is decidedly a part of the larger audience, not relegated to segregated seating. She seems to be enjoying herself as an engaged spectator, unaware of those around her.

While Zurier argues that "this mix of patrons conforms to period descriptions of the audiences at early New York nickelodeons and vaudeville performances," *Movies, Five Cents* is one of the very few material traces from this period that suggest Black audiences mixed freely with white moviegoers.[4] No one in the crowd seems concerned with the Black woman's presence.[5] This painting, rare as it is, hints at the existence of Black moviegoing in the medium's formative stages in the city and also the potentially complicated nature of that experience.[6] It resists the flat assumption that segregation meant Black New Yorkers could not experience cinema early on or that cinematic racism left Black audiences uninterested in the city's theaters. While the painting poses many more questions than it is able to answer, it serves as an important opening: one for deeper exploration and consideration of the city's Black film culture, which has yet to be undertaken by historians and film scholars.[7] In the face of limited source material, this chapter demonstrates that Black New Yorkers were definitely part of the city's moviegoing public and chose to develop their own film culture in ways that centered community-building opportunities, equitable access, and claims to the city.

Between the first Vitascope display in 1896 and Sloan's painting in 1907, Black and white New Yorkers witnessed formative changes in the city's cultural landscape while also experiencing visceral shifts in race relations. Immediately after the first film exhibition in the city, filmmakers and exhibitors alike flooded the market with content and new theaters. By 1907, when Sloan set his brush to canvas, there were close to two hundred nickelodeons in the city; a year later, six hundred nickelodeons in all five boroughs drew in three hundred thousand people daily.[8] At the very moment that movies were becoming permanent fixtures in theaters, the Black population in New York City was steadily increasing. Even as early as 1896, as the *Times* praised the

Koster and Bial's showing, its reporting suggested concerns with the rise of Black migrants arriving on the city's streets.

For example, the paper published multiple articles on the Atlanta University conference discussing "the condition of negroes living in cities" that year, which concluded that Black city dwellers should "improve [their] lot through better morals and harder work."[9] In the first of what was meant to be a series in the *Times*, W. E. B. Du Bois published a lengthy article on "The Black North" in 1901 that challenged this assessment. He pronounced that since the settlement of the area, "New York has had a negro problem," though its contours changed depending on white residents' fears and expectations of Black people, especially when Black migration turned from a trickle into a steady flow.[10] In 1900, and again in 1905, white New Yorkers met migration and population changes with violence, targeting Black New Yorkers after public skirmishes exploded. These events marked the city's streets as white and potentially violent, delineating a marked "geography of power" that affected the development of a robust Black film culture.[11]

In this atmosphere of violence, discrimination, and exclusion, film culture was fashioned with a desire for engagement with the medium and also for safety, belonging, and pride. Some of the earliest documented Black moviegoing experiences occurred in spaces outside of formal theaters, usually at annual dances and festivals specifically for Black communities, advertised for weeks in the Black press. At these venues, scenes of Black success and talent flashed across a temporarily hung canvas, where attendees celebrated into the night. Very quickly, though, theater owners throughout the city realized the potential for Black audiences. Theaters like the Crescent and Lincoln, both opened in Harlem in 1909, and the 59th Street Theatre, in Midtown, all operated in ways that appeared to center community welfare and support. Beyond offering nondiscriminatory seating practices and the latest race films, some of them worked themselves into the very fabric of the Black community through community events, financial support, and fundraising opportunities. These earliest of developments set the contours for what Black film culture, founded in the face of exclusion and with a desire to experience a modern entertainment, would look like throughout the remainder of the twentieth century.

Early Black Moviegoing: From Nickelodeons to Churches

Starting in 1906, the number of smaller storefront theaters offering moving picture performances (those typically referred to as nickelodeons) exploded in the city. Concurrently, some "legitimate" vaudeville and theater entrepreneurs turned their sights to moving pictures, converting their venues into nickelodeons and motion picture theaters or adding film to their higher-class vaudeville billings.[12] By 1909, small-time vaudeville, which offered a mixed bill of vaudeville and movies, was being "offered in large capacity theatres, many of which were ornately furnished and decorated in the styles of high-class vaudeville theatres."[13] This "trend toward larger houses," where balconies most certainly existed, cannot be ignored, particularly when considering the possibility of Black moviegoing in the city during this early period.[14] Indeed, scholars have engaged in rigorous debate on this period in New York City's film history, though often to the exclusion of potential Black patrons.[15] When Black moviegoing is taken into account, it is too often explained away as impossible because of the prevalence of segregation in the city's storefront nickelodeons.[16] However, not all early movie theaters could be described this way. Undeniably larger than storefront theaters, small-time vaudeville theaters would have been able to provide the necessary balcony and gallery space for segregated seating.[17]

This oversight of Black moviegoing is replicated, albeit through different means, in scholarship explicitly on Harlem's Black community in these early years.[18] Before 1910, the Black population of New York was still in flux. The mass movement of migrants and immigrants to Harlem was just beginning to take place and had not yet become a steady pour. In that year, a bit over 20,000 of New York City's 60,534 Black residents still lived on the city's West Side in clusters throughout San Juan Hill and the Tenderloin. Until mass migration to Harlem, most Black New Yorkers lived in densely packed pockets spanning a few streets and avenues throughout Lower and Midtown Manhattan. If, therefore, we are to take the possibility of early Black moviegoing seriously, it is necessary to look at Black New Yorkers where they were: spread throughout the city, not yet consolidated in Harlem, and responding quite vocally to the city's attempts to limit their lives, both inside and outside of theaters.

In 1900 and 1905, just before the nickelodeon boom and the rise of motion pictures' popularity, New York City experienced two riots that made it clear that much of the city's public space was contested territory. On August 13, 1900, a deadly fight between Arthur Harris, a Black man, and Robert Thorpe, a white undercover officer, broke out on the corner of Eighth Avenue and Forty-First Street and sparked nearly a month of violent skirmishes between white and Black New Yorkers in the area. "A mob of several thousands raged up and down Eighth Avenue and through the side streets from Twenty-seventh to Forty-second," wrote one contemporary, "Negroes were seized wherever they were found, and brutally beaten."[19] So pervasive was the violence, supported by the police, that *Harper's Weekly* explicitly called it out: "The worst feature of the late rioting . . . was the apparent disposition of many policemen to egg on the disorders, which it was their duty to restrain."[20] Another journalist writing on white feelings toward African Americans postriot elucidates how serious the struggle over claims to space in the city could be: "Negroes in New York do not constitute a very considerable proportion of the population," yet "I heard many native [white] Americans . . . after the riot that they would have been glad if many of the negroes had been killed."[21]

Five years later, in 1905, an argument between white and Black pedestrians in San Juan Hill led to weeks of interracial violence and a clear understanding that the police were unwilling to help Black bystanders. Lamenting the frequent and arbitrary nature of racial violence, one *Age* article complained that "race riots are too common in New York City, and the police department is largely responsible for them, as it manages to take sides with the aggressors in the mob, which is usually Irish people . . . who have a grudge against the Jews or Afro-Americans who live in their section or who stray into it."[22] Black New Yorkers traversed city streets and interacted with entertainment spaces that were certainly coded as white. To get to the theaters, especially those nickelodeons outside of neighborhood enclaves, it was necessary to walk along the city's hotly contested sidewalks.[23] Violence against Black New Yorkers in Midtown and northward continued as Harlem grew as a Black enclave in the 1910s. As historian Shannon King explains, "Blacks confronted territorial whites on a daily basis" in New York City.[24]

As the tide of migrants and immigrants moving into the city seemed unwilling to abate, Black leaders and intellectuals considered the dangers of city life. In an article titled "The Problems of the City Dweller" in *Opportunity* magazine, Mary McLeod Bethune described urban living as "unfavorable," offering "limits as pitilessly circumscribed as prison walls."[25] In her long list of affordances that Black city dwellers struggle for, Bethune explicitly cites access to cheap motion pictures and other amusements. Movies, she explained, "have lured many a grizzled homesteader to abandon home and ancestral acres and move cityward."[26] Yet segregation remained a reality for many Black New Yorkers who attempted to patronize the city's movie theaters, even as they struggled against racist justifications for its longevity.

As late as 1928, one theater manager outside of Harlem told an interviewer that segregation was a regular part of his business practice: "We try to keep Negroes upstairs in the balconies. They . . . feel more at home among themselves." "Besides," he continued, "they have their own theaters uptown."[27] At the same time, though, segregation was not always a given. In her novel *Plum Bum*, Jessie Fauset's main character, Angela, persistently questions the outcome of her positionality in downtown theaters as a light-skinned Black woman. On one occasion, she sits in a theater outside of Harlem, among white viewers, wondering: "Would these people, she wondered . . . begrudge her, if they knew, her cherished freedom and sense of unrestraint?"[28] On another, she considers the reaction of the white woman next to her had she revealed her racial identity: "Would she show the occasional dog-in-the-manger attitude of certain white Americans and refuse to sit by her or make a complaint to the usher?"[29]

Clearly, it was difficult for Black New Yorkers to feel welcome at some theaters throughout the city, especially before Harlem grew as a Black enclave. Yet, considering Black moviegoing at alternative venues, there is the potential for locations where Black New Yorkers might watch moving pictures without fear of discrimination. Take, for example, Prof. Moses M. Mimms, who, starting in 1907, began to exhibit movies in conjunction with his annual dances at the Harlem River Park and Casino. Located at 126th Street and Second Avenue, Harlem River Park had long served as a gathering place for Black New Yorkers to celebrate. Lodges, clubs, and associations, such as the Knights Templar, the St. Philip's Young Men's Guild, and the Young Cuban Social Club, all held regular picnics, musical performances, dances, and reunions there. Before the very first screening event in October 1907, Prof. Mimms promoted it as something unique, urging Black New Yorkers "not to miss this novel affair by any means."[30] He strongly emphasized the motion pictures in his promotional material, including an image of the projector itself in advertisements leading up to the event.

On October 18, more than three thousand people attended the show. In addition to a night of dancing, attendees were delighted with multicolored calcium lights that flanked the band, while behind the musicians "pictures of prominent people in the life of New York and vicinity were shown from an Edison kinetoscope." Those who ventured to Harlem River Park "were in no wise disappointed," the *Age* reported, "as the affair surpassed his picnic of August 29 by far," which notably did not have motion pictures on display. Audiences witnessed local businessmen like Barron Wilkins, a prominent nightclub owner; James Marshall, of the well-known Marshall Hotel; and cultural icons like Dora Patterson, a vaudeville performer who also sang at the event, moving across the screen. Considering the event a "monster success," Prof. Mimms continued to include motion pictures in his regular picnics and dances at Harlem River Park.[31]

From the start, as Mimms's events demonstrate, motion picture exhibition and consumption for Black New Yorkers was embedded in community celebration and advancement.[32] Taking place at a location regularly used by

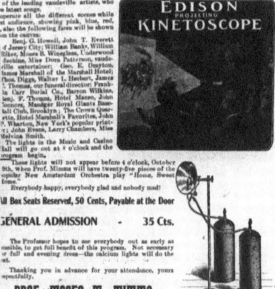

To all who intend to call on their friends on
Friday, October 18, 1907
Greeting from PROF. MOSES M. MIMMS

THE PROFESSOR begs you not to call on your friends on this Friday, the 18th, for nobody will be at home. Where will everybody be? They will be where all Brooklyn, Jersey and New York are going to be—at Sulzer's Harlem Casino and Music Hall.
A few people missed it on August 29, but no one will miss it on October 18. Everybody will attend and see the Professor operate his two calcium lights, see the moving pictures and all the PROMINENT colored business men's photo's appear on the canvas likewise views of the Jamestown Exposition, and much other attractive scenery.
Prof. Mimms has also secured a number of the leading vaudeville artists, who will appear on the stage and render some of the latest songs.
The Professor assures you that he will operate all the different scenes while the calcium lights are glittering upon the vast audience, showing pink, blue, red, green, orange, yellow, purple and other colors, also the following faces will be shown on the canvas:

Benj. G. Howell, John T. Everett of Jersey City; William Banks, William Riker, Moses B. Wineglass, Underwood Jochine, Miss Dora Patterson, vaudeville entertainer; Geo. E. Drayton, James Marshall of the Marshall Hotel; Thos. Diggs, Walter L. Herbert, James T. Thomas, our funeral director; Frank-lin Carr Burial Co., Barron Wilkins, Benj. F. Thomas, Hotel Maceo, John Connors, Manager Royal Giants Baseball Club, Brooklyn; The Crown Quartette, Hotel Marshall's Favorites, John P. Wharton, New York's popular printer; John Evans, Larry Chambers, Miss Melvina Smith.
The lights in the Music and Casino Hall will go out at 8 o'clock and the program begin.
These lights will not appear before 4 o'clock, October 9th, when Prof. Mimms will have twenty-five pieces of the popular New Amsterdam Orchestra play "Home, Sweet Home."
Everybody happy, everybody glad and nobody mad!

All Box Seats Reserved, 50 Cents, Payable at the Door

GENERAL ADMISSION - 35 Cts.

The Professor hopes to see everybody out as early as possible, to get full benefit of this program. Not necessary to full and evening dress—the calcium lights will do the rest.

Thanking you in advance for your attendance, yours respectfully,

EDISON PROJECTING KINETOSCOPE

PROF. MOSES M. MIMMS

Figure 1.3 Advertisement in the *New York Age* for Prof. Mimms's show at Harlem River Park, prominently showcasing the use of moving pictures. *(Public domain)*

Black New Yorkers for community gatherings and using a modern technology to center Black businessmen in the city reveals the intimate ties between motion pictures and Black New Yorkers' search for affirming, celebratory, and equitable space. When the event took place again, a year later, even more outright community involvement was included: Members of the Young Men's Progressive Club and the Ladies' Hyacinth Social Club were participants in an elaborate march over the course of the evening, and Black businessmen continued to flash across the large white canvas fitted for motion pictures. These linkages between community and motion picture exhibition were not necessarily unique to New York. As film historian Cara Caddoo has maintained, turn-of-the-century religious institutions and fraternal associations in the urban South used film as a means to promote racial uplift, entice members to join their organizations, and raise funds for institution building.[33] Southern migrants, who by 1906 made up the majority of the Black population in the city, undoubtedly brought these associations between cinema and Black institutions with them to New York, melding them with a growing Black film culture.[34]

The relationship between the Black church and the movies in New York City adds even more to the conversation around space, moviegoing, and community building. As early as 1908, there are mentions of an itinerant preacher showing motion pictures in a well-established church in the city. One hot July summer that year, Mr. W. R. Griffin, a member of the Washington division of the True Reformers, "gave a moving picture exhibition at St. Mark's Church," located at West Fifty-Third Street.[35] The show was held at the church's presentation space, known as St. Mark's Lyceum, founded "to attract the young people from the pool rooms and dives."[36] In addition to motion picture exhibition, the Lyceum hosted a range of events, including song and dance performances, mock senate events, and public addresses on topics ranging from public health to Black women in business. Later that same year, a member of St. Paul's Baptist Church gave another moving picture exhibition, described as "interesting and much enjoyed by a crowded house."[37]

The practice of showing movies, most likely containing religious themes, in churches was common in the city and spread into areas like New Rochelle, Flushing, and even New Jersey. These exhibitors, along with others like Prof. Mimms, who staged moving picture shows of "the latest dances [and] a good many of the leading colored businessmen of the city" to thousands in Harlem River Park, were part of a generation of Black entrepreneurs who, in Caddoo's words, "embraced the moving pictures as a symbol of black modernity and as a tool with which to publicize and raise money for mainline churches, fraternal orders, schools, and other organizations that espoused the ideas of racial uplift."[38] In New York, these exhibitors were also providing Black New Yorkers access to the modern medium in places that could be considered safe and communal and where, arguably, the content could be controlled.

Not everyone agreed with the close ties between churches and movies. One member of St. Mark's Church wrote a letter to the *Age* discouraging the use of film exhibitions at houses of worship. While the author, George Young, acknowledged the educational aspects of movies, he warned of "the harmful and danger [*sic*] side" of producing films with "holy and sacred" themes. In Young's view, "the moving picture shows have not added anything to the morals of any community, which they have invaded," and only made Christianity common, causing it to lose its power as "a soul-lifter and inspiration to holiness." Displaying his strong feelings on the matter, Young demanded, "Do not besmirge [*sic*] with filth, a thing so noble, perfect and beautiful."[39]

Despite, or perhaps because of, this strong concern, churches continued to debate their role in supporting, exhibiting, or condemning motion pictures during the nickelodeon period. In December 1910, a session of the Interdenominational Ministerial Conference in New York was dedicated to the relationship between motion pictures and church patronage. Rev. Mathew Clair, a Methodist Episcopal Church minister from Washington, DC, carried his distaste for moving pictures across state lines as he called for a crusade against movie theaters. Rev. Adam Clayton Powell, the popular minister of a New York church, challenged Clair's inflammatory rhetoric. "The Abyssinian Church is surrounded by theatres and nickelettes as is no other church in the city," he posited, "but I do not believe that they have affected our attendance in the slightest degree." He argued that people, especially the working class, were going to find cheap amusements somewhere, and if movie houses were closed, they would instead patronize "saloons, buffet flats and gambling houses, and the rest would stand on the street corners until midnight, which is about the most demoralized social diversion in New York City."[40]

Powell believed that censorship, not condemnation, was the best way to combat "any exhibition of plays deemed pernicious to the moral character." He urged parents and parishioners to visit theaters and protest when necessary. "When we do this something worth while will be accomplished and," he continued, "the people will be convinced the church is . . . not trying to destroy everything outside of its own walls." Ultimately, Powell was convinced that if the church was succeeding in its mission, there would be no need to consider motion pictures a threat. The reverend concluded with a fiery dictum: "The day has gone by when we can stop the ears of the people with the wax of tradition and lash them to the church by creeds and doctrines promulgated by the ecclesiastical councils of the Middle Ages."[41]

Powell's turn to censorship, instead of attempts at theater closure or community censure, shows his ultimate recognition that the medium was very popular among his nearby parishioners and that an alternative response to the changes wrought by migration and modernity was needed. The very necessity of a meeting such as this suggests that Black audience members were among the earliest of film exhibitions in the city, including those *outside* alternative settings like parks and churches, such as nickelodeons. That Black moviegoing in this period also caused such a stir in local church circles reveals its large numbers. Located on Fortieth Street, between Sixth and Eighth Avenue, the Abyssinian Church was at the heart of a Black neighborhood that housed almost seven thousand residents and was just steps away from the city's central entertainment district in Times Square.

Yet Black clergymen had long been negotiating their churches' position with regard to leisure and commercial amusements. Just a year after the first film was exhibited in the city, W. E. B. Du Bois lamented that he "heard sermon after sermon . . . thunder warnings against the terrible results of pleasure and the awful end of those who are depraved enough to seek pleasure."[42] Aiming for a more balanced approach to religion and recreation, Du Bois explained that the church could no longer be "the chief center of our amusement," insisting that the church allow other establishments, organizations, and spaces to take up the charge.[43] This remained a regular debate in the Black community during the early years of cinema's commercial popularity, even extending beyond the nickelodeon period into the 1920s.[44] Clearly, though, the city's Black churches were making attempts to respond to their congregants' desire to be consumers of cinema and participants in the development of a new aspect of leisure culture. Instead of wholeheartedly and decisively rejecting what cinema had to offer, some churches moved toward what film scholar Anna Everett describes as a "a pragmatic program of cooperation."[45]

Churches in the city continued to show moving pictures and take their services to movie theaters for at least the next three decades. In March 1910, the first of quite a few "big religious meeting[s]" was held in the Crescent, one of the first movie theaters catering to Black audiences in Harlem. The event made front-page news in the *Age* and was heralded as an "innovation in local church circles." The paper reported that almost three hundred men, ranging from young teens to elders, attended the service meant to "seek the sinners instead of waiting for sinners to seek the church." In addition to the services, a religious-themed motion picture exhibition was put on that proved both entertaining and educational. The joint meeting of the Mt. Olivet Baptist Church, Abyssinian Baptist Church, St. Mark's Church, and other smaller local churches managed to earn twelve converts and the recommittal of thirty men who had gone astray.[46]

And even as cinema developed toward a much more commercial endeavor, which included the race film industry, Black filmmakers, and theaters catering specifically to Black audiences, churches continued to serve as alternative venues for motion picture exhibition.[47] For example, Mr. Richardson, the "moving picture king," held services at the New AME (African Methodist Episcopal) Zion Church in Flushing, and the Society of Emmanuel Church "showed moving pictures of the Bible" in the late 1910s.[48] In Brooklyn, the Nazarene Congregational's youth group considered film exhibitions so powerful that they were thinking of buying a projection machine to help raise funds for the church.[49] Beyond religious services, some Black churches used motion pictures to boost morale during World War I. In March 1919, the *Age* announced that "real moving pictures showing 'Our Boys in Action Overseas,'" specifically featuring the all-Black Fifteenth Regiment, would be played at Mother Zion Church.[50]

In 1922, Pastor Summers gave a sermon at the New Douglas Theatre, while his congregation's Sunday School classes regularly took place in the theater's basement. In 1925 and again in 1926, the Harlem Federation of Churches held one of a "series of meetings to revive religious interest" at the Lafayette Theatre.[51] The initial of these two meetings was considered a great success as the *Amsterdam News* reported that over seven thousand people attended the services.[52] While it is unclear whether these services also had motion picture exhibitions, the significance of the meetings remains. As they had in 1910, a massive group of churches decided that the best way "to reach the churchless" was by meeting them at the supposed competitor.[53] Instead of waging "a crusade on the five and ten cent theatres," as Rev. Adam Clayton Powell had fought against fifteen years earlier, these church leaders continued to demonstrate that the church was malleable in the face of modern technology and urban amusements but also that churches were consistently viable venues for exhibition beyond the nickelodeon period.[54]

This trend continued well into the 1930s as motion pictures remained part of many Black church services. In 1930, the Rush Memorial AME Zion Church on 138th Street took "a new lease on life" as it promised "to do bigger and better things for its members and community in general." Part of this was the presentation of Sunday evening mass with movies, made possible by "the installation of one of the most modern and up-to-date moving picture machines."[55] That the church felt it warranted to operate a top-of-the-line machine suggests that moving pictures made up a significant aspect of the pastor's presentation. So connected were Black film culture and religious film exhibition that Reginald Warner, a Black projectionist at the nearby Renaissance Theatre, also ran the projection machine at Rush Memorial. As late as 1942, religious exhibitions were still taking place in churches in New York's Black communities.

A focus on churches evinces how Black New Yorkers were undoubtedly a part of the city's nickelodeon period, be that in small "nickelettes" or in houses of worship, but most importantly, they constituted part of the city's moviegoing masses. Whether in the theater spaces themselves or in alternative venues, Black New Yorkers found ways to explore this modern medium as it grew in popularity. In seeking alternative venues, like parks and churches,

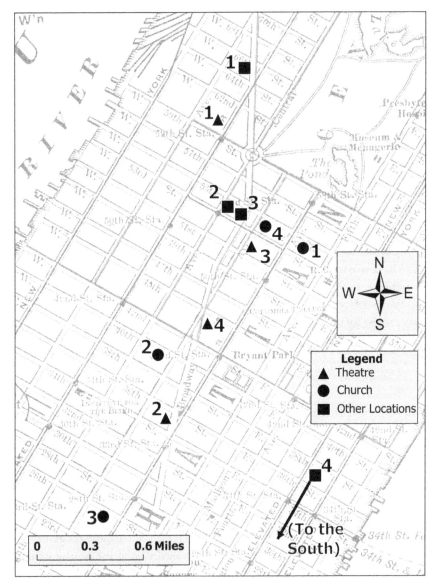

Figure 1.4 Black Amusement and other social centers in Midtown Manhattan, 1909–1930s. *(Created by Peter Rogers, base map by Rand McNally and Company [1897] from David Rumsey Map Collection, David Rumsey Map Center, Stanford Libraries)*

TABLE 1.1 MIDTOWN LOCATIONS		
▲	Theatres	Address
1	59th Street Theatre	313 West 59th Street
2	Koster and Bial's Music Hall	135 West 34th Street
3	Palace Theatre	51st Street and 7th Avenue
4	New York Theatre	1514–1516 Broadway
●	Churches	
1	St. Mark's ME Church	231 West 53rd Street
2	Abyssinian Baptist Church	242 West 40th Street
3	St. Philip's PE Church	161 West 25th Street
4	Mt. Olivet Baptist Church	161 West 53rd Street
■	Other Locations	
1	*New York Amsterdam News* office	132 West 65th Street
2	Maceo Hotel	213 West 53rd Street
3	Marshall Hotel	127 West 53rd Street
4	*New York Age* office	4 Cedar Street (not pictured)

Black moviegoers (and exhibitors) got creative in how they resisted white limitations on their existence, choosing venues that inherently centered community and safety.

Movie Theaters and the Black Community

The Crescent and Lincoln, both in Harlem, were two of the first theaters to
open their doors to Black moviegoers. Offering a mix of both vaudeville and
motion pictures, these theaters were working to cater to an influx of new Black
residents in the area around 135th Street. But as much of New York City's
Black population remained closer to Midtown in neighborhoods like San
Juan Hill and the Tenderloin, at least one Black-owned theater, the 59th Street
Theatre, continued to offer movies for those who had not yet left for Harlem.
By 1930, when most Black New Yorkers and their institutions had made the
move uptown, theaters, including the Lafayette and Renaissance Theatres,
could easily be found up and down the neighborhood's main thoroughfares.

These theaters were not simply places of amusement. In addition to offering the evening's entertainment, they also provided important community-
building opportunities. Local clubs and organizations held meetings in them,
theater managers provided patrons with groceries to meet essential needs, and
customers could feel good supporting Black-owned enterprises. The following
theaters, though not representative or descriptive of all the theaters in the city
that catered to Black New Yorkers, are some of the most significant in terms
of setting the norms for how theaters fit into the larger nexus of Black film

culture in the city. By patronizing these theaters, Black New Yorkers shaped the city's film culture, using it to their own advantage.

The Lincoln and Crescent Theatres

Addressing the needs and wants of the fast-growing Black population in Harlem, both the Crescent and Lincoln Theatres opened on the same block on 135th Street in 1909.[56] Maria C. Downs, a Cuban businesswoman, reversed the Lincoln's previous discriminatory policy to allow for Black performers and audiences, making it the first theater to do so in Harlem. For the next six years, oscillating between live performances and mixed bills, the Lincoln became famous for its fifteen-minute skits written and performed by Black comedians Eddie Hunter and Thomas Chappelle. The theater become so popular that in 1914, Downs renovated the theater, expanding its seating capacity from 300 to 850. That same year, the famous Anita Bush Stock Company opened at the Lincoln to rave reviews and packed crowds. Bush remembered that "all of the best people, some of whom had never crossed the sill of the Lincoln Theatre before, were there to welcome us. The house was packed and so were the sidewalks outside."[57] The group forged new ground as the first Black stock company established in a New York City theater and took their fame to the Lafayette just six months later.

After the loss of its stock players, the Lincoln remained committed to a regular mixed bill of vaudeville and motion pictures. By the 1920s, though, the theater had gained a somewhat unsavory reputation. In 1924, Theophilus Lewis, dramatic editor for the radical *Messenger* and eventually the *Amsterdam News*, described the general atmosphere at the theater:

> The Lincoln Theatre is a cheap movie-vaudeville house. Its audiences consist of the kind of people who kick the varnish off the furniture, plaster chewing gum on the seats and throw peanut shells in the aisles. The imperfectly disinfected odors of the lavatories somehow contrive to seep out into the auditorium to mingle with the scent of cologne and sachet powder and the body smells of people. . . . At night a strong fleet of cruisers . . . patrols the place looking for love-famished stevedores, and . . . sweet-back men without connections are wont to resort there for the servant girl shooting.[58]

Perhaps this is one reason why reportage on the Lincoln in the *Age* was rare beyond basic notes on who was performing and what was showing during the theater's earliest years. Advertisements for the theater did not even begin appearing in the paper until 1916. As the *Amsterdam News* explained, the Lincoln, when it first opened, "was not considered 'the thing' among so-called social elite."[59]

The Crescent Theatre and its management, on the other hand, were repeatedly praised by Lester Walton at the *Age* from the moment its doors opened in December 1909. Thomas Johnson, a Black businessman tied to a white theatre syndicate, managed the theater and, to Walton's satisfaction, gave "Harlem a first-class vaudeville and moving picture house which is thoroughly modern in every respect."[60] In associating the theater with modernity, Walton could have been referring to any number of elements, including the lavishly decorated interior, the shows that he generally described as "bill[s] of considerable merit," or the theater's eventual shift toward a reserved-seating policy that disallowed "some [to] find the little Harlem playhouse a haven of refuge from the refractory elements for hours at a time."[61] The discrepancy in reporting on the two theaters could depend on a number of additional things. When it first opened, the Lincoln was a shoddily put-together venue with "a dingy and gloomy interior, with its floor lower than the level of the sidewalk." The Crescent, on the other hand, was similarly sized but had a seating arrangement "much on the order of larger [more respectable] playhouses."[62] It is quite possible that Walton preferred to promote a business that catered to a "clientele [that] is far above that of the majority of theatres of its kind in New York," rather than a supposedly dirty nickelodeon.[63]

Both theaters, though, were a regular part of Black life in the neighborhood in various ways, offering means to uplift and support the community through multiple ventures. For example, both the Lincoln and the Crescent provided access to some of the earliest Black film efforts and strongly supported local Black talent. In 1910, the Crescent offered a private screening of George Broome's *A Trip to Tuskegee* (1909), which attempted to "show the industrial progress of the Negro along industrial lines by means of moving pictures."[64] Though this was a private showing, the fact that Broome, or those associated with Tuskegee, such as Emmett J. Scott, sought out this particular venue suggests its importance within the Black community. As film historian Allyson Nadia Field has argued, Broome's work at Tuskegee and the actuality footage that he usually included in the screenings, such as students at work on the school's campus, were some "of the earliest assertions of African American self-representation in cinema."[65] The Crescent, as one of the first theaters in the city to cater to Black audiences, became tied to this monumental advancement in Black cultural production.

The Lincoln followed suit in 1916 when it showed *The Colored American Winning His Case*, which "revolves around a colored boy who starts life on a small farm in the South and through sheer force of self-will rises from one position to another until he . . . enters a law school."[66] Importantly, the film was specifically made with the "idea of overcoming the effects of certain vicious photo plays which have created an antagonistic propaganda against the race."[67] In supporting the film, produced by the local Frederick Douglass Film Company, the Lincoln proved that it was interested in supporting community endeavors at self-representation and the ever-growing local race film industry.

The Crescent and Lincoln Theatres also assisted the local community through benefit measures. The Lincoln regularly offered complimentary attendance to the movies for those children who received free Thanksgiving and Christmas dinners and once, in 1928, even distributed toys to all the children in need that year. Contributions were made by the Crescent and Lincoln, alongside other theaters such as the Roosevelt, Franklin, Lafayette, Douglas, and Renaissance, to groups like the Salvation Army and the Fire Relief Committee of the Parents' Association of P.S. 89. The Crescent also offered a weekly country store out of the theater. Patrons were given lottery tickets, and if their number was called, they received a range of "free doings," such as sausage and ham.[68] Not long after, the theater inaugurated "poultry night," to the dismay of local butchers, who "complain[ed] that their receipts [were] smaller every Saturday night."[69] These efforts were not just about the entertainment value at each of these venues. Rather, they were attempts, usually by white or non-Black New Yorkers, to support the same Harlemites who were making their businesses profitable.

Furthermore, the Lincoln served as an important location for the presentation of local Black talent. The theater's various stock players between 1915 and 1929 went on to star in mainstream and race films, while jazz musician Fats Waller got his first job at the Lincoln at just fifteen years old.[70] Waller's sister, Naomi Washington, remembers that "people would go to the theater just to hear Fats play. There used to be a fellow who used to sit up in the balcony, and when Fats would play, this boy would whistle along, and when he did, you could hear a pin drop."[71] When Fats Waller began playing at the Lincoln, the *Age* considered it a performance "on the same order as that of the big Broadway Theatres."[72]

In 1928, the Lincoln also served as a location for a number of screen tests for a major motion picture company looking for Black talent, most likely for King Vidor's *Hallelujah* (1929). Four of the film's main leads were found in Harlem, but most exciting may have been that the screen tests were shown the next week at the theater, giving the audience "the double satisfaction of seeing themselves in action on the silver screen."[73] Given Vidor's stereotypical approach to Black religion in the film, the screening of local Harlemites takes on even greater representational power. It offered participants a chance to see themselves in (and as) a community of people committed to challenging racist representations in film by taking part in what was viewed as a potentially life-changing opportunity to affect the film industry through their talent. It also, in no small way, gave local performers significant publicity and residents the thrill of seeing themselves on the screen.[74]

Ultimately, the Crescent and Lincoln were a regular part of Black life in the neighborhood. Descriptions of the Lincoln and Crescent demonstrate the various ways that early Black theaters in Harlem were inextricably linked to the community and racial uplift. They provided stages for young Black actors to cut their teeth, served as meeting spaces for local churches to meet their congregants, and offered material that was meant not just to entertain but to educate and promote pride. Their contributions to relief efforts and attempts to support, in their earliest stages, Black filmmaking efforts make it clear that they were striving for community acceptance. While these moves can be read as mere marketing ploys for Black patronage, they can also be understood in light of the power that Black Harlemites held over these institutions vying for community legitimacy.

The 59th Street Theatre

William Mack Felton, a young migrant from Georgia, arrived in New York in 1898 full of ambition, with just "one dollar in his shoe."[75] When he finally saved enough money working as a longshoreman, he opened a repair shop for watches, bikes, and guns. "Gifted with mechanical ability," Felton was able to open an automobile shop and school in 1901.[76] Though he relocated the business a bit between 1901 and 1910, Felton always remained within Midtown, following the Black population's migration northward. In May 1913, Felton moved into the entertainment industry, opening the 59th Street Theatre between Eighth and Columbus Avenues.

Perhaps Felton had read about the many instances of discriminatory seating practices in the city's Black press, or maybe he recognized that there was a gap between those theaters catering to white New Yorkers and those willing to treat Black patronage fairly, especially in Midtown. Either way, Felton was undoubtedly a race man given his propensity for business ventures in modern technology, including cars and motion pictures. In a period rife with discrimination and violence against Black people, these types of large business ventures represented a significantly visible challenge to "a society that relentlessly denied black Americans both the material and ideological markers of bourgeois status."[77] Serving as a direct response to Jim Crow, the 59th Steet

Figure 1.5 William Mack Felton, owner of the 59th Street Theatre, featured in the *New York Age*. *(Public domain)*

WILLIAM MACK FELTON

Theatre was one of the few Black-owned or Black-managed theaters that directly appealed to race pride in an attempt to draw in their preferred clientele and meet community needs.[78] These spaces, including the Renaissance, which opened a decade later in Harlem, served as "coveted monuments of racial progress" that "exhibited optimism, capital, and a physical hold on urban space."[79]

The 59th Street Theatre was described as "one of the handsomest and most up-to-date small vaudeville and motion picture houses in Greater New York."[80] Having spent over $12,000 to renovate an old bank, Felton added a second floor, private boxes throughout, and an air-conditioning system for the coming summer months. The entertainment consisted of vaudeville acts, both drama and comedy, in addition to two- and three-reel films, all for ten to twenty-five cents. Before the 59th Street Theatre opened its doors, the

Palace Hall Theatre, at Fifty-First Street and Seventh Avenue, had briefly catered to Black audiences with Black vaudeville performances on Sundays.[81] When it changed its name to the Palace Theatre and began offering motion pictures a year later in 1910, it became clear how much the Crescent and Lincoln Theatres had an impact on Black entertainment desires in the city.

Felton operated the 59th Street Theatre in ways that were similar to the Crescent, suggesting an attempt to forge community and provide charity. For example, he ran regular contests three nights a week that drew in Black audiences from as close as next door to as far as 135th Street. These competitions ran the gamut; there were song contests and greased pole climbing and log-sawing tournaments for women. Prizes included a Buick Runabout, silk parasols and dresses, corsets, and watches. Beyond these gimmicks, Felton was "so deeply interested in reducing the high cost of living that he [was] giving away foodstuffs and clothing at his theatre three evenings of each week," in addition to holding weekly country fairs within the theater.[82] Though the *Age* poked fun at him for playing Santa Claus, Felton gave away over one hundred turkeys, chickens, and ducks during the 1913 Thanksgiving holiday.

In a neighborhood where racial tensions ran exceedingly high, the 59th Street Theatre offered up a space for community among San Juan Hill's Black residents, though not without limitations. Felton's trouble with the area's local white residents began almost immediately. On the theater's opening night, all performances were stopped after two shows because of a nearby theater owner, who became "apprehensive that the new theatre would make bad business for his house, [and] induced a friend to write to the authorities and give warning that as the theatre would be conducted by a colored man it would be used as a meeting place for the women and men of opposite races."[83] This kind of complaint was not uncommon of Black-owned businesses—even the *Age* noted that had Felton been white, his rival's "method of attack would have been different"—and it often resulted in their ruin.[84] For instance, the eventual fate of the Marshall Hotel, just six blocks south of Felton's theater, illuminates the devastating effect that controversy surrounding mixed-race establishments could trigger. Once targeted by the Committee of Fourteen, a private organization committed to fighting vice, for serving alcohol to Black and white patrons, the hotel lost its liquor license until promising to segregate its customers. As historian Jennifer Fronc explains, this "important gathering space for New York's emerging black cultural elite" and the Black businessmen who partnered with the committee "had been unwitting and unwilling hosts to Jim Crow."[85] Because he did not serve alcohol, Felton was in a much less coerced position. He refused to kowtow to local influences, the *Age* noted, "brand[ing] as false any rumors that have been put into circulation that he is anxious to dispose of the theatre."[86]

Beyond petty rivalries, Felton's desire for both Black and white customers somewhat restricted the 59th Street Theatre's ability to function as a truly free place for Black audience members to enjoy themselves. Despite protest from Black journalists, Felton hired only white employees for the manager and cashier positions, insisting that "it was absolutely necessary" because, according to him, "so many white persons would refuse to patronize the theatre" otherwise. Even after his first white manager and cashier were fired for discriminating against Black patrons and stealing, Felton insisted on the indispensability of white employees. In the midst of this, the Black press consistently advocated for Black employment at the 59th Street Theatre and all theaters catering to Black audiences, especially in the growing Black settlement in Harlem. Employment, of ushers, ticket takers, and even projectionists, was yet another way that proprietors tried to demonstrate their commitment to their Black clientele, though clearly Felton faltered here.

Felton intended, by all means, to make his white patrons comfortable in the theater, even when it was obvious that it was to the detriment of his Black customers. It was not until rumors began to spread about the true lack of esteem his white employees held for him that Felton decided to make a change. Mistaking a "colored girl of very light complexion" for white one evening, both manager and cashier felt comfortable making "disparaging references of Mr. Felton and wife" that included racist epithets. Learning of this, Felton made "a clean sweep" and replaced every single one of his employees with Black men and women "of that type which deceives nine white persons out of ten . . . even if colored people can tell when they are 'passing.'"[87] Rather than seeing this as a clear case of colorism on Felton's part, the *Age* poked fun at racist white people's ironic inability to ultimately distinguish between Black and white.

While Felton eventually found it necessary to dispose of his racist white employees, his reluctance reflects the limits of mixed-race theaters for Black patrons, particularly those outside of Harlem. It took a personal offense, not transgressions against his Black customers, for Felton to make changes at the 59th Street Theatre. These changes also resulted in a clear preference for light-skinned Black employees specifically so that white patrons would not be offended at the theater. Unfortunately, Felton was not able to see the lasting effect of his decisions. In January 1914, less than a year after its grand opening, the 59th Street Theatre suffered a debilitating fire. Without insurance, Felton lost a significant amount of his investment, and, notwithstanding promises that the theater would "positively open" again in February, the 59th

Street Theatre was closed for good by April.[88] From this point onward, most Black moviegoing endeavors and the expansion of a fervent Black film culture were centered in Harlem.

The Lafayette Theatre

Despite being "by far the most outstanding Harlem Theatre, the most successful over the long run, and the one whose legend, or perhaps myth, eclipses all other Harlem theatres of the period," the Lafayette Theatre opened on 132nd Street and Seventh Avenue, the southern border of the growing Black community, to immediate controversy in 1912.[89] Lester Walton recalled that he "felt downcast and . . . near to shedding tears" when he learned that the Lafayette, managed by Martinson and Nibur, previous liquor dealers and the former owners of the Crescent, would draw the color line.[90] Only "highly respectable colored people" could sit on the first floor of the nearly two thousand seat theater, but management still reserved the right to put the "riff-raff" in the balcony.[91] Just over a week after the Lafayette opened its doors to present vaudeville and motion pictures, Black theatergoers in Harlem became increasingly indignant about the management's determination to enforce segregation that made no distinction between the supposed riff-raff and "the most prominent Negroes of the city."[92] Recognizing that the management was not going to treat them with respect, Black patronage fell off. By 1914, the lack of Black business at the Lafayette, now becoming increasingly surrounded by Black residents, forced a new takeover that included Lester Walton, the *Age*'s cultural critic, as manager under white ownership.

Under Walton, the Lafayette forged its long-standing reputation for Black performances of legitimate drama, though not without the occasional motion picture exhibition. Walton convinced the Anita Bush Stock Company to leave the Lincoln for the Lafayette and become the famous Lafayette Players. He also continued the previous managers' practice of holding country fairs every Saturday evening (similar to the 59th Street Theatre and the Crescent) and adhered to the policy of showing only the "latest feature photo plays."[93] Known as "house beautiful," the Lafayette under Walton's management became integrated into the fabric of Harlem because of its up-to-date and interesting offerings and also because of its role in the neighborhood overall. Like the Crescent, which Walton held in such high regard, the Lafayette continued to serve as a community meeting space for religious and community groups, including those holding benefit performances to raise money "for a monument to be erected over the grave of the great heroine Harriet Tubman," the Howard Orphanage on Long Island, and the Boys' Camp of the

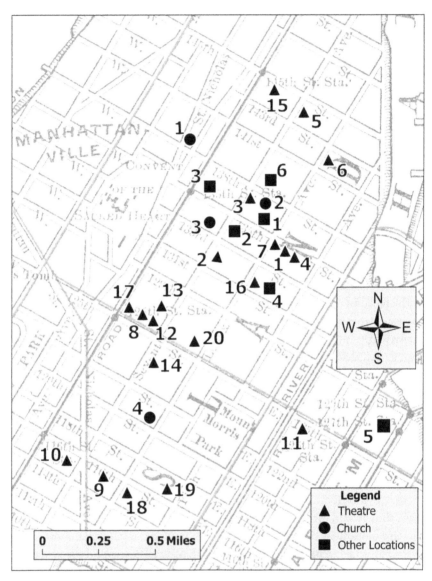

Figure 1.6 Black Amusement and other social centers in Harlem, 1909–1930s.
(Created by Peter Rogers, base map by Rand McNally and Company [1897] from David Rumsey Map Collection, David Rumsey Map Center, Stanford Libraries)

TABLE 1.2 HARLEM LOCATIONS		
▲	Theatres	Address
1	Crescent Theatre	36–38 West 135th Street
2	Lafayette Theatre	2225 7th Avenue
3	Renaissance Theatre	2347 7th Avenue
4	Gem Theatre	36–38 West 135th Street
5	Roosevelt Theatre	2497 7th Avenue
6	New Douglas Theatre	640 Lenox Avenue
7	Lincoln Theatre	58 West 135th Street
8	Loew's Victoria Theatre	233 West 125th Street
9	Loew's 116th Street Theatre	132 West 116th Street
10	Regent Theatre	912 7th Avenue
11	Keith and Proctor's 125th Street Theatre	112–118 East 125th Street
12	Harlem Opera House	211 West 125th Street
13	Alhambra Theatre	2110 7th Avenue
14	Loew's 7th Avenue Theatre	2081 7th Avenue
15	Odeon Theatre	256 West 145th Street
16	Franklin Theatre	440 Lenox Avenue
17	Hurtig-Seamon Theatre (eventually the Apollo)	253 West 125th Street
18	Regun Theatre	60 West 116th Street
19	Jewel Theatre	11 West 116th Street
20	Orient Theatre	111 West 125th Street
●	Churches	
1	St. Mark's ME Church	49 Edgecombe Avenue
2	Abyssinian Baptist Church	136–142 West 138th Street
3	St. Philip's PE Church	210–216 West 134th Street
4	Mt. Olivet Baptist Church	201 Lenox Avenue
■	Other Locations	
1	YMCA	181 West 135th Street
2	*New York Amsterdam News* office	2293 7th Avenue
3	*New York Age* office	230 West 135th Street
4	Oscar Micheaux's office	In the Franklin Theatre: 440 Lenox Avenue
5	Harlem River Park and Casino	2nd Avenue, between 126th and 127th Streets
6	Liberty Hall	120 West 138th Street

Urban League.[94] For a bit, the Lafayette's basement, known as Lafayette Hall, was used as a "temporary armory to Harlem's Negro National Guard unit" while also serving as a lecture venue for the likes of New Negro radicals like Marcus Garvey and Hubert Harrison.[95] One practice, a weekly Elks night at the theater, continued even after Walton left. Under the new owner-ship and management of Leo Brecher and Frank Schiffman, respectively, the

Lafayette continued to serve as the destination for Elks near and far, who came to "the popular playhouse . . . filled to capacity with members of the order and friends."[96]

By the 1920s, after changing hands a dozen times, switching often between Black and white management, the Lafayette's reputation in terms of its offerings tilted in the opposite direction. In 1924, Romeo Dougherty, the tough-minded dramatic editor of the *Amsterdam News*, pushed the Lafayette's newest manager "to reach the better class of colored people" with drama, as opposed to mixed bills of musicals, comedies, and motion pictures.[97] Yet, as the Lafayette fell again "into less dignified hands," as Dougherty cheekily referred to Brecher and Schiffman after their takeover in 1925, movies and tantalizing revues remained the norm.[98] The theater's regular audience was certainly not drawn from the supposedly better classes, as the weekly midnight show lured "sweetback[s] blocking the entrance en masse to show off their fine clothing"; people willing to shout names and whistle into the darkness in search of friends; patrons negotiating with hawkers selling candy, ice cream, and peanuts; and audience members catcalling dancers and passing booze from seat to seat.[99] The class and racial tensions at the Lafayette are evidenced here as mixed-bill shows, containing revues and moving pictures, were associated with "certain classes of Harlem folk," and specifically with white management.[100] As Wallace Thurman, a Harlem Renaissance author, saw it, the Lafayette, in all of its shabby provocativeness, was "the Jew's gift of entertainment to Harlem."[101]

From the start, white ownership of Black cultural and entertainment spaces caused issues in Harlem, including segregation and the exoticization of Black performers. Film historian Jacqueline Stewart considers this dynamic "one of the structuring tensions of Black film culture," where "owners and patrons . . . maintain a fiction of shared financial and political investment in Black neighborhood film exhibition as a corrective to the indignities of urban life."[102] While this is undoubtedly true, white proprietors' (sometimes uneven) willingness to cater to Black patrons and their desires also meant that they exhibited some semblance of control.[103] For example, the Lafayette nearly went out of business until it changed its seating policy. In later years, journalists, motion picture operators, and ordinary Black New Yorkers alike had no qualms about expressing their indignation at white proprietors who they felt crossed the line into discrimination or insult. Resistance gave Black New Yorkers the ability to continue to assert their freedom in the city, and especially in Harlem, and to make important claims to space that included movie theaters.

The Renaissance Theatre

In November 1911, news spread that the Johnson Amusement Company, a corporation run by Black men (including Lester Walton as secretary), was planning to erect a theater on 138th Street. The enterprise, they promised, would answer the "crying demand for a large colored theatre in the colored residential district in Harlem."[104] The proposed theater, described as a "work of art" in advertising campaigns, would hold around 1,300 people, contain a balcony section and a number of box seats, and present vaudeville for between ten and thirty cents. Recognizing the importance of the local community, the proposed theater would also have "suitable space" for fraternal organizations to hold regular meetings and banquet events.

For months, the company placed advertisements in the *Age* calling for investors among the Black community. For ten dollars a share, interested parties could take part in this momentous construction in Harlem. Historian Shannon King has noted that "black leaders asserted that black entrepreneurialism and racial consumer loyalty were the fulcra of the black community."[105] The proposed theater was no different. When the Crescent Theatre was sold to white interests just a few months earlier, Walton had been livid. He considered the sale "another instance in which white people possessed more foresight than the colored citizens relative to a business proposition regarded strictly as a colored enterprise."[106] He attacked the Black business community in Harlem for their failure to see the potential in the Crescent, lacking "striking evidence that the Negro was beginning to appreciate his own worth in the commercial world."[107] The Johnson Amusement Company's proposal was an answer to his frustration.

Near and far, Black theatergoers recognized the importance of the enterprise as even donors from out of state sent financial contributions and name suggestions. A man from Winston-Salem, North Carolina, suggested the Tuskegeean Theatre, insisting that "it stands for all that is greatest and best in the Negro-American," while Mrs. S. E. Ringgold from Atlantic City made a case for calling the prospective theater the Hogan Theatre, after Ernest Hogan, "who did his very best to bring the colored man to the front of the stage."[108] Making connections between the theater, entertainment, and community, the Johnson Amusement Company decided to name the project the Walker-Hogan-Cole Theatre, given these performers' "important part in solving the so-called race problem."[109] But after just a year, Walton found himself the bearer of immense annoyance: "Work on the 138th street theatre has not progressed rapidly because the colored citizens have been slow in seeing that the enterprise offers a splendid business opportunity."[110] Unable to withstand the lack of investment, and after many more months of false assurances, the W-H-C Theatre never came to fruition.[111] Even in the face of failure, the importance of the venture should not be lost. Located in the heart of a still-growing Black community in Harlem, the theater proposed cultural and geographical control for Black New Yorkers.[112]

Out of the slow-burned ashes of the W-H-C Theatre came the Renaissance. Nearly a decade after the failure of the Johnson Amusement Corporation, William Roach of the Sarco Realty Company decided to embark on erecting "the first and only Theatre in the City of New York built by Colored capital . . . owned and managed by Colored people."[113] The Renaissance opened in 1921 on Seventh Avenue and 137th Street to immense fanfare. The theater's initial and unchanging policy was to "furnish the best pictures at popular prices."[114] Considered the "cream of Harlem motion picture houses," the Renaissance contained 950 seats, a Wurlitzer organ, and small orchestra to accompany all films, which "attract[ed] the more select movie audiences."[115] In stark contrast to the nearby Franklin, Odeon, Roosevelt, and New Douglas Theatres, all of which showed movies as well, the Renaissance touted its ability to "meet the requirements of the refined and cultured in a standard of excellency."[116] So popular and refined was the Renaissance that it became an attraction for high-society visitors to stop by alongside trips to the Metropolitan Museum of Art and the Harlem Branch of the YWCA.[117] The Renaissance maintained this reputation well into the 1930s, when it was still regarded as "a real family theatre, with an atmosphere surpassed by none and superior to the majority in the community."[118]

The necessity of a community space was inherent in Roach's original commitment to audiences to "appeal to your sense of racial pride."[119] He purchased not only the lot to build the Renaissance but all the lots surrounding it on Seventh Avenue between 137th and 138th Streets. He thus was able to build not just the "modern, beautiful, and spacious moving picture house" but also storefronts for a number of Black businesses, including the popular Renaissance Casino, where Harlem's basketball team, the Renaissance Five, regularly drew crowds, and a large meeting space for lodge and fraternal organizations.[120] Like its predecessors, the Renaissance hosted community events and benefit performances. Beyond just offering the space for events like the Urban League's illustrated lecture series on social hygiene, the theater regularly hosted organizations that raised money for needy kids, such as the Utopia Neighborhood Association and the Child's Welfare League, the Madame Walker Agents Association, and even the fund for the Manassas School in Virginia. The theater also entertained groups of children for special screenings, such as one of *Peter Pan* (1924) given to one thousand children for free during a benefit event. The show was considered incredibly successful, "judging from the pleased yells of the happy children."[121]

The Renaissance's offerings also included important moments of reflexivity and resistance for Harlem's Black audiences. Even a few years after the war ended, scenes of the celebrated 15th/369th Regiment still made the news.[122] In 1922, the Renaissance screened footage of the group escorting Marshal Ferdinand Foch, a well-known French military leader, to his ship in the city. Similarly, the Renaissance also screened motion pictures of the more than two thousand participants and audience members at the annual Utopia Fashion show in 1923. In addition to the fashion show, which included dresses ranging from children's frocks to evening gowns, there were dances and choral performances showing off local debutantes and musicians. That the Renaissance, the first and only Black-owned theater in Harlem during its operational tenure, decided to film and then screen this event reveals its place in the community both socially and politically. As an institution, the theater exemplified race pride, but its offerings also occasionally provided moments of resistance to racism and stereotypes by highlighting the diversity, skill, and frivolity of Black New Yorkers.

The Renaissance proudly boasted its success as a Black-owned enterprise, and when, in 1923, Black nationalist Marcus Garvey tried to claim that it was Jewish owned, Roach published a scathing response in the *Age*. Roach "demanded a retraction of these words, to be printed on the front of the *Negro World*," the organ of Garvey's United Negro Improvement Association, "failing which 'will necessitate other means of redress.'"[123] Given the severity with which Roach took Garvey's offense, it is clear that the Renaissance's reputation as Black owned was a large part of its worth. Where other Black-managed, yet never Black-owned, theaters in the neighborhood had failed, Roach established a profitable business that elicited and promoted pride among Harlem's Black community—something that had yet to be done in any one single theater in the neighborhood. Roach and his managers worked hard to maintain that pride through its offerings and technological advancements. As sound technology precariously made its way into the industry, the Renaissance, alongside the Lafayette, was one of the first theaters in Harlem to offer talkies. Cited as an "epoch in the history of the Renaissance Theatre," the inclusion of a Vitaphone and Movietone, a decidedly early investment in this new technology, also meant expensive renovations to flooring, electrical equipment, and drapery to create the "perfect sound" for audiences.[124]

The Renaissance was the only theater of its kind in New York City between the two World Wars, operating for over a decade before being bought out fully by white interests. When the Sarco Realty Company went out of business in 1925, Black lessees maintained control over the Renaissance Theatre. During the early Depression years, they expanded their welfare efforts to include donations of free turkeys and chickens and participation in drives to raise cash for local unemployment funds, continuing to meet the essential needs of the community in times of crisis. When the theater transferred to white ownership in 1932, the *Age* lamented that it was "a serious blow at the progress and integrity of Negro business."[125] A reporter for the *Amsterdam News* wrote that "the failure [of Black ownership of that theater] should occasion keen regret."[126] Yet, certainly in an attempt to preserve its legitimacy as a Black theater in Harlem, the Renaissance hired multiple Black managers, including the *Age*'s cultural critic Vere E. Johns, to run business. Until it closed at midcentury, the Renaissance worked hard to maintain its ties to Harlem's Black moviegoers through fundraisers and "modernization" efforts like a new neon sign that "juts out majestically over the sidewalk" and lobby displays handcrafted by artists.[127]

By at least 1907, Black New Yorkers were watching films in local churches and parks. A couple of years later, there were two theaters that proudly refused to segregate their customers in the heart of the growing Black population in Harlem. Throughout the 1910s, more theaters opened their doors to allow for Black moviegoing, though mostly in Harlem and with mixed bills. The 59th Street, Crescent, Lincoln, Lafayette, and Renaissance Theatres, operating in and beyond the confines of the nickelodeon period, help outline the ways that theaters worked to appeal to audience taste and sought popularity and success in the Black community. Managers and owners offered up their venues for private meetings and public church services, held country fairs and contests, secured the most popular Black talents, and screened Black military and industrial triumphs. Through food donations, relief funds, and labor opportunities, they also sought to address some of the community's essential needs.

Black New Yorkers were unquestionably a part of the city's movie audiences as they shaped the culture surrounding the industry. White ownership of theater spaces sometimes complicated these efforts, particularly by the late 1920s when Leo Brecher and Frank Schiffman held a monopoly over Harlem's theaters, owning at least the Lafayette, Odeon, Roosevelt, New Douglas, and eventually Apollo Theatres.[128] Still, Black New Yorkers held firm that they had some say in what happened in them, "bolster[ing] blacks' feeling of freedom, and reinforc[ing] the idea that Harlem" and undoubtedly the film culture that blossomed within it "belonged to black people."[129]

This chapter forefronts the coming case studies of Black New Yorkers' use of these spaces to meet friends, strangers, and lovers in search of amusement, distraction, and relief; to watch the latest race film and all its intended messaging; to fight for the recognition of their labor; and to confront the city's widespread discrimination in theaters head-on. Though, as Carla Peterson notes, "the claiming of space is always a process, and the meaning of space unstable, contested, and in constant need of negotiation," the following chapters explore this uneven yet unrelenting endeavor.[130] Movie theaters throughout New York City acted as battlegrounds for acknowledgment and against discrimination, as escapes from drudgery and abuse, as the basis for careers, and, of course, as a chance to engage with a modern mass medium.

2

Fear and Fun at the Movies

Black Girls' Moviegoing and the Multiple
Lives of Movie Theaters

Yearning for its opportunities, Dora Ross probably heard about "the most popular and interesting section of contemporary New York" from her sister who had already gone north.[1] In 1924, after years of working as a laundress and despite her mother's protestations, Dora ran away from Lynchburg, Virginia, to Harlem, the "great black city."[2] While she may have been briefly disoriented by the "stream of dark people going to churches, theaters, restaurants, billiard halls, business offices, food markets, barber shops, and apartment houses" all along the main thoroughfares of Seventh and Lenox Avenues, Dora quickly adapted to the neighborhood's bustling leisure culture.[3] In Harlem for just three weeks, she was regularly attending movies and dances and, every "once in a while," going on picnics with dates.[4]

Shortly after her arrival, though, Dora and her sister "had words," and she left to lodge at another apartment on Edgecombe Avenue. Just a few days later, Dora was arrested for prostitution during a house raid. The twenty-year-old asserted that, while watching a movie at the Odeon Theatre on 145th Street, just blocks from her new lodgings, she met a woman and agreed to go home with her. Dora's case file from the Bedford Hills Reformatory, where she was sent after her arrest, notes that she claimed to be going to get her hair

---

A previous version of this chapter originally appeared as Alyssa Lopez, "The Dangers and Pleasures of Moviegoing: Black Girls in Harlem's Movie Theaters before World War II," *The Journal of African American History* 107.3 (Summer 2022): 370–396. Copyright © 2022 AS-ALH. All rights reserved. Published by The University of Chicago Press for the Association for the Study of African American Life and History. https://doi.org/10.1086/719962.

Figure 2.1 Odeon Theatre, where Dora Ross met a woman and followed her home. *(Courtesy Municipal Archives, City of New York)*

done "at a place where they do that and I don't know what else." It is quite possible that Dora followed the woman home for her hair, or perhaps she was procured at the Odeon and then lied to the interviewer at Bedford Hills Reformatory to speed up parole, which she was certainly "anxious" for.[5] Regardless of the scenario, the young girl's troubles began when she entered the movie theater that day.

Dora's story is illustrative of the ways that moviegoing was often intimately tied to how young Black girls and women navigated New York City's urban landscape. Dora was a migrant who supposedly fell victim to the perceived social ills inherent in popular leisure options in the city. Her experience at a Harlem movie theater beyond watching the film caused her run-in with the law and resulted in her institutional confinement. Further, her insistence on being independent from family by running away from both Virginia and her sister's apartment suggests the imaginative power of Harlem in young girls' minds as a symbol and means of freedom and unconstrained living.

Dora's experiences foreground the two main concerns of this chapter. First, how did movie theaters fit within the social landscape of Harlem? Research studies like the Payne Foundation–funded *Our Movie Made Children* often argued that the medium, by "affecting in various degrees their sleep, their conducts, and in a variety of ways, even their morals," had negative effects on children.[6] But the movies wielded a dual potential of danger onscreen and within the theater itself. Film historian Gary Rhodes posits that "perceived moral risks confronted audiences too, and not merely from questionable film content." "Physical risks," he continues, "abounded during the first 50 years of film exhibition."[7] This chapter, then, is mostly concerned with the physical aspects of Black film culture, which include actual theater spaces and the various actions individuals took in those theaters that blurred the line between private and public. Like rent parties and residential-based leisure during the 1920s, movie theaters offered, if only tangentially, "a measure of privacy from the gaze of whites, respectable blacks, and authorities."[8] Harlemites utilized movie theaters to engage in activities wholesome and harmful in an effort to escape an overcrowded tenement, to experience release after long hours of menial labor, or to make money in the underground economy, outside the confines of low-wage, discriminatory work. In embracing the physical elements of Black film culture—namely, claiming and then reinterpreting theaters through moviegoing—Black New Yorkers were engaging in a rereading of public urban space that allowed for economic freedom or personal delight.

But this potentially liberatory experience provided the very fodder for some within the Black community, especially parents, guardians, and reformers, to tie theaters and moviegoing to promiscuity, criminality, and incorrigibility and to enact restraints against their children and charges. The second focus of this chapter is young Black girls' and women's moviegoing experiences. The vast majority of the girls considered here, like Dora, were working-class migrants from the South. Thought to be especially susceptible to the dangers of the city, they and their behavior were "characterized as sexually degenerate and, therefore, socially dangerous."[9] The policing of Black girls and women in urban areas was not restricted to migrants. In fact, all Black girls and women lived life in a "double bind," forced to experience the inhumanities of Jim Crow's racialized violence while also expected to remain pure and respectable.[10] Locating, at least in some part, how Black girls and women experienced and navigated these tensions necessitates an expansion of the source material used in previous studies on Black moviegoing.

This chapter uses the archives of two New York–based carceral and reform institutions: Bedford Hills Reformatory (Bedford Hills), opened in 1901, and the Women's Prison Association (WPA), organized in the late nineteenth century. The turn to prison and institutional records does not necessarily reflect the girls' inherent deviancy as much as it reveals how their lives were closely monitored by family members, friends, and New York City's various penal measures.[11] Though not always engaged in the extracurriculars occurring in theaters, Black girls and young women's willingness to participate in public amusements was often perceived as criminal or immoral. In response to these constraints, some girls and women chose to emphasize personal freedom and independence in the face of those who condemned their moviegoing preferences.[12] They defied their parents' demands to stay home rather than go to the movies, exchanged sex for dates at the theater, and used the medium as an escape from the deeply traumatic realities of urban life.

This chapter starts by shedding light on the darkened interior of Harlem's theaters, tracing the presence of activities beyond movie watching, such as murder, theft, prostitution, and casual sex. Once the stage is set for a better understanding of the power of Black girls' and women's interactions with public and urban space, the latter half of the chapter moves into the specifics of their moviegoing practices: how often they went and with whom, what the movies meant for them, and how moviegoing fit within their lives as young urbanites. Through their stories, the intimate, liberatory, and potentially transgressive nature of Black film culture becomes exceedingly clear.

Harlem's Theaters: Dangers and Pleasures Within

Much like other movie theaters throughout America, Harlem's theaters offered patrons more than moving images on a screen.[13] But while the physical dangers and pleasures lurking in movie theaters were not necessarily unique to the neighborhood or even the front pages of the city's Black press, the drama that unfolded in them often matched the onscreen entertainment in both threats and thrills.[14] For example, one evening in October 1927, Joseph Masiah's pursuit of a better seat at the Lafayette turned violent. Masiah, whose ticket did not match the seat he wanted to take, claimed that an usher had struck him. When another usher got involved, supposedly to intervene, the fight got out of hand. Because "the balcony was crowded . . . a near panic ensued."[15] Masiah was sent to Harlem Hospital with a fractured jaw and a potentially fractured skull.

In 1933, another fight in the balcony resulted in a stampede of patrons from the Harlem Opera House. Two men got into a physical altercation over a seat, and, when someone screamed, "Fire!" the result was a rush for the exits. In the panic of nearly 1,600 people running toward the door, "women [were] trampled as they reached for lost shoes and pocketbooks," and "some one tossed a 4-year-old boy up . . . on the stage."[16] After it all, twenty-four people were treated by ambulances for minor injuries. A year later, a similar incident occurred when eight hundred theatergoers stampeded for the exit at the Renaissance after two men got into a fight in the gallery and someone yelled, "Fire!" Calling the event a "small riot," the *Amsterdam News* reported that a few people were trampled during the rush, including two young girls.[17]

On some occasions, moviegoers found themselves witness to some "true-to-life murder drama[s]" in Harlem's motion picture houses.[18] In these cases, the dark and crowded nature of theaters provided culprits with a sense of anonymity. Their violent acts often went unnoticed or obscured, leaving audiences and police officers questioning the true events of the scene. For example, "while theatregoers surged through the doors of the Lafayette" after a show one Saturday evening, they "were suddenly horrified to see [Taft] Rice staggering away from the arms of a 'mystery man,' who immediately lost himself in the crowd and escaped."[19] The famed vaudeville actor, who had been stabbed in the chest, stumbled to a nearby corner store before collapsing on the floor. Rice was pronounced dead at Harlem Hospital with his murderer still at large. The performer, who at one point traveled with Ralph Cooper's revue and brought thousands across the country delight through his "novel dance steps," or "hoofing," as one Black cultural critic called it, took his final steps at a theater in Harlem, the very neighborhood in which he had debuted just a few years earlier.[20]

Movie houses also made ideal locations for petty theft. As with murders, darkened theaters made it possible for small items, such as coats or purses, to be snatched from absorbed spectators. But movie theaters' receipts also made them likely targets. As one of the most popular amusements throughout the country, theaters made large sums of sometimes-irresistible money. In 1925, the Lafayette's ticket taker, clearly familiar with the theater's transactions, formed a crime racket around ticket sales. Instead of tearing the tickets in two and placing one half into a stub box as he was supposed to, William Scott kept the ticket intact. When he had amassed enough, he called some friends and sold the tickets throughout Harlem for reduced prices. Scott kept this scheme up for over a year before being caught by Frank Schiffman, the Lafayette's manager.[21]

Arguably, Scott was engaging in his own form of what Robin D. G. Kelley terms "infrapolitics," or the use of small, seemingly inconsequential acts of resistance to rebalance power inequities. He found a way to make more money off a white-owned business in Harlem while also providing a cheaper means for Harlemites interested in the latest tantalizing revue or well-reviewed movie to participate in the neighborhood's consumer culture.[22] This scheme, while undoubtedly a way for Scott and his friends to make money, can also be read as Scott's attempt to provide more accessible entertainment for Harlemites. Though the management tried to keep the prices purposefully low—tickets did not exceed more than fifty cents—many working-class

Harlemites may have found that out of their reach. In comparison, the *Age* sold their weekly paper at five cents, a loaf of bread cost ten cents, and rent parties, which included not only entertainment but alcohol and food, could be attended for between twenty-five and fifty cents.[23]

In February 1926, just months before Scott's scheme was exposed, the shooting of a Black lay officer made front-page news in the *Age*. Albert Cantor, a twenty-two-year-old who worked as a security guard at the Roosevelt Theatre on 145th Street, was in the middle of a chase when a police officer, unaware of Cantor's reserve status with the West 135th Street Police Station, shot him. The confusion began when "two women patrons screamed that a man was trying to steal their coats," pointing at a man exiting the theater.[24] Cantor pursued the supposed culprit, running down Seventh Avenue and shooting him in front of plainclothes officers. Before Cantor could show them his badge, William Dudley, a white officer, shot him three times. Cantor's position at the Roosevelt demonstrates that some managers felt compelled to maintain order in their movie theaters through the presence of armed security. The resultant police brutality incident, in which Cantor was mistaken for a criminal, also reveals the ways that movie theater happenings could easily spill out onto nearby streets, exacerbating already tense race relations in the neighborhood.

It was the presence of supposed "mashers," or men who conspicuously flirted, and sexual assailants, however, that made theaters particularly dangerous, especially for young girls and women.[25] In 1925, Captain Mulrooney of the Sixteenth Police Precinct warned Harlemites to be on the lookout for "mashers who spend much of their time on Harlem street corners or in front of public places openly insulting young girls and women." The *Age* warned that the men's "conduct has showed them absolutely devoid of respect for members of the gentler race." The paper pointed to the Renaissance and Lafayette Theatres as these mashers' "favorite hangout," where the offenders waited for female passersby to call out to or "insult."[26] Inside movie theaters, though, is where the threat of sexual assault lingered strongest.

For example, a 1926 *Amsterdam News* front-page article titled "Juvenile Vice Rampant" warned of the dangers of movie theaters for young girls. It recounted the story of a young girl of only thirteen or fourteen who had run away from home. She struggled to find shelter until a ticket taker at the Franklin Theatre took pity on her and rented her a room. After a few weeks, he failed to pay her rent, and "she went to another theatre and made advances to one of the attendants." Instead of helping her, he locked her in a changing room all night. The article provides no more detail than this, but the fact that "certificates from physicians were produced as evidence of the [girl's] serious condition" hints that the man may have sexually assaulted her.[27]

Though the article's anonymous author pointed to the culprit's arrest, the tone reads as condescending and accusatory. The title alone is enough to suggest that the author believed the girl was to blame for her assault. Moreover, the article's opening line reads, "Bad daughters and careless mothers suffered a great embarrassment Monday when they appeared" in court.[28] Instead of centering the assailant's crimes, the author directly tied the girl's assault to the fact that she had run away and attempted to find solace at the movies and with multiple theater employees. Stories like these, which hinged on the policing of Black women's bodies as central to the racial uplift project, were meant to serve as "cautionary tales" of what young Black girls should not do with their newfound urban freedom.[29] Their purpose was to warn readers, girls and their family members alike, of the possible dangers involved in moving through and acting freely within the city's various amusement opportunities, while publicly shaming those who transgressed respectable boundaries.[30]

Another admonition in the *Age* against working mothers and young girls just a few days later led to a partnership between New York's board of education (BOE) and the Roosevelt, New Douglas, and Odeon Theatres. The editorial pointed out that young girls lacking supervision while their mothers work "constitute quite a problem in Harlem." The author suggested that the BOE needed to do "real preventative work in safeguarding girlhood from the evils incident to roaming the streets, or going alone to a solitary apartment," by offering some after-school programming and discounted meals.[31] By the following week, the North Harlem Community Council had coordinated with the BOE and the local theaters to test out this possibility, starting first with school hours before moving into after-school. Every Friday, six hundred children were offered a discounted ticket to a showing of an industrial film, a comedy, or episodes of *The Chronicles of America* (all provided by the BOE) at one of the theaters, while half of the ticket proceeds were donated back to the school for the children's hot lunches. Importantly, the teachers also functioned as chaperones at the theater. This interesting experiment is an example of the ways theaters attempted to reject being labeled as inherently bad or dangerous and present the potential to serve as a moral good for the community.

But not all extracurricular events at movie theaters were violent or perilous. Some patrons engaged in activities other than movie watching for pleasure and fun. In addition to the thrills of winning high earnings on low bets in those theaters that promoted underground gambling, Black New Yorkers, including sex workers and would-be lovers, used movie houses to find potential sexual exploits.[32] In his 1931 memoir about life as a Manhattan detective, Cornelius Willemse explained that the Tenderloin district, a neighborhood that stretched between Sixth and Seventh Avenues from Twenty-Third to

Forty-Eighth Street and encompassed much of the city's early twentieth-century vice district, was "the happy hunting ground for unnumbered prostitutes."[33] As he witnessed it, many prostitutes, including Black women who acted as badgers posing as prostitutes to rob victims, "haunted the hotels, theatre lobbies, the restaurants, and the sidewalks" in attempts to pick up unsuspecting men.[34] Historian LaShawn Harris notes that "many freelance sex workers preferred indoor prostitution" in places like movie theaters because streetwalking prompted "fear of violence and even death."[35] "As an alternative geographical space for urban prostitution," theaters provided sex workers with a semiprivate and relatively safe space to ply their trade.[36]

Wallace Thurman, a novelist during the Harlem Renaissance, wrote extensively on the place of movie theaters in Harlem's sexual landscape. In his short story for the 1926 publication *Fire!!*, a literary magazine meant to "burn up a lot of the old, dead conventional Negro-white ideas of the past," Thurman narrates sixteen-year-old Cordelia's patronage of the Roosevelt Theatre on 145th Street (the theater that Albert Cantor stood armed watch over the very same year).[37] "It is the custom," Thurman writes, "of certain men and boys who frequent these places to idle up and down the aisle until some female is seen sitting alone, to slouch down into a seat beside her, to touch her foot or else press her leg . . . until, if successful, the approached female will soon be chatting with her baiter . . . helping to formulate plans for an after-theatre rendezvous." Cordelia willingly took part in "this hectic, entrancing game," being particular about the type of man she chose to fool around with. "Cordelia had not consciously chosen this locale," Thurman explains, "nor had there been any conscious effort upon her to part to take advantage of the extra opportunities afforded for physical pleasure."[38] The Roosevelt was simply the closest theater to her home, the program changed three times a week, and she remained open to the advances of the men around her.

Though Thurman describes Cordelia as "physically, if not mentally . . . a potential prostitute," the ending of the short story reveals that she was not engaged in sex work until an unwitting, nervous man shoved two dollars in her hand on the staircase leading to her apartment after a show. Instead, the rebellious young Cordelia, who refused to go to school or work, utilized "her favorite cinema shrine" for personal pleasure without, initially, the promise of money. Cordelia, whose "days belonged to the folks at home while the night . . . belonged to her," patronized the Roosevelt not only for its frequent rotation of film offerings but because she was able to explore her sexuality and experience pleasure on her own terms. Her life, as Thurman describes it, was circumscribed by her daily surroundings—namely, her responsibility to her migrant family in helping ensure that her siblings ate and made it to and from school. In attending the movies, she exercised a degree of autonomy, especially in spending her time there with "whoever will—let them come."[39]

Thurman once again explored Harlem's movie houses as sites for sexual liaisons in his 1929 novel, *Blacker the Berry: A Novel of Negro Life*. Emma Lou, the novel's female protagonist, finds herself in a Harlem theater out of boredom one evening, only to be approached by a young man. While watching a short that followed the feature, Emma Lou was surprised by "pressure on one of her legs, the warm fleshy pressure of another leg." She looked beside her to see a gentleman with "an impudent boyish smile [who] pressed her leg all the harder."[40] Initially torn over the advance, Emma Lou first "wished that the theater wasn't so dark" but quickly understood the necessity, observing that "if it hadn't been so dark this couldn't have happened."[41] Similar to the men courting Cordelia at the Roosevelt Theatre, Emma Lou's romancer used the dim light to his advantage, occupying an empty seat next to a young woman to test if she would be wise to his advances. She proved willing to play along, as the pair moved closer to each other in their seats, holding hands, brushing shoulders, all the while talking through the second showing of the feature film. When they finally decided to leave the theater, Emma Lou paid her date three dollars for the nearby furnished apartment that they went to together. Impressing the primacy of movie theaters as potential locations to pick up lovers, Thurman describes Emma Lou's subsequent visits to the same theater as a rotation of various men trying to pick her up.

Despite their liberatory potential, all these alternative activities—the illicit and undercover love affairs, the possibility of unwanted sexual advances, or the chance that one might be robbed or murdered—provided fuel for reformers' and community members' fears about the influence of movie theaters. This is especially clear in conversations about the darkness of movie theaters in the industry trade press. In 1910, at the height of the nickelodeon period, *Film Index* declared that "the dark picture theatre must go." James McQuade, a representative of the Chicago office of the paper, condemned the "baneful influences" that were drawn to the security of dark movie houses. Advocating for the use of a special screen that supported a lit theater, the article explained that with the new screen, "those who prey upon youth will find it impossible to carry out their vile designs in an auditorium where the safe and blessed light reached every bench and every corner of the room."[42] Only those patrons "who had been in the habit of going to these places, not to see the pictures, but to be unseen," such as Cordelia, Emma Lou, and their various lovers, would have a problem with the lights.[43]

By 1915, the undercover possibilities available to patrons of darkened auditoriums became so well known that *Pictures and Picturegoers*, a fan magazine, offered a joke about it in the Smiles section. In the joke, a woman sits down in a darkened theater, making a comment to her friend about how soft the seats are. A "faint masculine voice" responds from beneath her, saying, "If you're satisfied, madam, you're welcome to my lap," so long as she shifts so he can see the movie.[44] The cheeky exchange suggests a normalization of supposedly illicit sexual behavior in public spaces when it occurred in the dark, though it would not be condoned by more respectable standards elsewhere.

Fears, especially those held by middle-class reformers, of what occurred in theaters were also tied to concerns about Black southern migrants moving to the city. Victoria Earle Matthews, whose lifework was dedicated to ensuring the safety and propriety of young Black migrant women, considered most of her charges "ignorant," especially regarding the reality of life in the big city. Worried over their supposedly inevitable descent into vice and an immoral life, Matthews warned an audience at Hampton Institute to "let them stay home, it is better to starve and go home to God morally clean, than to helplessly drag out miserable lives of remorse and pain in Northern tenderloins."[45] Her contemporary Paul Laurence Dunbar, who wrote about the plight of Black migrants to New York City, called his subjects "vermin," lamenting their "search for pleasure, [which] they think they have found . . . when they indulge in vice." Clearly critical of migrants' choice to leave the South in search of a semblance of freedom, Dunbar explains, "They say that they have not their rights at the south; but better the restrictions there than a seeming liberty which blossoms noxiously into license."[46] Matthews and Dunbar connected migrants' trek to the North as a simple search for pleasure, leading them to link migrants' exploration of public amusements, including the movies, to moral ruin.[47]

In a series of articles on Black criminality, white reformer and sociologist Frances Kellor took this analysis a step further, arguing that "the social life of the negro lacks direction, restraint, and healthy interests." Time spent outside of work, including church attendance, she asserted, "consumes too much time with trifles, and increases the opportunities for committing crime." Focusing on Black girls and women, Kellor concluded that "judged by civilized standards, [they] are to a large extent immoral."[48] Eliding the institutionalized racism that subjected white women to a much more lenient and forgiving justice system than Black women, Kellor insisted that Black women and girls were environmentally prone to criminal and immoral activity, particularly in their search for pleasurable amusements.

Black reformers like Matthews may have disagreed with the idea of an inherent criminality, but they still maintained that Black girls' and women's interactions with commercial amusements would eventually result in a devolution into immorality. Edna Hunter, another Black reformer and the founder of the Phillis Wheatley Association, who engaged in work similar to Matthews's, believed the same. She considered young Black women who migrated from the South "helpless against temptation and degradation."[49] Reformers' concerns over young migrants can be read as an insistence that these girls and women did not actually belong in the city, often because of the dangers of city living, which included the ready availability of cheap amusements.

The crux of the issue was that young filmgoers, especially Black migrant girls and women, were believed to be the most susceptible to dangers and temptations at movie theaters.[50] Reform and vice agencies regularly canvassed these spaces, looking for children or immoral behavior, such as premarital sexual relations or prostitution, and some parents kept their children from attending at all. For example, when sixteen-year-old Naomi Washington, the sister of famed musician Fats Waller, went to the movies, she "was punished [and] couldn't go out for days." "The first time my parents learned I had gone to the Lafayette," she recalls, "you'd have thought I had gone to a house of disrepute."[51] As historian Cheryl Hicks explains, parents and "reformers were at odds with young working-class women who embraced personal independence and morally questionable coed public amusements and private entertainments."[52]

Family members' efforts to keep their kin away from theaters were informed by the very real dangers associated with them but also by the perceived immorality of young Black women trying to enjoy urban living on their own terms.[53] Various girls' statements to Bedford Hills Reformatory and WPA workers show the ways that Black families, in their desire to keep their daughters safe and ostensibly pure, attempted to mitigate the supposed harmful nature of cheap amusements. Some girls described themselves as "brought up strict" because they were always under the watchful eye of their parents or families.[54] For example, Jane Simmons, Mary Gibson, Joan Wilson, and Minnie George could go to the movies only under the supervision of a parent or sibling.[55] Jessie Smith, who was raised in a "quiet Christian house," was not allowed to attend the movies at all.[56]

It was common for families and reformers to tie the moral dangers of moviegoing to other popular leisure activities. The contemporary sociologist William Jones believed all "cheap cabarets and movie shows, unsupervised dance halls, and rowdy pool rooms" to be "notorious breeders of crime."[57] Similarly, most parents who restricted motion picture attendance or required supervision also did not allow their daughters, sisters, and nieces to go to public dances or even play cards. One family directly equated a sixteen-year-old's moviegoing habits with other alleged misbehavior, as her foster mother lamented that "she has always been a hard child to manage, very mischievous and full of fun. Seems to have no steadiness. Is fond of music and moving pictures. Has been associating with bad company for some time."[58] Already linked in her mind, her mother proved unwilling to divorce the girl's love for moving pictures from her supposed mischievousness.

Girls and women responded to the restrictions on their autonomy in a number of ways, employing what historian Erin Chapman calls "divergent strategies of self-determination."[59] Some followed familial and community expectations for their behavior, staying away from darkened theaters at the behest of those around them. Others, as Saidiya Hartman has eloquently argued, were "unable to fashion the world in their own terms, [but] they could, at the very least, resist the world imposed."[60] These girls refused the limitations placed on their leisure time, rebelled against strict parents, and challenged judgmental reform agencies. They disregarded their parents' rules and, in an attempt to have control over their free time, went to the movies or ran away from home. Their conversations with caseworkers reveal a myriad of experiences at the movies, which include daily visits to theaters, "treating," and sex work, and the ways these and other practices were part of their negotiation of Harlem's urban landscape. Indeed, their interactions with and shaping of Black film culture in the city illuminate quite clearly the linkages between the movies and placemaking.

Black Girls, Moviegoing, and Navigating the City

During the movie craze of the early twentieth century, Black girls and women forged a variety of moviegoing habits. For some, going to the movies every day or nearly every day was the norm. One girl at Bedford Hills explained that she had no savings because she "spent all her money on clothes and movies," illuminating the importance of not just cheap amusements but consumer culture as a whole.[61] Louise Rogers admitted to a caseworker that "she has always gone to the Moving Picture Shows almost every night."[62] Further, both Louise and Margaret Sweet, a young migrant from DC, worked at movie theaters for brief periods of time, revealing just one of the liberatory uses these spaces held for Black girls and women. Most gainfully employed Black women (nearly 70 percent in 1920) toiled in domestic and laundress positions.[63] Louise's and Margaret's decisions to work in a theater indicates not just their desire to escape this type of work, which often came with grueling hours and the threat of sexual assault, but also the chance to actually get enjoyment out of their labor. For example, Margaret was able to work as an usher for ten dollars a week, a wage that was fairly comparable to what household work paid, all while she was able to sneak in some free entertainment. On the other hand, Louise's hopes of a less demanding position must have been dashed at the Empire Theatre, as she quit after just one week as a scrubwoman because it was "too hard."[64] Still, theaters offered, even if in a limited capacity, some bodily and personal autonomy for women like Louise and Margaret. They served as alternative employment opportunities with a hint of pleasure for some, while acting as just one stop in the larger effort to navigate the urban landscape for others.

The experiences of Rachel Cane and Caroline Wilson shed light on Louise's and Margaret's decisions to work in theaters as opposed to white people's homes. The overbearing employer of nineteen-year-old Rachel "never [left] her out of her sight" in an attempt to "help her keep interested in her work and away from bad companions."[65] The teenager's free time was restricted to when she acted as chaperone for her twin charges at movies specifically shown for children. Some girls, such as Caroline, a teenager working as a live-in domestic on the Upper West Side, chose to ignore their employers' rules on their free time. Eschewing the 5:00 P.M. curfew they had imposed on her, Caroline stayed out until almost 10:00 P.M. to see a movie with friends. Her act of independence was not without consequence. Caroline was fired from her job the next day. Similar to their counterparts in the South, northern employers attempted to restrict the bodily freedom of their Black employees, often on the premise that using their bodies for personal pleasure and leisure would take away their energy for effective work.[66]

Black girls' and women's moviegoing practices were an extension of how they negotiated the ins and outs of living in the city. Movie theaters—their physical space as well as their actual geographical locations—were part and parcel of the city's social landscape. Historian LaKisha Michelle Simmons's work on Black adolescent girls in Jim Crow New Orleans demonstrates that Black girls created "mental maps" that helped them navigate the segregated city and their shifting geographically based subjectivities. Black girls' experiences were read and mapped as a complex web of their racialized bodies in various spaces that were internalized and acted upon when out in public.[67] Though New York City's Black girls and women were not necessarily navigating the Jim Crow South, their experiences in the city, and especially in theaters, were shaped by the arm of Jim Crow North. In cities like New York, Black girls and women often came face-to-face with a "system of segregation and oppression through law and policy without explicit racial invocation" that depended on popular discourses of their perceived inherent inferiority.[68]

Rachel, for instance, bore the brunt of her white employers' racism in the form of bodily control; she could not spend her free time on her own terms because her employer feared that her productivity would be sacrificed. Even when discrimination was directly against the law, white New Yorkers in the first half of the twentieth century rarely found reason to radically alter the nature of race relations across the city. Indeed, Elizabeth Clanton, a young woman who moved to New York from Alabama, insisted that when she "came North, it was similar to the same thing, just a different style."[69]

Seating discrimination was a regular practice in the city's theaters despite a nineteenth-century law that forbade segregation. While she fondly reminisced about the Lafayette Theatre as a space for Black patrons farther uptown, Mabele Mitchell, a migrant from Jacksonville who arrived in Harlem in 1926, felt differently about theaters just ten or so blocks away. She recounted, "When we would go to 125th Street, we would go way up there in that balcony 'cause we couldn't sit downstairs, believe me!" Sitting in the balcony at places like the Loew's Victoria, she insisted, "was just a thing . . . you just had to do that." But Mabele also explained that "all of the stores—the five and ten and what not—they were all white then," positioning the entire area as a location where her race was on particular display, requiring her to move in certain ways in that part of the city.[70] While Harlem, which held two-thirds of the city's Black population in 1920, was undoubtedly a Black neighborhood, its boundaries remained somewhat contested until the 1930s. In 1920, the southern border of Harlem was 130th Street; in 1930, that border shifted to 110th Street.[71] Maneuvering the particularities of segregated moviegoing required Black girls to be aware of exactly where in the city a theater was located, shaping their ability to comfortably go to the movies.

In other ways, the geography of Harlem encouraged girls and women to internalize how their bodies may be in danger in certain areas. The Lafayette Theatre, for example, was right near Connie's Inn. The nightclub, which was blamed for "the unsavory conditions in the neighborhood," drew a troublesome crowd that not only stood in front of the theater doors making crude remarks at young girls and women but also caught innocent Harlemites in its cross fire.[72] In 1932, Mrs. Lulu Willis, the wife of a respected real estate agent, was murdered when two rival gangs got into a shoot-out in front of Connie's and shot recklessly "into the crowd coming out of the Lafayette Theatre and hurrying home from other places."[73] Further, the Lafayette and other theaters, including the Franklin, the Roosevelt, and the Douglas, were, according to a 1924 *Age* exposé, all within very close proximity to underground "hootch joints" responsible for "idlers and hangers on."[74] Nearby theaters were often viewed as complementary locations and "points at which intense socialization goes on." Some, uninterested in the films, chose to hang outside to draw in moviegoers with "unconventional forms of 'showing-off' and display."[75] Aware-

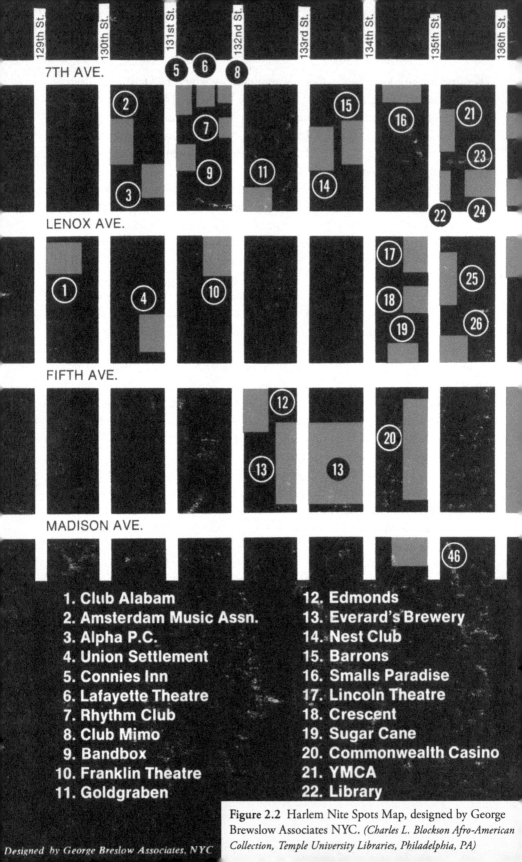

Figure 2.2 Harlem Nite Spots Map, designed by George Brewslow Associates NYC. *(Charles L. Blockson Afro-American Collection, Temple University Libraries, Philadelphia, PA)*

HARLEM NITE-SPOTS

CIRCA 1923-1930

23. Madam Walkers
24. Town House
25. Connors
26. LeRoys
27. Martin Smith Music School
28. Turf Club
29. Harlem Hospital
30. Olympic Field
31. Renaissance Theatre & Hall
32. Liberty Hall
33. Ideal Tennis Courts
34. St. Marks

35. Idlewhile
36. Bamboo Inn
37. World Chop Suey Rest.
38. 101 Ranch
39. Capitol Cabaret
40. Savoy
41. Cotton Club
42. Douglas Theatre
43. Happy Rhone or Lenox Club
44. Mike's Bar
45. Checker Club
46. Car Barn

ness of the dangers or lack thereof in the immediate area of any particular theater undoubtedly affected how girls and women chose when and which theaters to attend and, possibly, with whom.

In addition to keeping in mind the dangers that may take place in and around movie theaters, the mental maps of Black girls and women must have taken into account the reputations of certain theaters and areas in the city. Despite the earlier-mentioned report about hangers-on outside its doors, the Renaissance Theatre was considered the "cream of Harlem motion picture houses" because of its symphony, organ, and lack of vaudeville performances. The Franklin and Gem Theatres, on the other hand, were the "social outcasts" of Harlem movie houses.[76] In these latter theaters, audience members drank, smoked, and spoke over the run-down projection machines showing flickering films that were years out of date. Once familiarized with the typical atmosphere of various theaters, whether that included movie watching or not, Black girls and women could make informed choices about which ones to visit and when. Dora Ross, who was arrested after her visit to the Odeon Theatre, serves as an example of the potential risks inherent in navigating an unknown urban terrain and in utilizing movie theaters as an alternative means of pleasure.

Some girls, like Rachel Cane, found ways that may have helped to mediate any potential threats at or nearby movie theaters. Rachel, who bristled against her employers' restrictions, also resisted caseworkers' claims that she was "extremely childish concerning her expenditures" because she held no qualms about paying for tickets and snacks for her friends at the theater. On one occasion, though she had the money for herself to go, Rachel "cried and begged the worker to give [her] another dollar so she could take another girl to the movies and buy extras."[77] Another girl, Hazel Brown, was described by WPA caseworkers as only friendly "when she wanted company to go to the movies," which was rather often.[78] Rachel's and Hazel's insistence on having friends or acquaintances join them at the movies can be read as an act of protection. Traveling and sitting together in the theater space may have provided a modicum of safety and even propriety. Further, and within the context of their time at the WPA-run Hopper Home, their friendships could have easily served as a form of stability in a personal moment fraught with uncertainty. Girls at the Hopper Home were generally referred there after they had spent time institutionalized and while they awaited employment, usually as live-in domestics in white households. With this in mind, the young girls' efforts to maintain consistent friendships and partake in moviegoing together reflect the connections between Black film culture and community, allow-

Figure 2.3 "Harlem," John Vachon (1914–75) for *Look* magazine. *(Museum of the City of New York. X2011.4.11813.465)*

ing them to bond with girls in similar situations, perhaps "shar[ing] their joys, concerns, gossip, and heartbreak" over a movie.[79]

The experiences of Black girls and women taken at an aggregate level reveal much about the ways the moviegoing aspect of Black film culture played into their navigation of the city's landscape. Case studies, however, help illuminate the particularities of these moments in deeply intimate ways. The remainder of this chapter uses the experiences of Georgia Wright, Charlotte Parker, and Margaret Sweet to illustrate how moviegoing provided Black girls and women with a means for pleasure and excitement, personal autonomy, and escape from the sometimes brutal reality of city living.

Georgia Wright: Movies as Distraction

Georgia Wright was just fifteen years old when she was arraigned in New York City's Children's Court. On the day after Christmas 1933, her foster father Jeremy petitioned the court on the charge that Georgia "stayed out late at night."[80] In the days leading up to Christmas, Georgia had left home early in the afternoon and had not returned until 1:00 or 2:00 A.M. She was placed on probation for a year, but by April 1934, she was back in court for violation of parole, again for staying out late. At this point, her foster parents were willing to have her committed, but the judge placed her on parole again. Georgia lasted another five months before she ran away from home on September 10. She did not reappear until December 11, 1934, when she went to a police station "to report everything," specifically an "unnatural relationship" with her foster father. Though she "fully expected to get five years in jail" for running away, Georgia disclosed the fact that Jeremy had raped her.[81]

Despite what Darlene Clark Hine terms the "culture of dissemblance," in which Black women engaged in a "cult of secrecy" so as "to protect the sanctity of inner aspects of their lives," Georgia chose to report her foster father to the authorities. Her account of her abuse to WPA workers followed a long tradition of Black women "reclaim[ing] their bodies and humanity by testifying about their assaults."[82] As Georgia described it, one Sunday afternoon, while her foster mother Pauline was at church, Jeremy "tried to have sexual relations" with her. When she told Pauline what had happened, her foster mother "was furious and said that if her husband ever did it again she would 'knock his brains out.'"[83] Yet, after this first offense, Pauline chose to ignore her husband's abuse, claiming that Georgia's stories were "ideas that had been put into her head by bad companions."[84] Jeremy continued these advances on multiple occasions, sometimes getting into bed with Georgia or watching her bathe and dress.

Georgia's case file discloses that her family considered her arrests and the assault an embarrassing situation that required denial. In addition to Pauline, who assured the caseworker that she refused to let Georgia "brand her family," Georgia's aunt and current guardian felt her legal troubles "a disgrace to the family."[85] Furthermore, Georgia informed caseworkers that her sister was the only one who believed her regarding the assault, yet she refused to go on record "because of her love for her aunt," Jeremy's sister.[86] As with Black girls and women who came before and after her to publicly offer testimonials of sexual violence, from Harriet Jacobs and her *Incidents in the Life of a Slave Girl* in 1861 to Joan Little and her 1974 trial after she murdered her sexual assailant, Georgia's willingness to testify against her foster father suggests remarkable courage in the face of disbelief and secrecy.[87]

When asked how long she had trouble with her foster daughter, Pauline responded that "she had always been bad as far as she can remember . . . but that she became very 'bad' about two years ago," which aligned with Georgia's first appearance in Children's Court.[88] Georgia seemingly began to act out after her abuse. According to her, "her motive in staying out late at night was to get as much of the pleasure she had been deprived of as possible and to get away from" her foster father. She explained that at this point, "she 'went movie-crazy'" and sometimes came home so late that "she was afraid to knock on the door and would sleep on the roof or in the hall-way."[89] Georgia used the movies as an escape from a horrible living situation, in which she had no privacy and was subject to repeated sexual assault and abuse. Instead of remaining at home, risking the chance to become a victim of her foster father's advances, she sought distraction and pleasure at the movies. In doing so, she also resisted her foster mother's desire to treat her as "practically a prisoner."[90]

For Georgia, the physical and imaginative space of movie theaters, what reformer Jane Addams called "a veritable house of dreams," provided her with the safety and enjoyment the teenager so desperately sought after her abuse.[91] Historian LaKisha Michelle Simmons convincingly argues that "to consider black girls as full human beings, we need to understand their pleasures just as much as their pains."[92] To that end, movies should be viewed as one way, albeit a complicated one, that Georgia sought to take back her girlhood. Film scholar Jacqueline Stewart has asserted that Black spectatorship should be understood as a reconstructive experience that is always "oscillating between subversion and immersion" given "cinema's racist social and textual operations."[93] Operating as "a simultaneously liberating and constricting place," movie houses, if only for a few hours, took Georgia away from Jeremy into the fantastical shelter of love stories with their dreamy heroes or of westerns paired with riveting drama, giving her the space to forget her troubling home life.[94]

But her foster mother failed to understand Georgia's obsession with the movies. She strictly forbade her from going and believed that the girl's mind was "perverted by the movies."[95] On some occasions, she attended the theater with Georgia but only because she wished to prove that Georgia's "only interest in the movies was to see the love-making."[96] Relatedly, Pauline "would not say definitely that she thought [Georgia] was carrying on with young men," but she remained unsure "where [Georgia] got the money for the movies."[97] Georgia's battle with her foster parents reflects the fraught relationship between urban amusements, Black girls' personal autonomy, and familial desire to maintain respectability. Ultimately, Georgia wished to live in a home where she "would have some freedom."[98] Freedom to move around the city as she chose, freedom from the unwanted advances of her foster father, and freedom, of course, to go to the movies.

Charlotte Parker and Margaret Sweet: Movies as Freedom of Choice

Charlotte Parker, an eighteen-year-old migrant from Washington, DC, spent the first thirteen years of her life there under foster parents whom she considered "too strict to live" because she was never allowed out at night and "had to tell them everything she did." She and her mother moved to the Bronx after her foster father's death in 1912, but Charlotte ran away three years later and was eventually institutionalized as an incorrigible child. Upon her release in February 1916, her mother moved them to White Plains, which Charlotte considered "so lonely" because "the country was so dark and the theatres were so far off."[99] Interestingly, as reformers like Mary White Ovington, a founding member of the NAACP, were actively pushing events like "country week," where Black children were "sent away to the country" during the summer for their health, children like Charlotte were desperately trying to escape it.[100] Though Charlotte worked and contributed to the household income, her mother still forbade her from going out at night. Suggesting the imaginative pull of freedom that the neighborhood offered young Black girls, Charlotte ran away in October 1916 to Harlem, arguing that she "resented such strict supervision."[101]

While living on 134th Street in a single-room apartment away from her mother's watchful eye, Charlotte began "going to dances, moving picture shows, and theatres very often."[102] She used her newfound independence to do what she felt was justified after a long day's work. When she was asked by a caseworker whether her mother was right in not letting her go out, Charlotte responded, "In some ways, but, why shouldn't I go out some times if I worked?"[103] She particularly resented the fact that she, like many of the young girls at Bedford Hills and the Hopper Home, had left school early to help her mother pay the bills. Instead of recognizing Charlotte's contributions and, therefore, maturity, her mother restricted her free time and had her committed.

Margaret Sweet, a twenty-four-year-old charge at Bedford Hills, expressed sentiments similar to Charlotte's. Margaret's "unreasonably strict" mother "never allowed her to go anywhere in the evening," and even after Margaret started "earning her own money her mother would not let her go to a dance or the theater because she thought it was wicked."[104] It was not until Margaret moved to New York City when she was nineteen, free of parental supervision and with "no one to tell her what she could do," that she "began to go out nearly every night."[105]

Both Charlotte's and Margaret's case files show the prevalence of "treating" in the young girls' lives. According to historian Elizabeth Alice Clement, treating emerged at the turn of the century "from the tension between girls' desire to participate in commercial amusements and the working-class community's condemnation of prostitution."[106] In other words, it provided young working-class women with the means to participate in urban amusements without the negative stigma of taking money for sex. As one film scholar argues, dates at the movies "produced a commercial relationship between the sexes that rendered more ambiguous the connection between the exchange of money and the granting of sexual favours than the process of direct purchase assumed in the red-light districts."[107] Significantly, Charlotte challenged the caseworker's efforts to position her as a prostitute. Though she was arrested for solicitation, Charlotte denied multiple times that she was a sex worker. Instead, she argued that she "is not a prostitute because she has not taken money from them." She admitted, however, to accepting "presents" from men that included tickets to the movies and rent.[108]

Margaret, too, made careful distinctions between treating and prostitution. She told a Bedford Hills interviewer that "she has never prostituted" but had sex with "friends" from whom she took "presents," such as "candy, theatre tickets and invitations to dinner." Margaret believed that "prostitution is the worst crime anybody can commit because you have to do things that take away your self-respect," making it clear that the twenty-four-year-old did not believe her use of treating was immoral or wrong.[109] Despite caseworkers' attempts to place Charlotte and Margaret in boxes neatly defined by their supposed criminality, the young girls insisted on interpreting their actions for themselves, regardless of whether it ran counter to the various agencies, reformers, and family members that consistently policed them and their behavior. For them, using dates as a means to make their moviegoing and other leisure habits possible was simply part of being a young woman living in the city.

As with other girls, Dora Ross's interest in movies, exhibited by her visit to the Odeon after her move to New York, was tied to wider visions of personal freedom and autonomy. Though she was confined to Bedford Hills after her arrest, she attempted to run away, only to be reinstitutionalized. Upon her parole in 1925, she was sent back to her mother in Virginia. Less than six months later, she ran away again to Harlem. Her reappearance in Bedford Hills's records in 1926 and again in 1928 suggests not just that Black girls and women remained consistently surveilled but also that Dora was unable to live her life as unrestricted and unconfined as she pleased. Her defiance against confinement in the form of fleeing, threatening violence, and "screaming and yelling" sheds light on Black girls' and women's insistence on defining the contours of their lives, work, and play.[110]

During the first half of the twentieth century, as the movies shifted from cheap amusement to a staple of American cultural life, Black girls and women often used moviegoing to express independence, participate in consumer culture, and experience release from the grudging reality of tenement living or menial labor. Still, journalists, reformers, and family members frequently pathologized and criminalized their engagement with the movies. In many ways, this had to do with conflicting ideas of what acceptable public behavior entailed. Unfettered access to so-called cheap movies was envisioned as dangerous not only because of what was on the screen but also because of the many ways that movie theaters were repurposed for various needs and desires. Movie theaters provided a semiprivate space for all kinds of activities beyond moviegoing. Not all of these activities entailed danger and crime. While there are some cases when Black New Yorkers took advantage of the darkness to commit murder and theft, theater patrons also used it to experience the tantalizing embrace of a lover or swindle an unjust boss out of ticket sales.

Responding to these activities, parents and families tried to keep their daughters, sisters, cousins, and nieces from the movies. Their rules, which were an attempt to keep them safe and respectable, clashed with the girls' own hopes about how they would spend their free time. This entanglement of expectations and desires resulted in an exacting effort to monitor and police the movement of Black girls' bodies throughout the city, sometimes ending in their confinement. The records of Bedford Hills and the WPA illuminate this deeply intertwined web, undoubtedly connecting Black film culture to urban living, surveillance, and resistance. Most of all, though, the files shed light on the significance of moviegoing for Black girls and women. They understood their involvement in Black film culture as an escape into a fantastical world where their worries did not exist; it was an excuse to get dressed up and spend a night out of a crowded apartment with a group of friends; and, ultimately, they used trips to the theater to secure autonomy over their free time, bodies, and movement throughout the city.

Negotiated Resistance

*Oscar Micheaux and the New York State
Motion Picture Commission*

J ust two years after he began his filmmaking career, Oscar Micheaux was already thinking about the damaging effects of the censor's cut. In a 1919 article in *Half-Century Magazine*, he questioned the ability of white censors, even those of a liberal bent, to see Black people as anything other than a "good old darkey." Arguing that "the white race will never come to look upon [the Black community] in a serious light," he stressed that "our present environments and desires seem under a cover to them."[1] In other words, white censors just simply did not and could not understand the intricacies and realities of Black life, thus "only exacerbat[ing] the nation's already chronic racism."[2] To Micheaux, undue censorship from the country's various city and state censors was just one more thing added to "the already overburdening labors of the colored producer."[3] His time in New York certainly did not offer him any level of reprieve. From 1922 to the early 1930s, during which time Micheaux submitted at least fourteen films to the Motion Picture Commission for review, the director was at nearly consistent odds with New York State (NYS) censors. None of these films were approved without required eliminations.

Because, as Jane Gaines argues, the censor's cut "often produces a limp and tepid text," Micheaux fought steadfastly to have his films shown as close to their original form as possible in New York.[4] And, when his racially charged

---

Material from this chapter was condensed and revised for a chapter titled "Written Refusals: Oscar Micheaux's Confrontations with the New York State Motion Picture Commission" in *The Routledge Companion to American Film History*, edited by Pamela Robertson Wojcik and Paula J. Massood and published by Routledge.

narratives may have been absent or diluted, Micheaux remained determined to fight the censors, or sometimes completely ignore them, refusing to capitulate to censorship standards. Though "black filmmakers had to accede to the power these [censorship] boards exerted and the standards they established that were extensions of their own moral beliefs and principles," Micheaux was an overwhelmingly adaptative director.[5] He developed numerous methods to resist the censors' desire to cut his material, such as negotiating, simply screening the film without a license, and feigning innocence and ignorance in the face of accusations.

Micheaux's engagement with the Motion Picture Commission represents an essential aspect of Black film culture that includes filmmaking and also placemaking in atypical form. Not necessarily fighting physically, like Robert Thomas, to be in a space or using moviegoing to claim an urban, independent identity, Micheaux's negotiations still reflect a rejection of state-imposed power over his ability to show his race films to the country's largest Black urban population and have control over what images of Blackness circulated throughout the city. The battles between him and the censors over representation, tied as they usually were to race and sexuality, also occurred in a city with a legacy of inept white censorship. After the fruitless conversations surrounding the censorship of D. W. Griffith's *The Birth of a Nation* (1915), Black New Yorkers recognized the inability of white censors to meet their expectations. For Micheaux's part, his attempts to maintain artistic integrity were ultimately bound up in challenges to white supremacy, which the censors discreetly, if not always explicitly, worked to maintain. His form of resistance—negotiation and rejection—brought his race films to the city's Black theaters, giving locals the ability to experience a significant cultural development, while also actively challenging the power of local censors to impede that ability.

Movie Censorship in New York before 1922

The debate over film censorship in New York City began decades before the formal institution of the state censorship board. In the early years of the twentieth century, the regulation of film rested with the municipality and was enforced through its police department. The most typical example of such policing, which illustrates the connections between the state, progressive reformers, and concerns over seemingly influenceable populations, remains Mayor George McClellan's closing of over five hundred theaters on Christmas Eve 1908. After a very public battle about Sunday laws with the Society for the Prevention of Crime and the city's most vocal white clergymen, the mayor revoked the licenses out of concern for "the safety of their patrons." In particular, McClennan seemed concerned with those films that "tend to degrade or injure the morals of the community."[6] In Lee Grieveson's summation, this dramatic action demonstrated that the "policing of . . . cinema was [and would be] linked to broader concerns about morality, public order, and governance," particularly as it pertained to race and sex.[7]

In the immediate aftermath of the 1908 shutdowns, the city's exhibitors moved toward self-regulation. The National Board of Censorship of Motion Pictures, formed by the People's Institute, attempted to regulate the content of motion pictures through voluntary censorship.[8] When the board was created in 1909, it was supported by the Association of Moving Pictures Exhibitors of New York and the Motion Picture Patents Company.[9] The two groups believed that their financial interests were at stake if public opinion on cinema continued to be fraught with questions over propriety, and they considered the board a more lenient alternative to state supervision. The board aimed to identify troubling material at its source, from the manufacturers, rather than waiting for films to cause public outcry after being shown in theaters. The manufacturing companies were encouraged to submit their films directly to the board and follow any suggested recommendations. Any approved films would bear a seal of approval, thereby mitigating the need for state-sponsored censorship.

However, as historian Andrea Friedman explains, "The National Board's efforts to avoid state control facilitated [state censorship] expansion."[10] Despite its attempts to the contrary, the board was unable to acknowledge the vast differences in local censorship needs, as some audiences, especially in the South, considered their standards too liberal.[11] This was even the case in New York, where legal censorship was enacted not within the city but on the state level, where many lawmakers were responsible to small-town, rural constituents living north of the metropolitan city.

When NYS's censorship board, the Motion Picture Commission, was finally established under chapter 715 of the laws of 1921, the statute read:

> The commission shall cause to be promptly examined every motion-picture film submitted to it as herein required, and unless such film or a part thereof is obscene, indecent, immoral, inhuman, sacrilegious, or is of such a character that its exhibition would tend to corrupt morals or incite to crime, shall issue a license therefor.[12]

In 1926, reflective of continued debates surrounding film and impressionable youth audiences, the commission was transferred to the Motion Picture Division under the State Department of Education. Still, the censors' duties were the same. Almost all films, including theatrical, current event, and educational, came under the purview of the commission, which issued licenses for show-ings based on the criteria in the statute. As the standards make clear, the censors were particularly concerned with outward expressions of female sex-uality, interracial liaisons, and vice that could "incite to crime," all of which constituted common critiques leveled against Micheaux when he submitted his films for exhibition in New York.

Censoring Blackness in Early Film

Movie censorship in New York, and throughout the nation, was deeply tied to the perceived susceptibility of certain audiences to questionable or inciting material. This included not just children but also immigrants and ethnic and racial minorities who were considered "vulnerable and dangerous audiences" by progressive-minded elites.[13] As moral, sexual, and racial boundaries seemed to shift in the early 1900s, at least partially because of migration and immi-gration, reformers responded with a determined effort at the state-sanctioned monitoring of these signs of modernity. This resulted in the policing of urban spaces and particular populations, as well as the censoring of film content. From efforts to target vice in the city to censorship of moving pictures, "rac-ism was central to white progressive reform," which meant, in part, monitor-ing filmic representations of Blackness that challenged the racial status quo.[14]

When heavyweight fighter Jack Johnson defeated the "Great White Hope" Jim Jeffries in 1910, there was immediate resistance to the circulation of the film version of the fight. Even before Jeffries's loss, white audiences were wary of Johnson and his lifestyle. "A braggadocio and a dandy," as film scholar Dan Streible describes him, "[Johnson] gleefully and openly rebelled against white bourgeois standards of behavior."[15] But afterward, historian David Krasner argues, "Johnson's victory created a wholesale paradigm shift in what it meant to be African American."[16] Further, the win "offered a potent challenge to the social conceptions of race upon which segregation was built," prompting many to lobby for their cities to ban the film.[17] *Show World* reported that "one of the earliest protests was from New York," but other cities, including Chicago, Boston, and Washington, DC, expressed similar concerns about the film and Black reactions to it.[18] At the core of the argument against its exhibition were "fears of race riots and objections on moral grounds," particularly given the vio-lence that erupted in various cities after the fight's results were announced.[19] Yet Lester Walton, at the *Age*, decried "yellow journals [that] are endeavoring to work up race riots throughout the country."[20] Instead, he called for "all, irrespective or race or color [to] rejoice that the undisputed champion heavyweight of the world is an American."[21] Rev. Reverdy Ransom of the Bethel AME Church in

Figure 3.1 Jack Johnson working a movie camera, ca. 1914, as featured in *Cine Journal*. *(Courtesy of the Media History Digital Library)*

the city made similar remarks about Johnson's fight: "The negro is an American in every ambition, aspiration, and desire." He continued, "Johnson is not trying to win the negro championship, but to hold and defend his title against all comers, regardless of race or color."[22]

Yet after receiving hundreds of letters in protest from his constituents, New York City mayor William Gaynor decided that "he could see no impropriety in the exhibition of the [Johnson-Jeffries] pictures" and found no adequate reason to halt their exhibition.[23] Despite fears of bloody streets and racial unrest, the showings in New York City were met with nothing of the sort. *Film Index* noted that when the film was shown, including on Broadway at the Colonial, at the Alhambra in Harlem, and in multiple theaters on Coney Island, it was met with decent crowds who enjoyed the show. "Their morals," it was reported, "were none the worse for the entertainment."[24]

The movement to halt the distribution of the fight film was an attempt to censure "the undeniable image of Black power and white vincibility" and resulted in Congress banning the circulation of fight films in 1912. As Lee Grieveson puts it, "The fight films of Johnson became caught up in, helped usher in, a reshaping of governmental—at both the state and federal level—involvement with cinema."[25] Ultimately, after the 1912 Sims Act, an "evidently racist policing of disempowered population groups informed and shaped the policing of cinema."[26]

This is even true for the seemingly progressive National Board, which struggled with its decision regarding *The Birth of a Nation* (1915). Based on Thomas Dixon's racist novel *The Clansman*, the film dramatizes the fall of the South during the Civil War and blames northern carpetbaggers and newly freed Black men and women for its ruin. Griffith's South is only capable of being saved from the anarchy of Reconstruction by the Ku Klux Klan. The director opens his epic with the selling of Black bodies into slavery at auction, thus introducing viewers to the film's overall argument that "the black presence in the United States serves as a barrier to the firm establishment of a unified country."[27] This argument is woven throughout the narrative but becomes particularly clear in the second part of the film, which is dedicated to Reconstruction in the South. Here the audience is introduced to the worst of the Black image on film. Southern custom and propriety are bucked by Black men in power, who want to marry white women, drink while in political office, and refuse to bow to white people in the streets. To end "the agony which the Southern endured so that a Nation might be born," the Ku Klux Klan is formed to put insubordinate Black people back in their place and save the sanctity of the South.[28] Ultimately, as one scholar succinctly explains, the film "touched a sensitive political nerve."[29]

From the start of their actions against Griffith's *Birth*, Black protestors in New York drew important connections between Griffith's racist message and his use of the modern medium. In an editorial in the *Age*, James Weldon Johnson, future executive secretary of the NAACP, noted that, while the theatrical version of the Thomas Dixon novel was injurious, "made into a moving picture play it can do us incalculable harm."[30] Indeed, *Birth* took the nation's history of racism and, to borrow Elaine Frantz Parsons's words, "dressed [it] in the clothes of the modern."[31] Johnson boldly stated that the film "seriously attempts to hold the Negro up before the whole country as a degraded brute . . . to make him the object of prejudice and hatred."[32] Recognizing the draw of hundreds of thousands of individuals to the city's dime theaters, he asked his readers, "Can you imagine the effect of such a scene upon the millions who seldom read a book, who seldom witness a play, but who constantly go to the 'movies'?"[33]

Further, he acutely argued against the historicity of the film, asserting that its "representation is out of proportion to the history, civilization and development of the South" in that "there is not one single, decent, self-respecting, industrious and intelligent Negro represented in the whole production . . . there is not in it one credible thing attributed to the Negro as a race."[34] In an effort to resist the film and its racist imagery, Johnson called upon the "law-abiding" Black "citizens of this city [New York] to stand united and determined to see that this picture shall not be produced."[35] He pushed Black New Yorkers to pressure not only the police, who were responsible for regulating the boundaries of decency in the city's theaters, but also the mayor, to cut out the racist material or prohibit the film all together. By reinforcing the citizenship of Black moviegoers and describing them as law-abiding, Johnson argued for the protection of Black New Yorkers from the racism of Griffith's moving picture and directly challenged the authenticity of Griffith's narrative.

The editor of the *Age*, Fred Moore, similarly articulated his arguments against *Birth* in a public letter to Mayor John Mitchel. He succinctly argued, "We feel that we have a *right* to appeal to you as you appealed to us for our votes."[36] In positioning the Black community as voters with the license to call upon an elected official, particularly one who themselves appealed to the Black community, Moore asserted the agency of the Black community, as well as the duty of the mayor to respond to their complaints. Both Johnson's and Moore's demands in the *Age* are significant in that they reveal the particular ways in which Black spectators were positioning themselves as a moviegoing public that was, by necessity, also political. Black moviegoers were not, from the beginning of popular cinema, passive spectators enduring demeaning representations and storylines.[37] Rather, as Moore and Johnson demonstrate, Black spectators in New York were readily critiquing moving pictures and making important connections between history, the power of representation, and the lived realities of Black Americans.[38] It was undoubtedly this public action on the part of the Black community that *Birth* was responding to in the first place. As historian Davarian Baldwin has asserted, Griffith's film is "a history of the present," responding to fears of Black migration throughout the country and the resultant masses of Black urbanites ready and willing to challenge white supremacy.[39]

Despite the very clear relationship between Griffith's film, the racist re-writing of history, and the public protests against it, the National Board "felt that it was not its job to judge historical accuracy."[40] When it came time for the censors to decide on whether or not to screen *Birth* in New York City, it was at odds with members of the NAACP, who vehemently protested the film. After initially passing the film without any eliminations, the National Board agreed to do an advanced screening with members of the NAACP present, but only if they were white.[41] After a third screening, questionable material, such as a forced interracial marriage, a lynching scene, and a chase scene, was determined excessive.[42] However, the censors later determined that this decision was unofficial, and a fourth screening was scheduled where everyone in attendance, including some NAACP members and southerners, "agree[d] in condemning it."[43]

In the midst of this very public battle for censorship in the name of anti-racism, a group of "over five hundred colored and white citizens" occupied city hall in response to the film, demanding to be heard by the mayor.[44] There were a number of speakers present, including W. E. B. Du Bois; Joel Spingarn; Dr. William H. Brooks, pastor at St. Mark's Church; and Fred Moore, to contest the "cruel, vindictive, and untrue degradation of a part of the country's citizenship." On hand were clergymen, business and professional men, and women, whose "neat personal appearance was in itself a strong denial of the slurs made" in the film. Speakers not only reinforced Johnson's earlier view on the harmfulness of Griffith's narrative but also challenged the film with statistics on the successes of Black lawyers and doctors and the amount of real estate and bank deposits Black New Yorkers possessed.[45] Though the group was "advised by the mayor that he has been assured by the producers of the film that they will meet his wishes," the required cuts were never made, and the objectional and racist material remained in place.[46] The National Board's decision to approve the film with cuts and its powerlessness to enforce this decision revealed the limitations of voluntary censorship and "compromised its progressive credentials."[47]

The controversy surrounding *Birth* raises questions about the National Board's claims "to censor for the average person."[48] Andrea Friedman notes that before state censorship, the National Board argued it "respected the morals of the average American."[49] Nancy Rosenblum writes that its efforts reflected a concern for "cultural consensus based on greater tolerance for ethnic and racial diversity."[50] Arguably, the NYS censorship board, following the

Figure 3.2 Portrait of Micheaux, undated. *(Photographs and Prints Division, Schomburg Center for Research in Black Culture, The New York Public Library)*

general guidelines laid out by the National Board in terms of content restrictions and the middle-class reformers that made up its censors, also spoke for the average viewer. But who constitutes the so-called average person in early twentieth-century America? In the face of what Jane Gaines calls "the everyday racism of the local censor," how could the needs, desires, and expectations of Black viewers have been met by the standards of a majority-white censorship board (both the National Board and NYS included)?[51] Micheaux's own experiences with state-run censorship suggest that it was quite difficult for that kind of support to be the case. His clashes with the Motion Picture Commission reveal white censors' inability to grasp Micheaux's visions of Black life and their opposition to challenges to the racial status quo. The director, in the face of revisions to his work, learned the censors' expectations, often negotiated, and sometimes cut legal corners all in an effort to show New York's Black audiences his latest race film.

Oscar Micheaux Comes to New York

In 1921, after deciding that "Chicago is a dead one," the Micheaux Film and Book Company relocated its head office to Harlem.[52] According to his biographer Patrick McGilligan, Micheaux may have been affected by the racial violence that had shaken Chicago two years earlier, bringing the reality of continued racism into sharp relief for those who considered the North a so-called Promised Land. The city's "provincial censorship board," which had struggled to pass the provocative *Within Our Gates* (1920), and the "general feeling among black Americans that New York might succeed where Chicago had failed," McGilligan asserts, all led to his decision to move.[53] In a press release, the director argued that "better studio possibilities, together with the fact that the screen artists of the race are available in greater numbers in the big city," prompted his change of scenery.[54] In all sincerity, Micheaux seemed to hope that New York City would allow him to continue to expand his filmmaking business in a way that he believed Chicago simply could not anymore.

His new office's location at the Franklin Theatre, 440 Lenox Avenue, was ideal, given its proximity to his own apartment on 135th Street, other local theaters, and major thoroughfares. With just four blocks between his home and office, Micheaux could take in all that was Harlem in less than ten minutes. Two of Harlem's most popular theaters, the Lincoln and the Lafayette, were on the route to his new headquarters, making it easy to schedule showings of his most recent films or sneak a glimpse at some local talent.[55] Also nearby were the offices of two of the city's popular Black weeklies, the *Age* and the *Amsterdam News*. Neither of these papers had any qualms about praising or castigating (sometimes both) Micheaux's latest film—maybe he chose to stop by their offices once or twice to discuss a particularly bad review or the future of race films in the city. It is also possible, in his travels down 135th Street, that Micheaux overheard, among "the noises of Harlem," the proselytizing of a street orator or the murmur of some Universal Negro Improvement Association members leaving their meetings at Liberty Hall.[56] Had he left the office late one night, he could have easily bumped into slumming whites seeking illicit thrills or heard jazz music blaring from Harlem's infamous rent parties and cabarets. In other words, Micheaux's move to Harlem placed him at the cultural and political heart of Black New York and among fellow New Negroes.

Before moving to the Black metropolis, the thirty-seven-year-old already had a lifetime's worth of experiences that included homesteading, writing novels, and traveling cross-country to advertise and seek funding for his literary and motion picture endeavors. The self-made author and director was born as the youngest of eleven children on January 2, 1884, to former slaves Calvin Michaux and Belle Gough.[57] Micheaux's parents remained committed to his education until the family finances required his participation in the workforce. By 1902, Micheaux was tired of what he considered the limited ambitions of the people in his hometown and set off for Chicago to board with his elder brother. Like the many migrants who would follow in similar footsteps in the ensuing two decades, Micheaux initially considered the city a space for growth and opportunity. Chicago, and other northern cities at the turn of the century, like New York City and Detroit, offered African Americans access to the right to vote, increased wages, and potential freedom from racial persecution.

During his time in Chicago, Micheaux worked a number of jobs, including a position as a Pullman porter. At a moment of limited economic mobility for African Americans, becoming a porter was a particularly significant opportunity. Though they were paid meager salaries, the money was steady, and porters were given a "chance to escape both Reconstructionists and Klansmen, along with fields of cotton, [and] laws of segregation."[58] Not only were porters responsible for the dissemination of information about migration opportunities but they also facilitated the transmission of various cultural forms throughout the nation, including jazz and blues music. Micheaux's time as a porter allowed him to travel to a number of cities where he formed networks that would eventually serve him well when selling his books and exhibiting his films.

Despite his initial interest in the city, Micheaux was continuously drawn to the peacefulness of small-town living. After just two years, he realized his dream of homesteading as he paid the first installment on a 160-acre plot in

Chamberlain, South Dakota. Though he would, in less than ten years' time, give up homesteading after a drought and a failed marriage, Micheaux pushed for African Americans to move West and seek out these opportunities. In 1910, he published a front-page article in the *Chicago Defender* urging self-sufficiency within the Black community through farming. He argued that, despite the "openings galore for the lawyer, doctor, laborer, mechanic, and greatest of all, the producer," very few African Americans made their way to states like South Dakota, Iowa, Montana, Idaho, or Wyoming. Though he claimed his call for farmers was not a solution to the "Negro Problem," he asserted he could not "see a brilliant future for the young colored man unless he first does something for himself." The future of Black America, to Micheaux, "depends first on individual achievement."[59]

Micheaux's understanding of how African Americans could defy discrimination and succeed in their lives was shaped by his own experiences as a self-made man. Despite his modest upbringing and the strictures placed on Black life in post-Reconstruction America, the director believed that "a colored man can be anything," and he used his own success as an example.[60] This attitude was undoubtedly shaped by Booker T. Washington's own philosophy of individual achievement as example setting. The director was not shy about his admiration of Washington; he dedicated one of his books to him, and a framed image of the intellectual was not uncommon in his films.[61] These themes—of racial uplift based on self-help, conservative values, and education—were guiding forces in the films Micheaux would later make.

After a public divorce and a series of weather misfortunes, Micheaux's homesteading enterprise failed, and he began his career as a novelist. He traveled extensively to obtain the funds to publish from white neighbors who were interested in his stories. He did this for about five years until George Johnson, a Black postal clerk and secretary of the Lincoln Motion Picture Company, noticed "the steady flow of mail-order copies" of Micheaux's books.[62] When Micheaux received a letter from Johnson in early May 1918 offering to transform his novel *The Homesteader* into a movie, he jumped straight into negotiations. He was unimpressed with the company's newest releases, all of which were mostly three-reel pictures. This would not do for his story; Micheaux firmly believed that "this voluminous work could not be possibly portrayed short of eight reels, for it is a big plot and long story."[63] When the Lincoln Motion Picture Company resisted, Micheaux decided to produce the film himself.

This move, reflective of Micheaux's unyielding negotiation tactics, was the start of his nearly three-decade-long career as a race film director. As in his exchange with Johnson, Micheaux was often unrelenting yet strategic in his conversations with the NYS censors. While he did not always succeed in getting what he wanted from them, he grew exceedingly adept at forging excuses that calmed their fury over his various attempts to show his films when and where he wanted to and in the form he originally intended them to be.

Micheaux and the New York State Motion Picture Commission

The Motion Picture Commission reviewed every single motion picture that was to be screened in the state and issued a license unless any part of the film was found "obscene, indecent, immoral, inhuman, sacrilegious, or [was] of such a character that its exhibition would tend to corrupt morals or incite to crime."[64] No film could be shown without a license, and legal action could be taken against those filmmakers and distributors who tried to do so. The number of reviewers on the commission varied throughout its history, but it was not uncommon for just one person to review a film and make a decision. This made it possible for personal opinions to make their way into censorship choices, affecting the continuity of the censorship standards for directors. Further, older, middle-class white women were among the commission's earliest reviewers. These women, considered "moral guardians" in their progressive-minded attempts at social reform, tended to hold more conservative or traditional values, which were reflected in their censorship choices.[65] They frequently cut scenes of vice, violence, and female promiscuity or sexuality—anything that could supposedly lower the moral standard of a viewer. With Micheaux's penchant for the sensational, the director was frequently at odds with the censorship board and its decisions.

During his early years interacting with the state censors, most of his over-the-top films were immediately rejected. These moments served as important learning experiences for later, when he would challenge, debate, and compromise with the censors. For example, the first of Micheaux's films to flash across the screening room of the Motion Picture Commission, *The Dungeon* (1922), was rejected in toto. In a letter to Micheaux, the censors summarized the film as follows:

> The story treats of Gyp Lassiter, a villainous wretch, who employs a drug fiend to hypnotize a woman whom he wants to get possession of. The drug fiend brings the woman to Gyp who marries her while she is in a hypnotic condition. Gyp then takes her to a house which has been the scene of the murder of eight of his previous wives. By nature a killer, he then proceeds to asphyxiate her in a dungeon. From the clutches of death, she is rescued by a former lover who then kills Gyp.[66]

The censors failed to mention the film's subplot. In a critique of Black northern leadership, Micheaux has a Black politician abstain from voting against residential segregation in order to maintain his position in office. According to film scholar Charlene Regester, Micheaux also "heightens his critique" by making the politician a mass murderer.[67] The censors were either unable or unwilling to see Micheaux's message through the violence, despite the film's moralistic ending, in which the murderer is punished.

The commission rejected the film on the grounds that it was immoral and inhuman and would incite to crime and corrupt morals. While Micheaux had interacted with similar censors in other urban locales like Chicago, where a citywide censorship board had existed since 1907, this was his first experience with the all-white, largely female censorship board in New York. At this point, he did not negotiate with the commission and accepted their decision. In these early interactions, Micheaux was studying their expectations and standards in anticipation of his later negotiations.

This trend continued for the next three films, *The Homesteader* (1919), *The Virgin of the Seminole* (1922), and *Deceit* (1923), that Micheaux submitted for review. With each film, the censors required Micheaux to cut some reference to violence or female vice, such as drunken fighting or forced abortion. In all of these situations, Micheaux made the ordered edits without dispute, thereby gaining the official license to show his films in the state. However, only one of the first four films submitted to the commission, *Virgin of the Seminole*, was mentioned in the Black press in New York at the expected time of its release; this suggests the others were never shown in the city. It is possible that Micheaux, annoyed and discouraged by the censors' cuts, simply refused to show a finished product that was not his own in narrative structure and content. It could be this frustration that forced Micheaux to think through how to get his films passed by the commission without changes that deeply affected his stories. The feedback he received served as a significant learning curve that he eventually used to manipulate and push the commission's boundaries in order to get certain material passed.

Notably, the first four films Micheaux submitted to the commision were reviewed by one of two women, Mrs. Marian (Williams) Perrin Burton or Mrs. Helen May Hosmer. Mrs. Burton, who regularly gave lectures and wrote articles against women's right to vote, was a prominent antisuffragist and president of the Rochester branch of the NYS Association Opposed to Woman Suffrage.[68] This conservative outlook may very well have bled into her censorship work. Mrs. Hosmer was a member of the Republican Party and served as an alternate state delegate to the seventeenth Republican National Convention.[69] Her participation in party politics puts her on the opposite side of the spectrum from Mrs. Burton, suggesting she was for women's suffrage and was, perhaps, racially progressive.[70] Still, both women always objected to Micheaux's violence- and vice-filled portrayals of women, suggesting a common means, in the form of censorship, to "legitimizing women's participation in the political public sphere."[71] When they both retired by 1925, the female censors who followed them remained similarly committed to "mothering the movies," as historian Alison M. Parker terms it, until the middle of the Great Depression.[72] By then, most films submitted to the commission were already abiding by Hollywood's self-imposed Hays Code.

It was in 1924, when Micheaux released *Birthright* and *Son of Satan*, that the director finally stepped up to the censors and began to negotiate to keep some of his more racially provocative and meaningful material in his films. *Birthright* tells the tale of Peter Siner, a recent Harvard graduate returning to his southern hometown, Hooker's Bend, to start a school for Black children. The film reaches a climax after Siner gets duped by a local white landowner. It turns out that the plot of land he purchased for the school has a racially restrictive clause on the property, making it nearly impossible to use as Siner intended. After reviewing the film, the censors ordered two subtitle eliminations: the "underlined word from subtitle: 'How the *hell* can he arrest him when he just hit down'" and the entirety of "legal—hell—anything a white man wants to put over on a nigger is legal."[73] In a show of hands, the censors called for the elimination of this entire line, even though the racial epithet was not one that they customarily had any issues with.[74] Instead, the cut was most likely ordered because of its criticisms of institutionalized racism. While Micheaux did remove the second subtitle entirely, he simply changed "hell" to "h—l" in the first one.

Though the change seems insignificant and his more racially provocative subtitle needed to be removed because it would "tend to incite to crime," his subtle manipulation of words in the first subtitle maintained the power of Micheaux's original message.[75] In this scene, Tump Pack, another Black man recently returned to Hooker's Bend, had been arrested just after his arrival in town. In the subtitle, a Black man is expressing indignation at the arrest, particularly given that Pack is a World War I veteran with a medal of honor.[76] Maintaining the explicative, even in moderated form, allowed Micheaux to reveal the deep racial tensions running through Hooker's Bend and similar towns throughout the United States. Micheaux was acutely aware of the violence and poor treatment of Black soldiers in the postwar period, and this slight reworking of the censors' cuts reflected his determination to have this anger represented in his films.[77] In comparison, when the mainstream MGM was required to cut "hell" from *The Shooting of Dan McGrew* that same year, they submitted a new subtitle with the word completely removed, not edited as Micheaux's was. Micheaux, operating as an independent race filmmaker trying to get his films shown to anticipating Black audiences, was engaging in important, albeit small, acts of subterfuge.

Just nine months after *Birthright*, Micheaux became even bolder in his attempts to push NYS's standards. *Son of Satan* was summarily rejected by the commission because of "scenes of drinking, carousing, and . . . masked men becoming intoxicated. It shows the playing of crap [*sic*] for money, a man killing his wife by choking her, the killing of the leader of the hooded organization and the killing of a cat by throwing a stone at it."[78] A week later, Micheaux responded to the censors' disapproval of his film with a list of his own eliminations, arguing that "with these scenes eliminated, this picture has been approved by the Pennsylvania Board." He also added that "as this subject is only, in the main, the experiences of an ordinary Negro" and "all the characters, including the man playing Captain Tolston [the hooded leader] are colored . . . condemning it seems severe and unnecessary."[79]

Despite the fact that he still had to make some edits, Micheaux's negotiations were ostensibly successful. Not only did his appeal allow for a successful overruling of the commission's original decision but he also made edits that kept the "hooded organization," or what was certainly meant to be read as the Ku Klux Klan (KKK), in a negative light. Though the KKK's leader escaped persecution through murder, Micheaux maintained the group's incorrigible ways with the scenes of drinking and carousing. To him, the gratuitous violence that he voluntarily removed was, perhaps, too sensational, and he recognized that the scenes added "no special interest to the story."[80] In this case, Micheaux may have had to make changes, but they were by his own hand, and he successfully got the film shown despite initial rejection.

Micheaux's secondary argument that *Son of Satan* is about an average Black man is interesting here for a number of reasons. At first glance, it appears that Micheaux is telling the censors that they are overthinking the film. It cannot possibly be about racism, he seems to assure them, because all of the characters are Black. He also explained, in a postscript, that "because our business is confined to Colored houses we play only three houses in the state of New York."[81] Not only did he attempt to explain away the white censors' concerns about race; he also tried to minimize his impact in the eyes of the censors. In a manipulation of the censors, he pushed them on the idea that they were failing to see the film as ordinary Black life and also that his audiences were only Black and thus his themes would not be a point of contention in the city—this despite the fact that Micheaux knew his audiences would recognize the hooded characters as members of the KKK and that he had access to more than three theaters.

Micheaux may have also been aware of the inconsistencies within the commission's standards when it came to their treatment of white and Black directors of race films. Just three years earlier, in 1921, the white-owned Norman Film Manufacturing Company's *The Crimson Skull* was passed with only one elimination of a choking scene, despite the plot involving a town plagued by hooded menaces. Where Micheaux was targeted for his "hooded organization," Richard Norman, whose company had made the film, was decidedly not. Given that Micheaux was in contact with him, Micheaux may have known that Norman's film had no issue getting passed and pushed the commission accordingly.[82] The race film directors also approached the censors in different ways. After learning that Ohio censors cut out scenes of bulldogging from the aptly titled film *The Bull Dogger* (1921), Norman thought the censors "must be crazy," unsure "why they should make such cuts." However, he adjusted his next movie, which had similar scenes, arguing, "Now I have thought better of it and have left it out."[83] Micheaux, on the other hand, actively chose to be combative, seeking full control over his films. He aimed to revise them as he sought fit, to negotiate when necessary, refusing to relinquish editorial control over his product.

These early interactions with the commission are also suggestive of Micheaux's own dramatic representations of racial uplift, which were often at odds with more conservative uplift methods.[84] In showing, as he considered it, "the colored heart at close range," Micheaux's films sometimes portrayed characters that were not necessarily positive in service of his effort to teach a moral story.[85] These hustlers, gamblers, murderers, and cheaters, though immoral or criminal, always served the director's larger uplift project, but often in sensationalistic ways. It was not uncommon for the director to play up the drama in his films or even to use the word "sensational" when describing his work in advertisements in Black newspapers. His films frequently contained scenes of gambling, both intra- and interracial violence, bribery and murder, barely clothed female dancers, and uninhibited drinking.

Though it is possible that Micheaux toyed with the sensational to attract audiences and increase his income, this mode of storytelling also worked to visualize the lived reality of Black life in America.[86] "At the center of his [Micheaux's] sensational realist films," historian Davarian Baldwin argues, "was the recurring theme of black people confronting various pulp fictions in search of a livable social frontier."[87] Indeed, according to Micheaux, "the intricate studies and problem of human nature, all enter into the physical make-

up" of all motion pictures, even "the most lowly photo play."[88] Instead of simplifying race films to progressive images at all times, Micheaux pushed for the
"recognition of our true situation," in which not all of Black life was achievement and success; it also included poverty, violence, the lure of vice and pleasure, and struggles with Jim Crow. To Micheaux, this reality was the "stimulus
for self-advancement" even if it sometimes meant representing the immoral
in shocking ways.[89]

After Micheaux's measured wins with *Birthright* and *Son of Satan*, he continued to submit overly sensational films that barely passed the commission's
standards. On some of these occasions, as was the case with *Body and Soul*
(1925) and *The Spider's Web* (1926), Micheaux successfully negotiated with
the censors to get a license but failed to keep many of the important critiques
of racism and intraracial issues within his films. With *Body and Soul*, a tale about
a treacherous minister who preys on his congregation, the commisson called
for so many eliminations that Micheaux's critique of Black church leadership
was completely deleted from the film.[90] Trying to appease the censors in this
situation, Micheaux cut the film down from nine reels to five, added confus-
ing subtitles, and placed "the preacher in no position anywhere or having him
do anything that would be unbecoming the Clergy."[91] There are no reviews
of the film in either the *Age* or the *Amsterdam News* after it was released in
November 1925, despite advertisements for showings in at least three Harlem
theaters and a few prerelease articles that promoted it positively.[92]

As with *Body and Soul*, Micheaux was able to secure a license for *The Spider's
Web*, but not before some of its most critical material was removed. At the opening of the film, the viewer is introduced to a white man named Ballanger, who
accosts multiple Black women. While Micheaux was able to keep in the fact
that Ballanger ran a peonage ring, the censors made him remove any hint of
interracial sexual violence. Yet, four years earlier, the commission passed the
white-produced race film *The Burden of Race* (1921) without a single elimination, though the entire film revolved around the possibility of interracial romance between a Black man and a white woman. The difference between the
two is certainly motive. *The Burden of Race* "toyed with the theme of 'race
pride v. love,'" where that love was mutual yet necessarily suppressed.[93] *The
Spider's Web*, on the other hand, dealt with a white man's sexual assault of Black
women. Ballanger, it was explained, "is notorious and must sweetheart with
any colored girl that comes to town."[94]

Clearly, Micheaux's critique of southern racial and sexual violence, a theme
that was present in other Micheaux vehicles that struggled with censorship,
was too over the top for the censors. In demanding these eliminations, they
revealed the ways that censorship was "linked to concerns about race and

public order."[95] The director was also forced to eliminate all references to the numbers racket in Harlem. While some would argue that this was a positive elimination, Micheaux was speaking to his working-class audience in a number of ways with those scenes. First, he knew that gambling and its place in Harlem would be recognized by his viewers as a community institution that sometimes served to help those in need.[96] Second, his representation of playing the numbers, arguably, showed the negative aspects of it, such as desperation and the possibility of addiction, which played into his moral tale.

In addition to negotiating with the censors by suggesting his own cuts and asking for rescreenings, Micheaux sometimes chose to completely skirt the authority of the Motion Picture Commission and show his films without the proper license. This was a regular tactic Micheaux utilized—just one of his many entrepreneurial "survival skills," as film scholar Charlene Regester calls them—to have his films shown in their original form, unchanged by inept white censors.[97] It is unclear how many times Micheaux did this in New York, but it is possible that it happened on at least eight separate occasions.[98] On two of them, Micheaux had sought a license from the board but, most likely upset with the final result, chose to screen his film as he originally intended it, which landed him in legal trouble. For example, in late 1927, he received a license for *The Millionaire* (1927) after a record thirty-nine eliminations were requested by the censors, most having to do with scenes of gambling, prostitution, suggestive dancing, and violence.

By mid-December 1927, there was a bit of scandal surrounding the film. In a letter to the commission on December 12, Micheaux claimed he was a victim of insubordination. His brother and general manager, Swan E. Micheaux, "through the trickery of his associates . . . secured temporary possession" of the film.[99] Interestingly, Peter Eckert, the white owner of race film company Dunbar Film Corp., where Swan also worked, claimed that he was the rightful owner of the film and brought the legal papers and the print to the Motion Picture Commission to prove it.

While Micheaux, perhaps working to save his reputation, advised the commission that the approved version of his print was in Philadelphia, Eckert asserted that his print, which was obtained immediately after its run in New York, was "the very same film which had been exhibited at the Lafayette Theater."[100] When the censors reviewed the film with Eckert present, they found that it was in uncut form. It is unlikely that the film print Micheaux claimed was his own was actually in Philadelphia, mainly because Micheaux had insisted on keeping the cut reels. After he received the laundry list of eliminations from the commission, he requested that he hold on to the cuts rather than the commission keeping possession because they had previously been "lost or destroyed" when in its care.[101] After this incident, in which Micheaux briefly bested the commission to have his film shown as he preferred, uncut and with the original narrative and message intact, the NYS censors never gave Micheaux a license without asking for a rescreening of the edited reels.

Micheaux ran into more legal issues when he screened *Daughter of the Congo* (1930) three years later at the Renaissance Theatre. Micheaux's first sound film, as summarized in the *Age*, "deals with a beautiful mulatto girl who has been stolen as a baby and brought up among savages of the jungle. She is recused from the savages by members of the 10th United States Cavalry and taken by them into the republic of Liberia where the girl soon becomes the belle of Monrovia."[102] According to multiple depositions in the state's censorship files, Micheaux decided to forgo the censorship process once again, making up stories about having direct communication with the commission's director. After receiving a complaint about "an indecent motion picture . . . on exhibition at the Renaissance theatre," three inspectors traveled to the theater only to find out that Micheaux was showing the film under the license of another.[103]

After inspectors informed the manager, Cleo Charity, that the film was being shown illegally, he promised to take it down. When they returned the next day to find the film still available for viewing, they were told by Charity that Micheaux had spoken to the director of the Motion Picture Commission. Micheaux had told Charity that he had a phone call with James Wingate, in which the latter had "given permission . . . to continue to exhibit the picture until a license was issued."[104] Upon further investigation, the inspectors revealed that the phone call was impossible as "Director Wingate was en route to New York [by train] at the time." When they reached him the next day, Wingate "stated that he had no conversation whatsoever with Mr. Micheaux."[105]

In the midst of all this drama, Micheaux finally submitted the film to the commission. He secured a license, but only if he eliminated some of the more problematic scenes. These scenes included nudity and mentions of a Black man passing as white who takes a white lover. Despite the fact that New York never had an antimiscegenation law on the books, the censors took issue specifically with interracial sexual relationships. On an internal note regarding permissibility, "reference by title" to and "action" of romance between Black and white people was expressly forbidden, while for "others [it] depends on action."[106] This focus on white and Black lovers reflects the reality of racial segregation in the city and the heightened social anxiety surrounding race mixing in this period, particularly after the infamous Rhinelander case in

1924, in which a wealthy white man filed for an annulment after his wife's Black lineage came to public light.[107] The case was not settled until 1930, when *Daughter of the Congo* was released, making the film particularly relevant at that moment. While the *Age* commented favorably on the film, Theophilus Lewis, a dramatic critic for *Amsterdam News*, tore it apart in his review. He attacked it not only for its bad acting and casting but also for its depiction of colorism and its representations of native Africans as unintelligent and barbaric. Lewis argued that Micheaux possessed a total lack of understanding "of the progress of his race," and in light of the director's "kindergarten ethnology," the film had no silver lining.[108]

Micheaux received similar criticism from the Black press in New York after he screened *God's Stepchildren* (1938), a film that follows the tragic life of Naomi, a light-skinned woman desperate to pass for white. The Youth Communist League (YCL), led by well-known activist Angelo Herndon, protested the film and succeeded in having it withdrawn from any and all RKO theaters throughout the country on the basis that it promoted colorism and contained harmful stereotypes about Black intelligence and proclivity for vice. After three conferences with Micheaux himself, the group of picketers, which included members of the YCL, the National Negro Congress, the Harlem Teachers Union, and the Harlem Committee for Better Pictures for Children, was still unsatisfied. They planned to meet with representatives from the Motion Picture Commission for "future action in the matter." Seemingly, Micheaux's own promises to remedy the situation by cutting out the suggestive material was not enough to bring a "progressive and enlightened type of Negro motion picture to movie audiences," as the group so desired.[109] Perhaps Micheaux's reputation for skirting his commitment to censorship had become well known by that point.

That these incidents, dealing with both *Daughter of the Congo* and *God's Stepchildren*, escaped the ire of the censors is significant. The commission found barely any fault with *Daughter of the Congo*—the scenes that were removed dealt with nudity and racial passing. Lewis's complaints of poor representation of Africans and dark-skinned African Americans were not addressed at all with the required cuts. The same is true of *God's Stepchildren*, where no eliminations were required at all, despite the fact that it depicted the enraged, malicious nature of Naomi's white husband when he learned she was Black and Naomi's eventual suicide because of her inability to navigate life as a light-skinned Black woman. By 1938, some Black audiences in the city were tired, not only of the censors' inability to see offensive material, even from Black directors, but also of what they perceived as Micheaux's inability to address Black life seriously and deliberately, without sensationalism or offensive material. Toward the end of his career, it seemed, audience tastes were shifting, and Micheaux was not necessarily keeping up.

By the early 1930s, the Motion Picture Commission had begun to cut less of Micheaux's material. More and more, the censors simply did not eliminate scenes of dancing, gambling, or female intoxication, thereby making it unnecessary for him to correspond with them. This shift may have occurred because of the ushering in of a younger, more lenient group of censors or because, in the near decade since the formation of the commission, certain material was no longer seen as particularly offensive. Either way, the more liberal standards resulted in more of his sensational material remaining intact. For example, the plot surrounding a female character in *The Exile* (1931) is entirely based on her position as a femme fatale—she "ruins" a young migrant and runs a lowly dive in Chicago, where men and women can freely drink and gamble. In addition to vice, the censors let inflammatory dialogue slide on a number of occasions. The main female character in *The Exile*, for example, goes on a rant about the futility of Black higher education. In *Murder in Harlem* (1935), also known as *Lem Hawkins' Confession*, a character comments on how educated African Americans were starving, particularly in DC. In yet another instance, from *The Notorious Elinor Lee* (1940), the censors did not cut a conversation at a bar in which one man goes into detail about how Black men, fully capable of finding employment, fool the welfare system by refusing to work because of their laziness. Even as the commission became more lenient in terms of monitoring vice, it remained unlikely to be critical of Micheaux's commentary on intraracial issues and debates such as higher education and self-help.

By this time, the director was already falling out of popularity among Black audiences. His films, as they had since they first started appearing in the city, continued to contain material that not everyone found favorable. For example, *Murder in Harlem*, loosely based on the lynching of a white Jewish man, Leo Frank, for the murder of a young white woman, was lambasted for its use of a pejorative racial slur. As Lou Layne explains in his review of the film in the *Age*, "Alex Lovejoy is pictured writing a note being dictated by his employer, who uses the term 'Negro.' Four times, Lovejoy makes it" the more derogatory epithet. "Micheaux may be pioneering in Negro theatrics," Layne continues, "but when he does so by holding himself and the rest of us up to nationwide ridicule, we can well do without him—and gladly."[110] Ten years earlier, fellow race filmmaker Richard Norman had predicted Micheaux's plummet: "The man, who was in a position to do most for its advancement, due to his color, has due to the propaganda nature of his pictures and his business methods, seriously retarded the popularity of this type of picture."[111]

Two more reviews of *Murder in Harlem* suggest that audiences were growing weary of Micheaux's inability to maintain the same technical standards as Hollywood films. One reviewer noted, "While the sound recording is definitely a great improvement over past releases, the continuity has again been ignored as one of the most vital elements of a good motion pictures." The acting, he added, "is decidedly overdone."[112] Another reviewer agreed: "To say that the picture is entertaining would be a misrepresentation." In addition to the acting, the lighting, editing, and humor were poor, making the film "an effort which can be praised only as an effort."[113] It certainly did not help Micheaux that large Hollywood studios were picking up Black actors for roles in mainstream films, such as Louise Beavers and Fredi Washington in *Imitation of Life* (1934), and showing interest in creating their own all-Black films, like *Hallelujah* (1929), *The Green Pastures* (1936), and later, *Stormy Weather* and *Cabin in the Sky* (both 1943). In 1939, one commentator decided, "The most we can admire about Micheaux is his 'sticktoitiveness.' We don't recall anything else praiseworthy."[114]

Figure 3.3 By the 1930s, Micheaux's films were most often screened at second-run theaters in Brooklyn like the Banco Theatre. *(Photographs and Prints Division, Schomburg Center for Research in Black Culture, The New York Public Library)*

Despite the decline in his popularity, Micheaux continued to produce and screen films in New York City. Usually, though, they were shown at second-run theaters in Brooklyn or at the meeting places of professional associations, no longer the glamorous Lafayette in Harlem. Some critics even continued to defend the director and his legacy. In a two-part story on the history of Black film, a writer in the *Age* noted that Micheaux was one of the only Black filmmakers still working in the industry dominated by white interests. "Mischaux [*sic*] . . . puts what Negroes want to see in his pictures," he noted, "while his rivals shy away from Mischaux subjects and suffer losses." The article also cited a racket that developed in the city that kept Micheaux's pictures from Harlem's theaters in favor of larger-box offices drawn from mainstream studios. The author was most likely referring to the fact that Micheaux and his films were banned from all Leo Brecher and Frank Schiffman establishments in Harlem after he got into some very public squabbles with them.[115] "If this is true," the story continued, "every theatre-goer and performer should squawk to the high heavens to nip in the bud a situation that may have ugly developments."[116] And, indeed, it did have ugly developments for Micheaux and his career. In the months leading up to his death in 1951, despite releasing both a handful of books and films, the director never had more than a few hundred dollars in his bank account. When he passed away while on the road promoting his new material, he left his wife Alice B. Russell with just $7.06.[117]

Notwithstanding the roadblocks placed in his way, Oscar Micheaux was the most successful Black filmmaker in the first half of the twentieth century. In the 1920s, he was one of just a few Black directors working and showing films in New York City, and this remained true into the 1930s.[118] The roadblocks that Micheaux navigated as a Black director reveal the truly complicated nature of his efforts to get his films shown locally and also his insistence that it happen on his terms. His efforts, tied as they were to criticisms of white power over Black film, serve as an important microcosm of the resistance inherent to Black film culture in the city.

Motion Picture Operators and
the Struggle for Recognition

During a late afternoon showing on April 14, 1930, Reginald Warner and Christopher Monroe, projectionists at the Renaissance Theatre, "heard a slight cracking sound" while in the projection booth.[1] Though their first investigation proved fruitless, they heard the sound again and left the booth to survey the situation. Almost immediately after their exit, the projection booth crashed down on the seats behind them. "Instantly," explained the *Amsterdam News*'s report on the collapse, "the theatre was in pandemonium with the three hundred patrons fighting their way through the darkness to the exits."[2] The booth's collapse, caused by the snapping of its support beams, resulted in almost thirty injuries to theatergoers ranging in age from five to forty-seven and the death of one middle-aged woman.

In their assessments of the tragedy, both the *Age* and the *Amsterdam News* pointed to the operators' role in minimizing the death toll. In its front-page reporting on the disaster, the *Age* cited the projectionists' "rare foresight" in shutting off the projection machine as a "miracle."[3] "If they had not done this," the article accurately explains, "there is no doubt that a serious fire would have ensued."[4] The *Amsterdam News* credited Monroe directly with the task, explaining that "before deserting the booth, Monroe . . . turned off the electric current . . . [which] probably saved scored of lives."[5] Indeed, "so absorbed were they in all the drama" of the western playing out on the screen in front of them that the audience missed the cracking noises that prompted Warner and Monroe's investigation in the first place. The local Black press's championing of Warner and Monroe for their work with the projection machine is significant given the general obscurity given motion picture operators. As one film industry expert noted, despite the operator's role as "an important function for the entire industry," he remained "unnoticed by the thousands who view his work" and was "accorded no publicity or glamor."[6] The Renaissance tragedy, however, came on the heels of a mass movement by Harlem's Black projectionists to publicize the essential nature of their skilled labor to the film industry and their right to unionization.

Just five years earlier, in 1925, eleven Black motion picture operators had decided to challenge what they perceived as a general ignorance of their difficult, skilled labor. Decrying the employment discrimination that they were facing at the Lafayette Theatre, they insisted, "We want a union: we want to live. . . . We call upon the colored theatre-goers who suffer daily from the exploitation of bosses. We call upon them to back us in this fight for the rights of colored labor."[7] Before striking at the Lafayette, these men were members of an independent organization of Black projectionists working in Harlem, the United Association of Colored Motion Picture Operators (UACMPO). After its formation, the group first appealed to Harlem's theaters for employment, subsequently fought their way into Local 306, and, once members, advocated for union standards at those Harlem's theaters that chose to employ Black operators.

First in 1926 and then again in 1930, at the Lafayette and Renaissance, respectively, the Black members of Local 306 demanded the same wages and working hours as white union men in theaters across the city. By the early 1930s, independent Black projectionist unions had begun to form as well, challenging the primacy of Local 306 while still showing the significance of Black employment in the trade. These intense battles, which included physical and verbal assaults, were waged publicly on street corners and within the city's Black weeklies with moderate success.

By focusing on Harlem's Black motion picture operators and their struggle for recognition, this chapter traces the deeply intertwined relationship between cinema, labor, and race in the city's Black film culture. As film scholar Anna Everett notes, "Part of the new reality [of Black modern life in the urban North] was the creation of a specifically African American niche in . . . the popular media of film."[8] The desire to be part of this developing modern cultural tool, then, resulted not only in filmmaking efforts and theaters appealing specifically to Black patrons but also in employment opportunities. For the most part, labor options for Black New Yorkers were limited. Racism kept the bulk of African American workers out of many jobs, including manufacturing and white-collar employment. Moreover, many of Harlem's white-owned businesses refused to hire Black labor, and if they did employ Black workers, it was in the least desirable positions. By 1930, most Black men were still working as either elevator operators or porters.[9]

For Harlem's Black projectionists, their skilled labor challenged the boundaries placed on their employment prospects, even during the Great Depression, when Black men and women remained disproportionately out of work or in service positions. Their union demands and eventual membership also makes them a part of a significant moment in the New Negro movement, one focused on Black unionism in the postwar years that included the guidance of Frank Crosswaith, an activist dedicated to organizing Black workers. Despite Local 306's resistance to their membership and Black workers' overall distrust of unions, these operators pushed for admission in the service of a fair wage and the recognition of their work, often unnoticed by theater audiences.

From 1925 to around 1935, the operators—both those independently organized and members of Local 306—waged their public battles on the basis that their labor was essential and they, therefore, held a certain power within the industry and deserved a place in Harlem's projection booths. With rhetoric similar to that expressed in trade presses and by industry experts, the operators argued that the show quite literally could not go on without them. Hidden in elevated and fireproof booths, they could be neither seen nor heard. However, as they make clear in their own public statements and protests through the pages of the *Amsterdam News* and the *Age*, their participation was active, essential, and exceedingly dangerous.[10]

Their activism reveals that, as "the final technological link between filmmaker and audience," the motion picture operator served a vital purpose.[11] They wanted recognition not just as employees but as full-fledged members of a cultural industry that needed their expert, skilled labor. Further, they insisted that they should be able to conduct that essential work in Harlem, where the majority of Black New Yorkers lived. Fighting on both the cultural and local level, Harlem's operators used Black film culture to command respect for their labor and assert a physical claim to Harlem for the city's Black laborers. In the face of an industry that often ridiculed and maligned their participation, most commonly by using racist caricatures or sidelining Black filmmakers, these operators stand out as an important challenge.

The Operator's Role

In a 1926 article in *Transactions of the Society of Motion Picture Engineers*, Lewis Townsend, a projection engineer, explained the multifaceted duties of a motion picture operator. His job started when he received a film's reels, combing through the film to ensure its integrity, searching for any worn-out portions or "punch-holes" made by previous projectionists to mark a reel change. It was also sometimes necessary for the operator to hand-clean the reels, as they were easily covered in oils, grease, and dirt. Then, if possible, he previewed the film with a musical director to arrange a proper score. This was all before the film was actually ready to be watched by the hundreds or thousands who would visit the theater. At showtime, Townsend notes, a projectionist's work depended, ultimately, on his machine. Distance from a screen varied, forcing a variation in arc light, which could affect the brightness and clarity of a film's image. Occasionally, an operator needed to adjust a machine's focus depending on the heat levels emitted from a particular arc.[12] By 1930, an additional mastery of sound technology was considered "an integral part of motion picture projection" with its own "rigid requirements" for electricity, voltage, and mathematics.[13] The transition to sound "necessitated the redesigning and reconstruction of projection rooms," and projectionists also needed to be more mindful of changeovers, which if done wrong could diminish sound quality and throw off the entire show.[14]

It was not uncommon for a nonunion operator to work twelve-hour shifts, in which he had a variety of responsibilities. According to one report in *The Nickelodeon*, moving picture operators had sixteen responsibilities in the typical song-and-picture variety program, which characterized many of Harlem's theaters, including the Lafayette.[15] A few of these, aside from actually cranking the projection machine at the appropriate speed and changing reels at the right time to ensure proper continuity, included rewinding films for the next projection; signaling for the next performer, such as a singer or a lecturer; turning the theater lights on and off; displaying intermission slides; and maintaining the theater's ventilation fans. After the nickelodeon period, in which some theaters continued to offer variety acts, the role of the projectionist varied by location. For example, a theater like the Lafayette, with mixed programming, could depend on their operator to conduct most of these responsibilities, while an operator at the Renaissance, which only showed films, would most likely be limited to projection.

After the 1910s, the labor of a motion picture operator occurred in a fireproof room above or behind the audience. These rooms were required by law, but the various aspects of them, such as the thickness of walls, the dimensions, and the items that could actually go in the space, depended on the size and reputation of the theater. Out of all of the operator's responsibilities, from the nickelodeon period until the switch from nitrate film to cellulose acetate "safety" stock in the 1950s, the most constant remained the continuous monitoring of the carbon arc lamp on the projection machine, which, if ignored, could light the film reel on fire and cause a dangerous stampede out of the theater or worse. The trade press frequently reported on a number of horror stories, reflecting the danger of the profession and the absolute necessity for projectionists to be trained—not only for their own safety, but also for patrons. For example, in a January 1908 *Moving Picture World* editorial, the necessity of having an experienced operator was made clear by a tragedy in Boyertown, Pennsylvania. A fire caused by a knocked-over kerosene lamp on the same stage as a stereopticon machine resulted in the death of 171 men, women, and children in attendance.[16]

In yet another shocking story, the editors of *Safety Engineering*, a publication dedicated to the prevention of needless waste by fire and accidents, shared a "sad example of the discouraging contest against indifference and stupidity" in an operator's booth in Newark, New Jersey. The projectionist failed in respect to a number of safety protocols expected of someone who was properly licensed with five years of experience. First of all, the operator's booth was equipped, by law, with tin fire shutters on the wall shared with the auditorium, which were set to close automatically in the case of a fire to protect the audience. For some reason, the operator had taken them down and had not yet put them back into place, even after the theater manager warned him to. When a film caught fire, the operator panicked and attempted to save the whole reel, which was not in danger.

As was reported, "A temporary obstruction stopped the film as it was going through the film trap in the picture machine long enough for the concentrated rays from the lamp to ignite it. This happens frequently. When it does cool-headed operators stop machines, safety shutters close, films burn a few inches and the flames die out." When, instead, the operator removed the reel and "flicked" out the fire, a spark landed on five uncovered reels, which should have been in metal containers with spring lids. The reels instantly combusted, and the operator's clothing caught fire. Not only did this operator not follow protocol that could have prevented his untimely death but the safety shutters failed to close, causing the audience to panic and stampede out of the building upon seeing the flames. The author of the report questioned just what would have happened if this had been in a "storefront theater, as many are in New York."[17]

These sordid tales of operators' miscalculations provided fuel to reform efforts targeting the burgeoning film industry.[18] As nickelodeons gained traction as a cheap amusement, "one of the avowed goals of the newly organized industry was to clean it up."[19] The industry trade press played a large role in this process in a number of ways, including offering uniform standards for things like lighting, advertising, and, of course, projection. From his earliest appearances in *Moving Picture World*, F. H. Richardson, an "expert operator" and eventual technical editor of the magazine, attempted to standardize projectionist work.[20] Richardson's first series with the magazine was titled "Lessons for Operators" and offered monthly columns, starting in February 1908, on basic rules such as preparedness in the booth and detailed electrical and wiring instruction.

A few months later, it became clear that Richardson considered fair wages and proper training for projectionists central to the economic and artistic success of any theater. "The operator is the man who puts on the show," he wrote in May 1908, "and you might as well say that a cheap barnstormer can play Hamlet as well as the best talent as to assert that a cheap, careless, ignorant operator can put on a credible show."[21] Richardson criticized managers who aimed to save a quick buck by paying cheap wages to unqualified operators, thereby offering a poor show and keeping capable men out of the booth. By September 1909, Richardson was much more direct in his castigations: "You invest from two to fifty thousand dollars in a house and then place the operating room, on which depends absolutely the income from your investment, in the hands of a $12 a week man. Is that common sense?" "What I mean is that by paying decent salaries you will be able to get good operators," he explained, "which you cannot do for $12 per week in New York, or elsewhere."[22] Almost twenty years later, as Richardson and others continued to advocate for the centrality of projectionists' labor, Harlem's motion picture operators used this same rhetoric in their attempts to seek employment and union membership, firmly grounding themselves within the industry's concerns over their labor.

Beyond the writings of men like Richardson, two other events provided the grounds for the operators' activism in Harlem two decades later: licensing requirements and the formation of a motion picture operator local. Starting in mid-1908, the New York City Board of Water Supply, Gas, and Electricity began licensing requirements for motion picture projection. To obtain a license, one needed to pass an examination that included questions testing technical knowledge of electrical currents, operation of a projector, and safety precautions. An exam, which in New York was conducted orally, could easily ask, "What mechanical defects will cause travel ghost on the screen when framing lever is moved above center?" or "Design an operating room which embodies your ideas of what [one] should be, naming six principal points to be considered in the construction thereof."[23] Of the 332 people who applied for a license and of the 200 examined the first year it was required, less than half passed.[24] By 1922, the number of licenses granted reached well over two thousand. In addition to the examination, which was kept relevant in terms of technological advancement, the applicant was required to have at least six months' worth of an apprenticeship under the direction of an already licensed operator. There were no clear-cut racial restrictions in terms of the city's licensing procedures, and the lack of a licensing fee made it more accessible to people interested. The apprenticeship, however, could prove prohibitive for Black operators in a new market.[25] Though it is not clear when he earned his license, Thomas Johnson, a vocal advocate for Black projectionists, was an operator in Harlem since at least 1910, making him, most likely, one of the first licensed Black operators in the neighborhood.[26]

Also in 1908, the International Alliance of Theatrical and Stage Employees (IATSE) formed an affiliation with the American Federation of Labor (AFL), with Local 306 eventually representing the Greater New York area.[27] Suggesting the union's hold over the area, 65 percent of motion picture houses in that jurisdiction used union-affiliated operators less than a decade later.[28] More generally, as film historian Donald Crafton notes, IATSE, and Local 306 by proxy, "found itself with much greater power, because without a projectionist, the show couldn't go on."[29] In 1922, *Exhibitor's Review* ran a profile of Local 306 and its president, Samuel Kaplan. The piece proudly announced that Kaplan ran a "successful leadership of a band of men representing virtually every race and creed," which purportedly made him "tolerant and just."[30] In his interview, Kaplan remarked that his "life work" was to advance "the cause and improve the status of the moving picture machine operator."[31] Despite the publication's high praise and Kaplan's own thoughts on his work, Local 306 remained prejudiced against Black operators. The AFL was historically discriminatory against Black workers, often invoking individual locals' autonomy in deciding their own membership rules, even when they were created to the detriment of nonwhite workers.[32] In New York, Local 306 attempted to unionize theaters that employed nonunion Black operators, thereby threatening to remove them from employment, while at the same time refusing Black operators entry into their organization.[33]

Harlem's Black operators, in many ways, rested their activism on these important developments. In defense of their work and significance to the film industry, they mirrored the points made by Richardson during the rise of cinema's popularity at the turn of the century. They seized upon earlier calls for better wages and the centrality of the operator's role to a successful show. Indeed, their own struggles for unionization and fair employment coincided with continued industry efforts to emphasize the deeply essential labor of the projectionist and were built off a surge in Black unionism after World War I.

Supported in Fight by All Harlem Theatres, Except Lafayette

Members of the Motion Picture Operators' Union Employed in Harlem Theatres — (Left to Right, Standing)—Samuel Brown, Eugene Satterfield, John Gibson, Bert Staples, Fred Cannon. Middle Row. L. to R.—Thomas Johnson, Walter Simms, Charlie Hankerson, Bennie Proctor. Bottom, L. to R.—Granville Dick, Reginald Warner.

Figure 4.1 Black members of Local 306 and former members of UACMPO. *(Image published with permission of ProQuest LLC. Further reproduction is prohibited without permission. Used with permission of* New York Amsterdam News *from September 29, 1926 issue; permission conveyed through Copyright Clearance Center, Inc.)*

Employment and Unionization for Harlem's Black Operators

In 1925, after having tried unsuccessfully to gain access to Local 306, at least eleven Black operators decided to create their own organization of operators, the UACMPO.[34] Though some of the first motion picture operators in Black film history were women, the entirety of this group was male.[35] Census data reveals that almost all of the men were born in the United States, with only Granville Dick born in the British West Indies. Some of the men were migrants, such as Bennie Proctor and Walters Simms from South Carolina, Thomas Johnson from Maryland, Charles Hankerson from New Jersey, and John Gibson from Delaware. The oldest of the men was Reginald Warner at forty-six, while Samuel Brown was the youngest at just twenty.[36] Interestingly, only Walter Simms and Johnson were lodgers, while the rest rented their own apartments or lived with their parents. Six of the men were married, and all of their wives were afforded the ability to stay at home, uncompelled to join the workforce. Finally, and perhaps most importantly, all of them at one point between 1925 and 1930 lived in Harlem. It is unclear when the men of UACMPO decided to come together, but they sought the help of Black labor activist Frank Crosswaith in 1925.

By then, Crosswaith had a well-known reputation as an activist committed to Black involvement in the labor movement and socialist politics. Born in St. Croix in 1892 and having lived in the United States since his teens, Crosswaith cut his teeth learning and organizing with other Black intellectuals and radicals like A. Philip Randolph, Gloria Campbell, Cyril Briggs, and Richard B. Moore.[37] The same year that the UACMPO approached him for help in their unionization battle, Crosswaith was at the head of the newly formed Trade Union Committee for Organizing of Negro Workers (TUCONW). The purpose of the organization was "not only to organize Negro workers, but also to secure justice for them inside the unions, and to educate both Negro and white workers toward a realization of their common economic interest."[38] Crosswaith truly believed that the "reputation of the Negro as a scab is unjustified," and this misgiving sullied the potential of interracial labor organizing. If given a fair chance, he stressed, Black workers would participate in trade unionism, thereby making labor stronger.[39] With Crosswaith by their side, the UACMPO's fight was twofold—they wanted employment in Harlem's Black-patronized theaters and official union membership, which would grant them standardized and improved wages and hours.

The first part of their fight started in mid-1925, when the UACMPO began using Harlem's weeklies to make "no demand upon theatre owners and managers . . . [but] simply coming forward, asking for a fair chance."[40] As only a few Black operators were hired in white theaters outside of Harlem, it seemed "no more than just that they should seek a livelihood in a community where the support comes from their own people."[41] At the start of their fight, Black operators were only employed in the Lafayette and Renaissance Theatres, but the Roosevelt, Douglas, Franklin, Lincoln, and Odeon were actively being petitioned. For the next decade, the *Amsterdam News* and the *Age*, both weeklies with wide local and national readership, played significant roles in keeping readers abreast of the operators' concerns, struggles, and triumphs. The coverage and editorials within these two papers afforded the operators and their struggles a large public audience and, sometimes, reporters willing to advocate on their behalf. The *Amsterdam News*, in particular, was aware of its own role in the fight.

"As the Negro has no other paper but those conducted by his own people to air his grievances," one article read, "the *Amsterdam News* felt that it was doing its duty by those colored men working at the motion picture trade when we asked (no, even demanded) that theatres supported by Negroes should at least give Negro picture operators a chance."[42]

In their appeals to the public, UACMPO members echoed trade press concerns about projectionists. Just a few years before UACMPO set out to get employed and unionized, *Exhibitor's Review* ran a five-part series arguing that "the operator is the prisoner of the booth, unnoticed by the thousands who view his work."[43] In a letter published in the *Amsterdam News* almost a year into their struggle, the operators lamented that "because the operator in a theatre is hidden away from the view of the public," the injustices they suffer, like white men taking their jobs, go unnoticed.[44] Harlem's Black operators were not asking for fame or notoriety but the chance to ply their trade. They reasoned that "the theatre-going public of our race is not aware of the treatment" they received "or they would . . . help us in some way to secure these positions."[45] In a reminder of the stringent licensing requirements, their letter explained, "We have sacrificed too much in our efforts to pass the rigid examination in order to get our licenses."[46] This reference to their hard work was just the first of quite a few mentions they made about the labor they conducted in the projection booth. The operators' letter, then, was an attempt to force Harlemites to reflect on the men who were behind the booth's doors, to recognize their work, and to make conscious, race-first decisions in their patronage of motion picture theaters in Harlem.

In the midst of this, Crosswaith began negotiations with Local 306, despite the latter's constant resistance. The union only gave Black operators the chance to join when it needed their help: When they did not want the Black operators to break strikes, they handed out membership cards that were then taken away after the strikes were over.[47] UACMPO's public demands for more work in the neighborhood and the realization that Black operators already worked in some Harlem theaters, which precluded Local 306 from unionizing there, led the union to consider membership for Black projectionists under restricted circumstances. Like other unions that sought to limit Black membership, the local offered the Black operators a separate auxiliary unit. Members of this auxiliary could not participate in regular union meetings and, instead, would be granted a white representative who would speak to their needs and grievances at these meetings. Black members would, however, still be required to pay regular union dues and other fees, which were steep at upward of one hundred dollars. While granted union wages, they were "confined as far as physically possible to working in the colored belt [Harlem],"

Figure 4.2 Frank Crosswaith at work in the offices of the Negro Labor Committee, undated. *(Photograph by Hansel Mieth; Collection Center for Creative Photography. © Center for Creative Photography, The University of Arizona Foundation. Image provided by Photographs and Prints Division, Schomburg Center for Research in Black Culture, The New York Public Library)*

not permitted to work outside of the neighborhood.[48] In a final attempt at some form of agreement, the local claimed that the Black operators could eventually, at an undisclosed date in a "reasonable amount of time," apply for full-fledged membership but could never attend regular meetings.[49] The operators justifiably rejected these terms.[50]

The *Amsterdam News* and the *Age* often reported on labor issues in the city, which included the efforts of Black workers and organizations to unionize. With the exception of the Black-run Brotherhood of the Sleeping Car Porters union, the papers held a mild attitude toward unions and a decidedly critical stance toward the AFL.[51] The papers' main focus was the overall well-being of Black workers throughout the city, and they remained wary of Local 306 and its restrictions on Black members. When one reporter learned of Local 306's proposed membership policies, he asked:

Can . . . [you] please explain why, in the name of all that's holy they [the union] would foster a Jim Crow organization in this part of the country where outstanding white Americans, born and bred in this and other countries, have led a valiant brigade . . . who fought and succeeded in doing away with the Jim Crow practices of that benighted section of this country where ignorance runs rife and lynching is the chief outdoor sport?[52]

The author directly confronted the union men with their own racism and demanded that "the black boys get a chance in their own community," where eleven white men were already working, despite its label as "the black belt."[53] At this early stage in their battle, both the press and the operators were already linking Black film culture to the local, equating their demands with eradicating the city's Jim Crow restrictions and the operators' entitlement to Harlem's theaters.

By June 1926, the Black operators and Local 306 had come to an understanding, most likely because Local 306 was trying to unionize more theaters in Harlem, some of which had already employed Black operators. Essentially, the union needed Harlem's Black operators' participation and cooperation in order to extend the union's monopoly over the city. Despite claiming that "we are not at all averse to stating we would like to see our motion picture operators earning a livelihood WITHOUT the union" just a month earlier, the *Amsterdam News* joined the "battle for recognition of the union" at the Lafayette, which was just stirring up.[54]

After a year of fighting for union admittance and publicly calling for employment in Harlem's theaters, the Black operators were able to call their two-pronged campaign a success. The operators had finally won the right to join Local 306 on what, at first, seemed like equal ground. Black operators were also employed, since at least March, in the Gem, Renaissance, and Lafayette and, after union membership, the Roosevelt, Douglas, and Lincoln Theatres. Further, those Black operators who chose to join the union received a massive pay raise. Unionized operators received $63.02 for thirty-five hours of work, whereas before membership they had received $45 for sixty-six hours.[55]

Once the Black operators joined the union, their priorities changed. Now capable of being paid union wages and working union hours, the men realized the unfair working conditions they were subjected to in nonunionized theaters. Their fight, then, shifted from employment and union recognition to the employment of unionized Black operators in those theaters—specifically the Lafayette and Renaissance—that already hired Black operators but at overworked, underpaid standards.

Local 306 and the Strike at the Lafayette

On Monday, September 6, 1926, "without any notice or warning whatsoever," two of the newly admitted Black members of Local 306 failed to show up for work at the Lafayette.[56] Hours after skipping work, the Black operators, with the help of other white and Black union members, "appeared on Seventh Avenue in the vicinity of Lafayette Theatre, picketing the house" after two Black operators had been fired after asking for the same pay wage as white union members at a different establishment owned by Leo Brecher.[57] Demanding the same scale of wages as the white operators in union houses, the operators were, they explained, only trying to "save a little money and perhaps secure some of the comforts of life to which we all aspire at some time or other in our lives."[58] The fight became "open warfare" as both the Lafayette management and the operators took to Harlem's Black weeklies to defend their respective claims.[59]

In an interview with picketer Thomas Johnson, a Black member of Local 306 and former member of UACMPO, the *Amsterdam News* recounted how strongly these men felt about their right to equal pay in their own neighborhood. Johnson explained, "Two of our men, who had worked faithfully for years, were thrown out of work because we had the audacity to ask for the same scale of wages as the same owners of the theatre in question have been paying to white operators in another one of their houses." The operators, as Johnson made clear, were simply asking for fairness, and they were using union membership to do so. Aware that he and the operators needed the help of the Lafayette's consumers, Johnson exclaimed, "Make it clear and ask the colored people of Harlem if they think it is right for any theatre owner or manager to assume that because we are Negroes we should be satisfied with a smaller wage and longer working hours than those white boys."[60] He continued:

> The race is on trial and if they want to continue to give their dimes and quarters to those who would deny us a small share of the returns for our labor, let the black residents of Harlem announce to black people all over America that they are against those of us who would use our God-given right . . . to agitate in an orderly manner to better our condition.[61]

In this ringing denunciation of those Black Harlemites who continued to support theaters that refused Black men and women equal employment opportunities, the Black projectionists made clear how serious they were about their fight against Brecher, whom they deemed unreasonable and racist.

Thomas Johnson and the rest of Harlem's Black operators were also acutely aware of the connection between their good work and the entertainment and economical value of the evening's entertainment. On a number of occasions, Brecher insinuated that motion picture operation was "a comparatively simple and easy job" and that "any colored man with a slight mechanical bent can do it."[62] Simplifying the nature of the labor, Brecher claimed that anyone "can learn to operate a motion picture machine in the course of a week, and be able to pass the requirements to enable him to obtain a license."[63] The Black operators quickly challenged Brecher and his careless assumptions, laying out the demands on a projectionist in a letter printed in the *Amsterdam News*.

In addition to the fact that projecting is actually "arduous and eye-straining work," they explained to readers that the operator "must have an excellent knowledge of mechanics, electricity and optics, and is in charge of a delicate and complicated mechanism, made with scientific accuracy to handle a fragile and inflammable material."[64] Directly confronting Brecher's simplistic analysis of their work, the operators framed their labor as a detailed process, necessitating great care, training, and expertise. Perhaps most significantly, the operators drew an important relationship between their labor and the entire film industry: "The projectionist has a great responsibility, for a failure to measure up to the right standards means that all the producer, director, actor and cinematographer have striven for loses much of its artistic and commercial value."[65] "The pleasure of the audience is lessened," the letter continued, "the exhibitor is subject to constant expense, and lives and property are endangered."[66]

Indeed, a similar sentiment was expressed in the trade presses. "A motion picture machine operator," one column exalted, "is essential to the conduct of every motion picture theatre."[67] The article continued, "The operator or projectionist . . . often is an important factor in the sum total superiority in entertainment value, which the discriminating exhibitor offers his patrons."[68] The Black members of Local 306 recognized their worth in Harlem's theaters and, using the language of the industry, challenged Brecher's "efforts to place the colored operators on the par of a porter."[69]

Following the breaking coverage of the strike, Leo Brecher and Frank Schiffman, owner and manager of the Lafayette, respectively, issued statements to the *Amsterdam News*. Brecher argued that, with the exception of the manager, the entire workforce at the Lafayette had been Black since he took over the theater in June 1925. He maintained that "at no time was there a condition, either as to surroundings or wages [which they claimed were on par with union standards], to which [the Black operators] raised any objection."[70] Yet, when they joined a union that "did everything possible to keep a colored man from getting work as a motion picture machine operator," they decided to picket the one theater that handed them the best opportunities in Harlem.[71] Despite Brecher's claims that he was paying his Black operators higher than union wages, it seems unreasonable to imagine that the Black operators would strike for equal pay if they were already receiving it.

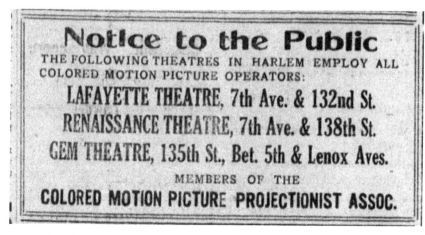

Figure 4.3 The UACMPO placed notices in the city's Black weeklies, advising audiences on which theaters to attend and support. This one was printed in the *New York Age* in 1926. *(Public domain)*

Taking personal offense to the strike, Schiffman condemned the protest as a "campaign in which pickets, platform orators, circulars, and other means of propaganda were used . . . in which malicious falsehoods flowed free and fast . . . which was calculated to deceive the residents of Harlem."[72] He argued that he and Brecher "brought about a substantial improvement in the entire tone of the theatrical entertainment which this community enjoy" and that they had always employed Black labor in doing so.[73]

Local 306 did not remain quiet on the matter. In a letter to the *Amsterdam News*, the union claimed that Brecher and Schiffman were moving "heaven and earth to help out-of-town Negro operators to secure their New York licenses and work at the Lafayette" only so the claim of racism could not be made against them.[74] The union even went so far as to maintain that Brecher would rather close the Lafayette than acquiesce to union demands. The operators also refused to hold back against Brecher and Schiffman's claims about how well they treated their Black employees. They argued that not only was Brecher lying about the Lafayette already having eight-hour workdays ("colored operators . . . were always made to work 11 hours a day, seven days a week") but the wages were significantly lower than those demanded by the union ("under union conditions the payroll for the Lafayette operators would be $141.40 a week . . . as against $74 the management pays").[75]

The strike against the Lafayette was complicated by a number of developments. First, a month after the Black operators started their campaign at the Lafayette, the white members of the union began to strike other Brecher establishments in the city, including the Washington, Olympic, and Verona The-atres. When Brecher and Schiffman agreed to the union stipulations at the Lafayette, the Black operators would not give in unless the other (white) hous-es were unionized. As they framed it, "they would consider themselves curs" if they accepted, leaving "the white men with whom they became affiliated to paddle their own canoe."[76] Second, it was revealed in an *Age* article that the Motion Pictures License Bureau, under the Department of Water Supply, Gas, and Electricity, was led by a union man. It was suggested that "many competent colored operators who have taken the examination have been made to fail in order to bar them from jobs."[77] Third, it became somewhat clear that while Harlem's theaters were employing Black operators, they were hiring them mainly as relief operators, who received fewer hours and less pay. As the battle waged on between the union and the theater, two of Harlem's street orators, Professor S. R. Williams and Hubert Harrison, got involved and ad-dressed some of these complications.

Despite his distrust of AFL-affiliated unions, Harrison promised to stump for the Black operators in Harlem during their strike, which he did until an injunction on street oration forced him to stop. After deciding to conduct his own investigation, Harrison met with Schiffman and suspected "something fishy about their [the union's] claim that they had Negro workers' interests primarily at heart."[78] He learned that even after Brecher agreed to the Local 306's stipulations at the Lafayette, the union would not halt the strike unless Brecher unionized the rest of his theaters, which only employed white opera-tors. Schiffman also informed Harrison that the union invited Black members into its fold just as their contracts at Brecher theaters were up, suggesting that the union did not want the Black operators to act as scabs.

Here was Harrison's biggest contention: Local 306 was using the Black union members to satisfy their own interests, those of the white union mem-bers working in theaters outside of Harlem. Harrison also discovered that, in unionized theaters across the city, the chief operators employed were always white. In a personal search of the projection booths in three Harlem theaters (Odeon, Lincoln, and Roosevelt), Harrison found only three Black opera-tors—all of whom were relief. After this, Harrison apologized to Schiffman and decided to no longer advocate for the union. He warned the Black op-erators: "a record of facts stares them unblinkingly in the face," but "what they may choose to do . . . is their business."[79]

Professor S. R. Williams, another respected orator, also visited with Frank Schiffman. Upon learning the same information that Harrison did, in addi-tion to the fact that the union was apparently forcing the Black operators to continue on with the strike against their will in order to support white operators outside of Harlem, Williams considered "the union's position in this case absolutely indefensible."[80] The Lafayette, Williams explained, "is an institution in Harlem" and "the fact that the public has continued to pack the theatre daily is to my mind a sufficient answer to what the community thinks."[81] Still, the union and its newest Black members refused to back down, and the battle waged on.

By June 1927, nine months after the fight against the Lafayette began, the strike was anticlimactically called to an end. After a few months of no reporting on the matter, the *Amsterdam News* informed its readers that the union and the Lafayette had settled their issues outside of court "to the satisfaction of all parties concerned" and the Black operators had returned to the theater on union standards.[82] The paper recounted that "although Negroes did not respond as it thought they would when the news went through Harlem like wild fire that a real strike was taking place in our midst," the Black operators still came out on the winning side of the situation.[83] Even in the face of the apathy of Harlem's theater patrons, who continued to attend nightly shows, the operators had managed to secure more equitable wages and hours at the Lafayette. In a final letter to the paper, the Black members of Local 306 recognized the essential role that the *Amsterdam News* had played in their fight against the Lafayette. Walter Simms, an original UACMPO member, wrote, "With gratitude to you, our present condition is all that could be hoped for," and "We take the liberty to say at this point that the 'N.Y. Amsterdam news is as valuable as time.'"[84]

In the years following the Lafayette strike, Black operators across Harlem began to be hired at more theaters. Already employed at the Lafayette, Renaissance, Lincoln, Gem, Roosevelt, and Douglas Theatres, by the end of 1930, they also worked in the Alhambra and Orient. Yet the positions in these theaters were not always secure. As contracts expired and the Great Depression hit, Local 306 found itself going on strike more frequently in Harlem. After the successful strike at the Lafayette, the operators targeted the only other theater in Harlem that had employed Black workers, including projectionists, from the beginning of their demands for recognition—the Renaissance.

As opposed to the earlier strike, which lasted about nine months, the operators' fight against the Renaissance lasted on and off for years because of management changes and financial issues. Similar to previous efforts, though, the Black operators who challenged the Renaissance through Local 306 or formed alternative unions to do so centered their significance to the film industry in very particular ways. They still continued to defend their status as skilled laborers, who not only went through arduous examination processes

and apprenticeships but who also needed to adapt to changes in the industry—namely, the coming of sound.

Sound Transitions and Alternative Unions
at the Renaissance

After a rocky experimentation period, sound films, iterations of which had
been demonstrated as early as 1906, became mainstays by 1930.[85] The transition to sound, media studies scholar Steve Wurtzler has argued, prompted an
"industrywide concern with both the labor and the identity of the motion
picture operator."[86] Much as during the nickelodeon period, the projectionist
became a central character in standardization efforts as sound technology
became more widespread. In the early years of sound technology's rise, F. H.
Richardson continued to defend "the very vital part which the theater projectionist and his work plays in the success of any production."[87] He connected good projection with the ultimate economic success of all theaters,
arguing that any manager who refused to "appreciate and recognize efficient
work on the part of the motion picture projectionist" would, in the end, lose
the loyalty of his patrons.[88] Sound technology, he further theorized, encouraged operators to imagine themselves "to be very largely responsible for the
general effect—for the putting on of the entire show."[89] Decades-old concerns
about the motion picture operator as the final step in the industry, with "artists on the screen and audiences in the seats . . . at their mercy," were also
reignited.[90]

Organized labor, too, embraced the operator's continued importance in
the midst of technological change. In 1929, William F. Canavan, president
of the IATSE, insisted that a projectionist was an artist, "mechanically etch-
ing upon the silver screen a series of beautiful photographic images that are
unfolding to his movie audience a visual impression of a beautiful story told
with the aid of his mechanical pen."[91] Ultimately, the coming of sound imbued projectionists with a "new power within the industry" that the operators
in Harlem utilized to their defense.[92]

In 1930, almost four years to the day after the start of the Lafayette strike,
white and Black members of Local 306 began to picket the Renaissance
Theatre. Its manager, Cleo Charity, refused to sign a new contract with the union
when it expired on September 1, and any attempts at striking a deal were denied.[93] Charity argued that sound technology, recently brought to the Renaissance, changed labor practices within the union. Since 1927, five men had

been required to work at any movie house, given hour and workday restrictions, and two men needed to be in the booth at all times to ensure the safety of the projectionists and the theatergoers. A union official speaking to the *Age* reminded readers about the particularities of projection, which required not only one man to maintain full focus on the projection machine but another "to rewind, examine films, and make ready and look after the sound volume."[94] With highly flammable film reels, another Black operator explained, "there are times when it is impossible for one man to handle [the] talking picture apparatus with any degree of safety."[95]

Again framing their argument in terms of skill, the operators pushed the fact that projection, especially with sound, was an extremely tedious and arduous process that required constant supervision. Even Frank Crosswaith, who was working with the Black operators again, decried the Renaissance's "economic lynch program" where "two men are compelled to do the work of five."[96] He urged that "the management of the Renaissance theatre must not be permitted to re-establish in Harlem the cruel practice of under-paying and over-working Negro motion picture operators."[97]

Still, Charity found it impossible to maintain that many operators in the face of a "general business depression."[98] "The union," he declared, "has assumed an arrogant, unfair and dictatorial attitude which, if allowed to continue, could wreck any business enterprise that runs counter to its demands."[99] In his criticism of the union's seemingly extraneous demands on the theater, it is quite possible that Charity was referencing the Lincoln Theatre. Owned at this point by Leo Brecher, the theater had been closed because of financial issues "after a fight had been staged" by the Black members of Local 306 just a few months earlier.[100] The question remained, according to Charity, "whether a business must hire more labor than he needs to maintain a payroll at times greater than for which he has the money to pay."[101] It took two years, but the answer to that question was a resounding "maybe."

Unable to meet overhead costs from white property owners, the Renaissance transferred from Black management to white in early 1932.[102] Forced to pay $500 per week in rent, not including repairs like those needed after the projection booth disaster, Black management at the Renaissance could no longer hold their stake in Harlem's entertainment landscape. After its takeover, the new white ownership reinstated a contract with Local 306, only to refuse to renew it in 1933, sparking a new round of tensions that simmered for over ten years.

As with the previous strike, race and employment in Harlem's movie theaters played a major role in both sides of the on-and-off fight against the Renaissance. When Charity refused to hire projectionists from Local 306, he did not snub union labor altogether. In fact, he hired Black operators from another union in the city, the Empire State Motion Picture Operators Union.[103] Though the union was not formally recognized by the AFL or any other national labor body, it presented stiff competition for Local 306.[104] To the dismay of Local 306 members, including those Black men who fought hard to be admitted, Empire State seemed to offer work for longer hours at lower wages. They also continued to undermine Local 306 standards by not requiring a theater to maintain two men in a booth.[105]

Around the same time, another unofficial union, the Motion Picture Projection Association (MPPA), was established in Harlem and added to the rivalry. When white management at the Renaissance later realized it could cut costs and also get recognition for hiring Black projectionists, it dropped Local 306 and picked up the competitor union. Black projectionists in these competing unions worked in the Franklin, Orient, and Renaissance indefinitely and the Harlem Opera House until 1933. Black members of Local 306 were keenly aware of the consequences of these actions, asserting that hiring non–Local 306 men was "an attempt to force Negroes to work for much less than white operators with no opportunity to earn enough for a living wage."[106] The gains that the UACMPO had made just seven years earlier were at stake. Without Local 306 standards, these men argued, the wages of all Black operators would be unfairly lowered beyond a livable salary, and all of them, regardless of any particular union, would lose out in the end.

Squabbles between these competitor unions continued for years inside and outside of Harlem and, mostly because of racism within Local 306, were still not resolved by the mid-1930s. Though the *Amsterdam News* and some of the Black operators swore on the union's willingness to do right by its Black members, Local 306 remained discriminatory. Granville Dick and Charles Hankerson, both original members of UACMPO, were in contact with the NAACP in 1934 concerning the racism they experienced as members of the union. In addition to being "safely bottled up in Harlem," Black operators were not allowed to work in Loew's or RKO chains in the neighborhood and made significantly less pay than white operators in other theaters in the city.[107] When negotiations between the AFL, Local 306, and the Renaissance faltered, Dick went public with his complaints. During an interview with the mayor's commission on conditions in Harlem, he testified that the now twenty-five Black members of Local 306 "were allowed to work only in certain smaller theatres in the Harlem district and were barred 'altogether' from working in any theatre outside of the district."[108] The larger theater chains in Harlem, Dick maintained, were entirely staffed by white union men. Black union operators were also making significantly less than white union operators at thirty-seven dollars per week versus sixty-five dollars per week. "Powerful enough to disregard justice and right," Local 306 continued their discrimination mostly unabated and in the face of Black protest within their ranks.[109]

Since the early 1930s, Local 306 had also refused to grant new Black members admission to its organization on the grounds that it had no room, forcing the hand of Harlem's other Black projectionists who desired recognition for their hard work and, perhaps, less restrictive working conditions.[110] They, too, were licensed and experienced and wanted the same wages granted to those Black projectionists in the official union. These other organizations, though unofficial, served as significant alternative spaces for Black projectionists to fight for their right to work in Harlem at fair wages and to ply their chosen trade. For example, in 1935, members of the MPPA won higher wages and lower hours at the Franklin Theatre.[111] In 1940, the same group was responsible for forcing the Regent Theatre in Brooklyn to hire a Black projectionist, the first in the entire borough. It was not until 1945, when Local 306 finally agreed to accept every single member of the MPPA into its fold, that the competition and, most likely, the continuous strikes against the Renaissance and other Harlem theaters came to an end.[112]

In spite of almost two decades' worth of constant reporting in the local press on the issues at stake in the operators' struggles, Harlemites seemed to generally ignore the picket lines at the theaters. "The *Amsterdam News*," explained Romeo Dougherty, "did everything within its power to arouse the people of the community to the necessity of supporting the operators, but they were dormant."[113] Even Frank Schiffman noted that the Lafayette remained packed during the 1926 strike, and one editorialist in the *Age* in 1932 observed that "people in Harlem don't care a hoop in h . . . l about picketing—not even when they are really justifiable."[114] Despite Harlemites' resistance to the operators' picketing, the strikes and public demonstrations were not necessarily a failure.[115]

Starting in 1925, the Black members of UACMPO successfully convinced a number of Harlem theaters that Black operators should be employed in those theaters that served majority-Black patrons. Once they were employed in these places, the operators then forced the hand of Local 306. If the union wanted those theaters unionized, which it absolutely needed in order to maintain its desired monopoly over the city, white union men would have to cooperate with Black operators. In this way, and in the span of less than two years, UACMPO projectionists secured themselves more employment in Harlem's booths and union membership. Though Local 306 continued its discriminatory policies, it is clear that most Black members believed union membership was the way to go for recognition of their skilled labor.

Further, the men were not limited in their union options; Reginald Warner left Local 306 and subsequently joined the Empire State Union after the latter struck the Renaissance. Thus, despite arguments that Harlem's Black leadership failed to recognize "the impact of the developing American cultural apparatus on the economics, the politics, and the creative and social development of the black community," the neighborhood's Black operators actually centered their relationship to the film industry in their struggle.[116] They utilized the rhetoric of industry specialists, insisted on the recognition of the skill and expertise, and publicly demonstrated on the grounds of their essential labor in their own neighborhood.

Harlem's Black motion picture operators, then, are important examples of the myriad ways Black film culture was shaped by and constituted calls for equality and justice. The labor of these men, largely ignored until they presented it to the public by way of the local Black press, was key to the success of any movie house in Harlem that gave them a chance to occupy their booths. In waging fights against those that refused, they demonstrated that they were not discouraged by restrictions on their employment prospects or racism within the ranks of organized labor. Their demands also reflect a desire to be treated fairly and to live their lives as others do: "We have the same obligations to our children as the white workers have. We too want our children well-fed and decently clothed. We, too, want to educate our children. Theirs is the future, ours the duty to defend that future."[117] Challenging discrimination within the operator's booth, these men were part of a larger culture of organization and protest against the film industry's continual disregard for Black humanity, which also included New York City's Black film critics and ordinary Harlemites alike.

Black Film Criticism at the *New York Age*

In 1909, the *New York Age* issued a call to action regarding New York City's antidiscrimination laws. The paper brought attention to a New York statute, which dated back to 1873, by reminding Black New Yorkers that they were "entitled to full and equal rights and privileges" in places of public accommodation and amusement. Citing a Black patron's recent court victory over a sightseeing company, the article insisted, "The date is far too late for respectable colored men and women to be humiliated in public places." Explaining that the offenses continued "because examples have not been made of offenders," the *Age* promised to no longer be "lax and negligent" and to report more on "other instances of [the law's] violation." In a rallying cry to resist violations of the antidiscrimination law, the anonymous author exclaimed, "We call upon our citizens to accept no humiliation, we call upon our public men and women to awake!"[1]

That very same year, the dramatic editor of the *Age*, Lester Walton, wrote his first in-depth article on film in New York City. The piece, scathing in its critique of the sensationalist tactics used by exhibitors to lure in audiences, was the first of many written by Walton and his successors at the paper dedicated to the relationship between New York City's Black film culture, the fight for civil rights, and Black New Yorkers' right to enjoy the medium. Their protests were often aimed at two specific kinds of discrimination: racist discrimination within the city's theaters and the persistent dehumanization of Blackness in film. And while filmic representations were not subject to the state's civil rights laws (or the Motion Picture Commission's responsibilities), journalists actively tied racist representational practices to larger patterns of discrimination, including lynching, throughout the country and city.

While other local newspapers such as the *New York Amsterdam News* and the *Inter-state Tattler* offered film commentary and criticism, their coverage remained spotty, less critically developed, or more focused on drama. The *Age*, which had a reputation as "one of the most constructive influences for the betterment of conditions among the Negroes of all groups in the United States," by contrast, covered film in detail from very early on.[2] Journalists at the *Age* were explicit in their connections between racist cinema and its proprietors and the debilitating effects of racism on Black New Yorkers. Thus, their writings speak to the power of cinema as a medium and also to the significance of theaters as they related to Black life in the city. For them, debating and delineating the consequences of cinema went beyond just pointing to negative images on the screen to critically assess their relationship to theaters as institutions with power and meaning.

This chapter traces how journalists at the *Age*, specifically Lester Walton and Vere E. Johns, wrote about racist practices in theaters. As the first Black journalist in the country to discuss film on a deeply critical level, writing from around 1909 into the 1920s, Walton offers readers an intimate glance into responses to the growth of cinema from its early stages to its solidification within American culture. Johns's own rhetoric, appearing as it did in the 1930s, reveals the lasting significance of film culture in the Black community. Their writings, taken together, should be read as a continuation of T. Thomas Fortune's founding efforts at the *Age* to "imagine and create community" through the activist efforts of Black journalists.[3]

The *Age*'s writings on film make it difficult to disconnect critiques of mainstream cinema from Black New Yorkers' demands for equality. To report on, to chastise, and to detail an offender's missteps and mistakes while celebrating those brave enough to resist was not just an answer to the 1909 call to action but a way to make a city that insisted on limiting access for Black New Yorkers more hospitable to Black life. Ultimately, in much the same ways that theaters served as sites of labor activism, community development, pleasure, and danger, theaters were also arenas of protest. Black New Yorkers forged these by fighting for their right to equal treatment and positive representation in theaters throughout the city, arguing that the consequences otherwise were dire.

Lester Walton, "Music and the Stage"

Though historian Susan Curtis argues that Lester Walton "has gotten lost in the swirl" of Black New York's most stunning achievements, such as the

Harlem Renaissance and New Negro activism, the journalist was on the scene even before these feats.[4] A migrant from St. Louis, Missouri, Walton arrived in New York City in 1906, as one of many transplants who shifted the city's population. In the same year he arrived, most Black residents were not native New Yorkers.[5] Walton was in the city only a short period of time before he was hired to be the paper's dramatic editor by Fred Moore, who had recently taken over as editor of the *Age*.

When the *Age*, known previously as the *Globe* and the *Freeman*, was started in the last two decades of the nineteenth century, it followed a long line of Black journalistic endeavors in the country. The very roots of Black journalism began in New York City with the founding edition of *Freedom's Journal* in 1827 and continued to spread throughout the state with publications such as *Rights for All*, *Colored American*, and Frederick Douglass's *North Star*. Central to *Freedom Journal*'s role, and to much of the Black press later, was to "implement the drive for racial unity, full citizenship rights, and self-development" and essentially act "as the agency or vehicle of a cause."[6] Black journalists continued to orient themselves toward these goals so diligently that over one hundred years later, the Black press was still considered "the most loudly impatient agency for immediate, fundamental change in the status of the race."[7]

T. Thomas Fortune, himself a southern migrant and a descendant of slaves, started the *Age* in 1880 and quickly secured the paper's reputation as one of the nation's most esteemed Black newspapers, working as one of "the foremost molders of opinion in [his] day."[8] Fortune was unrelenting in his criticisms of racial injustice. He consistently devoted a large portion of his paper to editorial space, where prominent Black leaders from Frederick Douglass to Booker T. Washington could share their opinions on the state of American race relations and politics.[9] And while the paper was eventually beat out by the *Amsterdam News* in circulation numbers, Fortune and future editors maintained the "tradition of journalistic outspokenness" that the *Age* was founded on.[10] As Black migration to the city in the late nineteenth century and into the early decades of the twentieth century stoked the fears of racist white New Yorkers, resulting in increased racial antagonism throughout the city, the *Age* continued to offer its readers a beacon of hope and knowledge.[11] In 1925, *Opportunity* still ranked the paper among "the most outstanding" Black newspapers in the country.[12]

When Moore became editor of the *Age* in 1907, upon Fortune's retirement, he quickly made important changes to the paper's content. In addition to continuing to report on civil and political issues that affected Black life in America and the city, Moore diversified the paper's offerings by including

Figure 5.1 Lester Walton, ca. 1910s. *(Photographs and Prints Division, Schomburg Center for Research in Black Culture, The New York Public Library)*

reportage on sports, literature, music, and theater. In this way, theater scholar Artee Felicita Young suggests, the *Age* began "reflecting the whole of black society" in meaningful ways. It is under these circumstances that Walton came to work at the well-respected paper; his first article under his own column "Music and the Stage" was published in February 1908.[13]

As one of the first Black journalists to offer consistent and vigorous film commentary, Walton is, to use Anna Everett's words, "African America's first major mass-culture griot."[14] He used his position as editor to write incisive reviews of musical, stage, and film productions inside and outside of New York and offered cutting analyses of race relations as they were often reflected in the country's theater spaces. From the start of his career at the *Age*, Walton consciously linked culture to civil rights. As he extensively explored American culture, his criticisms and feedback were "not just limited to the dynamics of the theatrical stages"; they "extended beyond the footlights and into the broad arena of the social and political environment."[15] His articles on film examined a range of aspects within film culture, including censorship, the encroaching popularity of film over the stage, and the mass medium's position to maintain or radically alter race relations in America. In particular, Walton excelled at calling out racist cinematic practices both on the screen and in theaters.[16]

Walton's first article on film, "The Degeneracy of the Moving Picture Theatre," interrogates the extreme and offensive advertising strategies used by theater managers and production companies coupled with early cinema's penchant for exploiting African American pain and trauma for profit. "While passing a moving picture theatre on Sixth avenue" one January day in 1909, the editor was bombarded with the "offensive as well as repulsive-appearing" advertisements for the screening of John Smith's lynching in Paris, Texas.[17] Just days later, Walton witnessed the same at a theater in the Bowery, farther downtown. To Walton's disgust, both theaters were selling, for just a penny, "the sight of a human being meeting death by burning, with moans and groans," for enjoyment.[18]

The details of Smith's lynching provide necessary context for Walton's outrage. Ida B. Wells, a prominent antilynching activist, called the 1893 event "indescribable," as "never in the history of civilization has any Christian people stooped to such shocking brutality and indescribable barbarism."[19] Henry Smith, who was incorrectly named by the advertisements as John, was accused of raping and murdering the four-year-old daughter of a Paris police officer who had recently arrested and mistreated Smith. After briefly fleeing to another town before recapture, Smith was returned to Paris and subjected to immediate torture. After being paraded through the streets, he was stripped and held down as male members of the young girl's family took hot irons to his entire body, saving his eyes for last, before setting him on fire. A pastor present at the lynching remembered that "20,000 maddened people took up the victim's cry of agony and a prolonged howl of maddened glee rent the air." "The people were capable of any new atrocity now," he described. "It was difficult to hold the crowd back, so anxious were the savages to participate in the sickening tortures."[20]

Historian Amy Louise Wood has pointed to a lack of evidence suggesting Smith's murder was actually filmed. Instead, she posits that the film was composed of a number of still images paired with a phonographic recording, all of which did circulate in various formats nationwide after 1893.[21] Still, it was the carnal and primitive response to violence against a Black person demonstrated with the events in Paris that Walton feared the most. He noted that the film was most likely not reserved to these two theaters and warned of the "planting of the seed of savagery" by the "mass communication of these incendiary images."[22] In pointing to the wide reach of these pictures and sounds, usually reserved to southern provinces and antilynching efforts in various publications, Walton revealed his unease with early cinema's transportability. With the release of this film on a potentially citywide (or nationwide) scale, Walton grew concerned with the power of these images to transform even so-called liberal, northern white viewers. As New York was less than a decade from its most recent race riot and lynching numbers remained steadily high until midcentury, Walton was justified in his concern for "those whites who even in this enlightened day and time are not any too far from barbarism and to whom such acts of inhumanity would appeal."[23]

Walton remained critical of the cinema's ability to erase the actual horror of lynching and desensitize white viewers to violence against Black people. As the theater marketed the atrocious images and sounds of the lynching, Wood has noted, "for the shock and marvel of perversely curious spectators," it functioned to minimize the pain and suffering of the victim while monetizing that same trauma.[24] Walton expressed his deep concern about how the film helped viewers ignore the "shame and horrors of black lynchings" in the service of casual entertainment.[25] Here, Walton is making important (albeit not necessarily explicit) connections between modern technologies and anti-Blackness. Just as lynching photography served as "seemingly indisputable graphic testimony to white southerners' feelings of racial superiority," so, too, was cinema demonstrating its potential for such in its infancy by offering viewers this multisensory experiment on a much wider distribution scale.[26]

Walton's criticisms also reveal his worry over the impact of film on potential claims to city space. The signs, as Walton points out, were "prominently displayed" right at the front of the theaters, so passersby could not miss them. In addition to the big bold letters informing pedestrians that inside they could see "JOHN SMITH of PARIS, TEXIS, BURNED at the STAKE" as well as "HEAR HIS MOANS and GROANS," there was a "crudely-painted picture of a colored man being burned at the stake."[27] As this aggressive and grotesque advertising suggests, Black New Yorkers need not even be in the theater to become subject to the potential of cinema's violence. Assaulted, as Walton may have felt, by this advertising, Black passersby were placed in a confrontational situation by the very sites of the theater without actually entering its doors, stretching early cinema's racism into the very streets of Manhattan.

The film, released as it was in 1909, coincided with rapid developments in New York City, not the least important of which included mass numbers of southern migrants moving into and around the city. Film scholar Sabine Haenni points out that "physical circulation created much anxiety" in New York City in this period, even at the same time that it "gave people a new sense of self . . . and social relatedness."[28] More and more people, including European immigrants and Black migrants, experienced the "simultaneously utopian and dystopian nature of urban circulation."[29] For Black New Yorkers, though, that relationship was made all the more complicated by the sights and sounds of the city. In this case, the conspicuously placed advertising materials worked to circumscribe Black New Yorkers' space, obstructing any possible denial of their existence, while also expanding the reach of southern violence into the North. Ironically, as Walton lambasted the filmmakers for claiming the film had educational purposes, the manager's promotional techniques proved instructional for Black passersby and their understanding of the city streets and theaters.

Within a few months of his first article on film, Walton wrote a piece on a second topic that preoccupied many of his writings on New York's theaters: racist seating practices. Seating issues remained a significant issue in New York for most of the twentieth century, as Robert Thomas's story made clear at the start of this book. This trend continued despite civil and criminal laws preventing such practices. Walton's commentary on multiple occurrences provides insight into the discrimination Black theatergoers experienced throughout the city. He not only explains what happened in these instances but also recounts the means he deemed appropriate to seek justice and damages for the humiliation of being refused a particular seat. Not a proponent of protests or what he considered radicalism, Walton advocated for more conservative avenues, mainly the court system, to combat racism in New York City's theaters.

In November 1909, Walton reprinted an article from *Life*, in which its white dramatic editor James Metcalfe opined on seating discrimination against Black New Yorkers. Ignoring the realities of lax enforcement of the law, Metcalfe went so far as to assert that because of civil rights protection, "the Negro has more rights with respect of the theatres under the laws of the State of New York than the white man has." Metcalfe argued, "If they [Black theatergoers] set out to assert their legal rights they could make it very uncomfortable and very expensive for managers." Though Black audience members may have been able to obtain better tickets through "subterfuge," Metcalfe explained, "an ingenious solution has been found" to remove them from the theater regardless. The manager and his bouncer would create disturbances in the immediate vicinity of Black patrons, pick a fight with them, and, when the police were called, all were taken to the station.[30]

Metcalfe's insistence that Black customers be limited to certain areas of the theater or not allowed in at all is another example of the relationship between racism in theaters and a circumscription of Black movement in and throughout the city. The final line of his article, following the assumed arrest of unwitting Black theatergoers, reads, "The rest, of course, is easy."[31] "The rest" can certainly be assumed, at the very least, to include the typically tense, sometimes violent, interactions between Black New Yorkers and the police. Most likely aware of this dynamic, managers used these schemes to limit Black mobility not just in theater spaces but also in the city. Black audience members aware of discrimination in certain locations might fully avoid them. Walton, however, was firmly against this. When a "white theatrical man" asserted that "colored theatre-goers should not try to go where they are not wanted," Walton defended Black movement as its own justifiable desire. His response forcefully explained that Black life was not about "conform[ing] to every wish and desire of the Caucasian." "The fact that it was presumed that we were not wanted," he protested, "did not necessarily mean that we should not aspire or make an effort to realize our ambition."[32]

Still, Walton remained shocked at Metcalfe's shameless praise of the violation of antidiscrimination laws. "What is particularly galling to us," he wrote, "is the thought that we who are native-born American citizens are discriminated against solely on account of color, and that an organized effort is being made to deprive us of rights and privileges which we are justly entitled by law." Walton believed that, guaranteed rights as citizens, just as white New Yorkers were, Black theatergoers should be able to "walk about with a feeling of pride and self-esteem, knowing full well that it is your prerogative to sit wherever you desire." To him, the freedom to "enjoy the satisfaction of knowing we can sit downstairs when we so will" was deeply intertwined with African Americans' rights as Americans and New Yorkers. Clearly, the imagined space of a body politic is important here. Though white theater managers' and employees' were resistant to a Black presence in the city's theaters, Walton rejected this stance on the basis of citizenry, whereby belonging is grounded in public access and claims to political rights. He uses the word "citizen" numerous times throughout the piece, insinuating that skin color should not erase equal opportunity in amusement opportunities. By referencing "pride," Walton also insisted that the seating policy was dehumanizing, as Black New Yorkers sought to occupy theaters without being snubbed or herded to a particular seat on the basis of race. Yet Walton remained dejected. "It will be a long, long time," he lamented, "before the box office will cease receiving protests from prejudiced whites against being seated beside Negroes."[33]

Though he remained puzzled over Black New Yorkers' lack of initiative to take recourse against discriminatory theaters in 1909, just two years later Walton was reporting on a handful of instances where individuals chose to fight for their entitlements under the law. In late 1911, Mrs. Hattie Roberts, the wife of a prominent Black dentist in the city and a Midtown resident, was awarded civil damages for being discriminated against at the New York Theatre. Despite purchasing tickets for the area, Mrs. Roberts and her husband were both ejected from the orchestra section of the theater during a vaudeville and motion picture program. When they refused to leave or be reseated, the manager called the police. Showing the ways in which local police officers chose to serve and protect only certain people, the officer threatened to arrest the Robertses, though they were well within their rights. To be sure, the policing of Black New Yorkers in this case, respectable as they were, spilled out of the theater onto the streets, running the risk that they could be publicly shamed and arrested simply for wanting to attend a show. The next day, the couple retained L. C. Collins as counsel and filed individual civil suits against the manager; Mrs. Roberts eventually won her suit.

The structure of Walton's article is deliberate in how it asserts the respectable reputations of its subjects. Within its three columns, Walton placed three significant images—one of each of the Robertses, Hattie and her husband, Dr. Charles, and one of their lawyer—that reflect each individual's respectability. Dr. Roberts and Mr. Collins are both wearing suits and ties, while Mrs. Roberts, a light-skinned Black woman, sports a fashionable top with her hair tied back neatly in a lace ribbon. Looking off camera, her relaxed gaze and poised upper body exude grace and esteem. These images cement each person's class standing and, therefore, their justification for bringing and winning their suits. Though Walton asserts that all Black New Yorkers are protected under the civil rights law, he quotes Collins, whom he praises, as believing "any *reputable* colored citizen" to be capable of recovering damages for discrimination.[34] Walton also used these images to challenge some of the claims raised by the defense that the Robertses acted "boisterously" during the showing. In fact, Mrs. Roberts's image is directly in line with the paragraph that describes these statements, further illustrating Walton's point that these particular Black New Yorkers ought to have been protected by their class status.

In visually demanding the respectability of the Robertses and their lawyer, Walton was engaging in a long history of what Jasmine Nichole Cobbs calls "picturing freedom."[35] Started during slavery as "a site wherein free Black people organized new ways of existing within the domiciles of slaving nations," picturing freedom, or the purposeful use of visual culture, continued to serve as a means to quite literally visualize Black freedom in the United States.[36] This practice was used by race leaders in the Reconstruction period to assert the arrival of the "New Negro" and was sustained into the twentieth century as assaults on Black life continued in a range of visual forms.[37] Walton's use of the visual here, then, takes on added significance when one considers the regularity with which blackface was used by so many white performers on New York City's stages and the dehumanizing ways that Black life was handled on the screen in the city thus far.[38]

Walton was also critical of those who preferred to "talk! talk! talk!" instead of taking action.[39] Still, he was adamant that a particular kind of action was necessary. Praising the Roberts couple, he wrote, "Instead of spending their time telling friends and acquaintances of the humiliation to which they were submitted, they . . . aired their differences in court."[40] Walton, it seems, believed using the courts (as opposed to, perhaps, direct protests) also served two purposes. First, it allowed for redress for the humiliation and embarrassment Black New Yorkers experienced when theaters discriminated. Second, according to Walton, making use of the court system also garnered white respect. He opined, "The respect for the colored citizens of Greater New York will be greatly increased when the whites learn that the members of the race have made up their minds to take advantage of the laws passed prescribing against discrimination."[41] It is possible that Walton was using the prospect of white respect as another way to promote conservativism, but this also reflects Walton's belief that white approval was a precursor to the successful end of racist discrimination.

In this same edition of "Music and the Stage," Walton briefly mentions the arrest of the Lyric Theatre's manager, Harry A. Levy, for discriminating against Louis Baldwin. While he notes that the victim is a real estate agent, a lucrative profession, the focus here is less on the man's respectability and more on the unprecedented decisions made by the district attorney's office and Court of Special Sessions. Until this point, law enforcement in New York had failed to bring criminal, as opposed to civil, charges against individuals who discriminated on the basis of race. Given this, Walton's initial reportage is decidedly cautious, but as the case wove its way through New York's court system, he expanded on the case's massive significance in the city's theater circles. Three months later, when the Court of Special Sessions handed down its unanimous decision to charge Levy with a misdemeanor, the editor was elated over the case's potential to alter the pattern of discrimination in the city.

Though the Lyric was only occasionally a movie house between the 1910s and 1930, the ramifications of the case against Levy extended to all theaters in the city. This is particularly true as the Shubert Organization, owners of the Lyric, eventually held over one thousand theaters throughout the country by the 1920s. As Walton details, the court was packed with theater managers who anxiously awaited Levy's fate, knowing full well "that the decision was of more than passing consideration." He describes these men as being filled with "widespread alarm" upon recognizing that Black New Yorkers would certainly bring criminal instead of civil charges. Walton proclaims, "The spectacle of some of the Broadway managers being hailed to court daily at the instance [*sic*] of colored playgoers who have been denied the right to occupy the first floor is quite probable." In transferring the humiliation from Black patrons to managers who were "emboldened and indifferent to the law," Walton successfully reverses the normative narrative of who should bear the embarrassment and shame in these situations and highlights a potential way that Black New Yorkers could reclaim space throughout the city.[42]

Figure 5.2 Lafayette Theatre, ca. 1920. *(Photographs and Prints Division, Schomburg Center for Research in Black Culture, The New York Public Library)*

Walton's vision of white managers in handcuffs and Black theatergoers unscathed by racism failed to materialize. In January 1913, he was again reporting on discrimination in theaters, and this time it was occurring "in what might be termed 'a colored neighborhood.'"[43] The newly opened Lafayette Theatre in Harlem refused to allow Black patrons to sit in the orchestra, and, as Walton delightfully relayed, business was suffering. Maintaining that "self-respecting colored people refuse to patronize the place" and white people were in the minority, Walton not so subtly implied that the theater had made a "suicidal" choice by drawing the color line. Perhaps it was Walton's ringing of the death knell for the Lafayette—"All indications are that the count of ten is about to be called on the Lafayette Theatre"—or the managers' realization that the bottom line was more important than prejudice, but less than one month later the theater's policy on segregated seating changed.[44]

After these astute observations on New York's seating policies, Walton's commentary on film shifted back toward concerted observations of filmic representations. During the remainder of his tenure at the *Age*, Walton wrote vigilantly against mainstream cinema's tendency to caricature Blackness and the implications of these representations. His first of many diatribes against the French Pathé film company was printed in June 1913, after he viewed one of the company's weekly newsreels known as *Pathé's Weekly*.[45] In a Harlem theater, Walton watched as the French company attempted to turn scenes of Black misery into pure comedy. The director, Walton posited, failed to sympathize with a group of refugees from a Memphis flood. Instead, "under these depressing conditions he was light of heart and wanted to laugh." Thus, the director "arranged three little black, half-starved pickaninies [*sic*] in a row, sat a bowl of mush and a piece of bread before each and then waited to see the fun." The children scrambled to eat the food, showing no care for the camera in front of them as they laughed with their mouths full and ate food off the floor. Another scene of a grown Black woman "subjected to vigorous disinfecting by health officials," in which a cleansing agent was "squirted down her throat in large doses," was also meant to spark humor with its absurdity. Though Walton quickly segued into a discussion "on Negro stage types" (which these arguably were not), his descriptions of these particular images indicate his continued concern for the treatment of Black representations in cinema.[46] Questioning the relationship between Black trauma and white laughter, Walton's admonition against Pathé makes it clear that the earlier lynching film was just the first of many such violations on the screen.

In his article, Walton was explicit in his lack of faith in mainstream cinema's ability to create empathetic, relatable Black characters, but he was also insistent that Black theater managers had a responsibility to "prevail upon the manufacturers of motion picture films to present the Negro under more favorable conditions." While Walton was worried about the harm these images would have abroad for those across the globe who had no way of knowing the lived realities of Black Americans, he was also expressing a desire to rectify these incidents right in New York. It was, after all, in a Harlem theater that Walton had watched these "harmful" images of the "lowest types of the race."[47] Essentially, Walton was calling on Black theater managers to yield whatever influence they had over the industry to insist on more accurate, fair representations of Black life to be screened throughout the city, or at the very least in Harlem, where many Black New Yorkers were consuming the medium.

As the United States entered World War I, Walton frequently reflected on the various ways that Black contributions to the war effort were ignored or minimized. By August 1918, Walton found himself quite fed up with the mainstream motion picture industry. After about a decade of film screenings, he lamented, "I have not noted a single picture wherein the colored American has been shown at his best. It is always at his worst." His four-part article began with a remonstration against the Hearst-Pathé company for its failure to show Black soldiers as loyal, heroic, and worthy of honorable coverage. "AT NO TIME HAS THE COLORED SOLDIER BEEN SHOWN AS A MAN!" he exclaimed. Instead, Walton witnessed two scenes on two separate newsreels where Black soldiers were ridiculed. In the first, a Black soldier is shown trying to learn French, "scratching his head and gazing into the book in a bewildered fashion." In the second, two scared men "were figuring on the less dangerous way to serve the country," comparing naval and military service. Walton was deeply offended by these images as they erased the "generosity and loyalty" shown by Black soldiers abroad, clearly eliding their role in the war effort.[48]

But Walton's purpose with this article stretched beyond his castigations of the Hearst-Pathé newsreel. He was largely concerned with lifting the cinematic veil—revealing to his readers once more how cinema was capable of replicating and spreading white supremacist ideology. For example, Walton posits that, despite their academic and literary accomplishments, some "would make a [W. E. B.] Du Bois or a [William] Braithwaite use 'dis' or 'dat' on the screen, although these litterateurs know more about the use of English than all the white movie picture producers combined." Walton makes it clear that, despite the facts, the film industry insisted "on a propaganda of misrepresentation," educating "the general public to judge twelve million native Americans by the worst and lowest types of the race." But this ideology, Walton believes, stemmed from the individual movie producers themselves. These white men were infected, he argues, with "over-burdened self-conceit and false notions on the race question" that gave away their "superficial notions about race superiority." "And it will ever be thus," he warned, "unless more sanity is shown on the part of those laboring under such hallucinations."[49]

Ultimately, Walton considered it necessary to lay bare the film industry's blatant participation in the spreading and teaching of Black inferiority. He denounced its continued use of disrespectful and malignant representations of Black life and, in doing so, proclaimed Black America's awareness of such: "We the colored people of the United States, are tired of being maligned; we resent being misrepresented."[50] The Committee of Public Information, who was responsible for the production of wartime propaganda newsreels, eventually agreed to show accomplished Black soldiers, but only in Black theaters. Walton rejected this "'Jim Crow' method," as it would fail to show white audiences how Black men "helped to save the 'white man's civilization.'"[51] To be sure, Walton was insistent that it was white audiences who needed to see images of Black heroism, mainly because the alternative had the potential to promote ill will and misunderstanding. Less than a year after this article, for example, the New York Times reported that a disagreement between a white and Black man in Harlem, specifically over the war, led to a "race riot," where bystanders were shot and Harlemites attacked the police.[52] While the Age did not mention this Harlem-based incident, its focus that week was on a race riot in Washington, DC, after uniformed white military men attacked Black men and women in the nation's capital without discretion.

Perhaps his adamant promotion of the war effort and his concern for Black soldiers served as representation of his potential, but in four months' time, Walton was in France covering the Peace Conference in Versailles for the *Age*.[53] By 1922, Walton left the *Age* for the *New York World*, a position that came with a byline and the ability to "place more boldly stories of his people before a white reading audience."[54] He would not return to the *Age* until briefly in 1932, and then as a political correspondent and general editor, before embarking on his career within the Democratic Party (first as publicity director, then as appointed envoy and minister to Liberia).

His early articles in the *Age* on cinema reveal his distrust in the medium, particularly in the hands of white producers, to promote positive race relations and favorable representations of Blackness. Walton was regularly concerned about the very real consequences of these visuals in the lives of Black Americans, both in the city and nationwide. Like the men who were to follow him in New York City's various Black publications, Walton was more devoted to drama as the most effective avenue for Black progress in the arts. Still, he remained critical of those public spaces where these dramas, onscreen and onstage, took place. Ultimately, Walton was devoted to the progress of African Americans in New York and the nation at large, and his cultural criticisms of discrimination in theaters and on film contributed to this larger vision of racial equality.

Vere E. Johns, "In the Name of Art"

In Walton's absence, William E. Clark took over as the more regular dramatic editor of the *Age*. However, his articles rarely provided the same critical engagements with cinema that Walton's did. Instead, the void left in Walton's departure was later filled by Vere E. Johns, but not until 1932, when he began his short tenure at the *Age*. Johns was a Jamaican migrant who arrived in the United States in June 1929 with his wife, Dorice. Just "a few days after his arrival . . . he appeared at the office of The Amsterdam News with a letter of introduction to the dramatic editor," Romeo Dougherty, who hired him on the spot.[55] After a handful of articles and a few years, Johns began writing for the *Age* instead. It is possible that the *Age* gave him the freedom to express his opinions in a way that the *Amsterdam News* did not, but a public feud with the *Amsterdam News* suggests that it was more personal than that. Starting in 1933, just a year or so after he began writing for the *Age*, Johns and the dramatic editors at the *Amsterdam News*, including Theophilus Lewis and George Schuyler, consistently lambasted one another in very public ways with their journalism, revealing the diversity of the city's press.

Whatever the reason for his departure, Johns wrote hundreds of articles for the *Age* during his three-year stint at the paper. Johns's articles covered a range of topics that reflected his talents and his interests. He wrote editorials on Marcus Garvey, the Universal Negro Improvement Association (UNIA), prostitution in Harlem, colorism in Jamaica and America, Black business, local politics, racist employment practices, the intellectual merits of Washington and Du Bois types, and racial solidarity among immigrants and Black New Yorkers. Of particular importance are his articles on New York City's theaters, as they illustrate how he grappled with them as spaces for the liberating potential of cinema.

Some of Johns's earliest articles questioned the film industry's inability to provide Black actors with meaningful roles. While he noted that a few Black entertainers, including Louise Beavers and Clarence Muse, were "flowers now growing in our motion picture garden," he asserted that most movie parts were "persistent burlesquing of the Negro."[56] Critiquing a film recently removed from the Renaissance Theatre at the behest of the president-general of the UNIA, Dr. Lionel Francis, Johns describes the ways that Black characters were added to stories simply for comedic effect. The Black bodyguard in *Haunted Gold* (1933), who "was an unreal, frightful monkey, [who] jumped at his shadow . . . with his eyes popping from his head, teeth chattering," Johns asserted, was an unnecessary addition to the plot and only served to reify white audience's stereotypes of Black people. Johns stood ready to challenge those who argued that a white audience would not have taken issue with the bodyguard's actions had he been white.

He noted that because whiteness was varied in film, objection to negativity was unnecessary, whereas Blackness was always ridiculed or criminalized. Like Walton before him, Johns pointed to the ability of cinema to negatively affect race relations, as white audiences with little or no contact with African Americans form "instant and unfavorable conclusions" based on stereotypes.[57] Johns's reference to Dr. Francis and his local activism also provided a successful model for other Harlemites to emulate in efforts to hold the motion picture industry accountable to the Black community, even if it meant just limiting the distribution of the film on a smaller scale.

In addition to what Black actors looked and sounded like onscreen, Johns was concerned with the ways that Black people were spoken about in popular media. On April 29, 1933, Johns found himself confronting an old enemy of Walton's: the Pathé company. Johns was taken aback when, in its partnership with RKO, a Pathé newsreel used "the offensive word 'darkey' to indicate a man of color and for no apparent reason than to belittle and vilify."[58] Johns made it clear that this was a deliberate choice of words, given the fact that the voice-over was undoubtedly scripted. He called out the industry's continued mistreatment of Black subjects by asserting that the slight was not accidental and came from a "careless and inconsiderate executive," rather than the absentmindedness or nervousness of the commentator.

In yet another display of support for a local activist, Johns cited the work of Mrs. Clara Burrill Bruce, of the Dunbar Apartments on 150th Street, as exemplary for her complaints of the racist term in mass media. Mrs. Bruce had, according to Johns, "whipped the managing editor of the Herald Tribune to his knees over that same word." Indeed, it was her argumentative framework on the unfair use of demeaning terms that Johns appropriated in this specific, filmic, case. He argued that the only time other racial epithets were used was in an effort to insult and debase, but when it came to African Americans, "it is made common practice of and at that to classify the entire Negro race without exception." This was particularly insulting as the man whom the commentator referred to as "darkey" was a Black doorman and barber at the White House with years of experience. To Johns, it was horrifying that the RKO-Pathé company would choose to debase an individual who, given his position, was respected and admired. To elucidate his point and to maybe be a bit provocative, Johns asserted that if he called the Jewish mayor of New York City, Herbert Lehman, a "kike," the slight would be no different than "the action of the raucous voiced, impudent commentator of Pathé News, who dared to refer to the colored employee at the White House as a 'darkey in uniform.'"[59]

It was also in this early example of Johns's work that readers became familiarized with the author's preferred form of protest. Not a fan of "ostentatious demonstrations in the shape of pickets and mass meetings," Johns preferred a more economic and less dramatic challenge to racism in Harlem's theaters.[60] Instead, he advised Black Harlemites to "threaten the film moguls with a curtailment of their filthy lucre and see how speedily they listen to reason." He believed that to interfere with Hollywood's income, of which he estimated African Americans contributed $25 million, meant forcing the industry to think more cautiously about its treatment of Blackness. But he pressed that this could only occur with "a loud voice and a collective voice"— something he would again insist on when he demanded the removal of all Will Rogers films from Harlem theaters.[61]

On the evening of January 21, 1934, Will Rogers, an actor and radio personality of white and Cherokee descent, was discussing cowboy songs on his radio show. While doing so, Rogers referred to Black spirituals as "nigger spirituals" and used the word three more times during the show.[62] Less than two weeks later, Johns provided an urgent demand for protests in the face of Rogers's "confounded impudence."[63] Johns quickly tied Tom Mix, a white actor who had recently praised California's governor for encouraging mob law, to his protests against Rogers, confirming his belief in cinema's ties to racism, politics, and local race relations.[64] In challenging one actor's use of a derogatory term and another's praise of lynching, Johns makes important claims about how Black audiences can use mass media, or the rejection of it, to demand fair representation and treatment. Johns was convinced that the most efficient and effective way to stop the industry from producing something "detrimental or insulting to the Negro" was "by hurting them where they will feel it most, and that is in their pockets." Thus, he asked theaters in Harlem to pull all Rogers and Mix films from their offerings. And if the theater managers did not act "in the proper relation to [their] patrons," who were mostly Black, Johns warned, then "we will stay absolutely clear of their theatres."[65]

The editorialist did not give advice frivolously; he also took it himself. After hearing about the incident, he entered himself into the fray with others who were protesting Rogers, such as the NAACP, which was privately asking NBC and Rogers for a public apology.[66] He succeeded in having the managers of the Roosevelt, Lafayette, and Harlem Opera House Theatres, which ran straight down Harlem's main thoroughfare of Seventh Avenue from 145th Steet to 125th Street, halt their showings of Rogers's latest film at his personal behest. Yet not everyone in Harlem agreed with Johns's angle. The dramatic editor of the *Amsterdam News*, Romeo Dougherty, advocated for a more aggressive demonstration of protest against Rogers, including hissing, howling, shouting, and tearing down movie screens.[67] Johns was quick to sense Dougherty's dismissal of his work and argued his means were "far more practical than dreaming absurd 'castles in the air' that you know will never be realized."[68]

Perhaps Johns had little faith in the roughly two hundred thousand Black Harlemites who might happen upon a Rogers film and exact their contempt upon the physical space and those around them. But Johns also favored less aggressive displays of protest. He preferred the real damage to be felt by the production companies or "the people who have to pay Rogers his salary," and not the local theaters willing to cooperate with Black activist demands in Harlem.[69] Johns's economic threats to the film industry struck a special chord, coming as they did during the Great Depression. He advocated for thrift in the face of disrespect, hoping that Black New Yorkers could force the hand of an already struggling industry to make film a more democratic art.

Like Walton, Johns was successful at flipping the script on typical racist narratives to reveal the lack of civility and decency among white people in New York and the nation. One example took place after an incident at the Loew's Victoria, which had recently discontinued its segregated seating practices in 1933. One of Johns's friends had taken a seat with his wife in the orchestra section and laid their coats down in the seat next to them. When a white couple sat down and Johns's friend could not move the coats fast enough, the white man simply sat on his wife's belongings. The man refused to get up upon request, insisting, "You don't pay for the whole theatre, you only pay for one seat." When his friend responded by throwing the man off his wife's coat, another white woman who was uninvolved in the situation shouted, "The nerve of those Negroes! They come into a white theatre and want to boss it." Instead of focusing on his friend's physical response to the white man's rudeness, Johns chose to emphasize the actions of the white people in the theater. He believed their display, a response to Black Harlemites' ability to sit wherever they chose in the theater after years of embarrassing discrimination, was a "slip back into savagery."[70] Their inability to act like decent human beings to people of a different race was enough for Johns to deem them backward and uncivilized—descriptors that were often weaponized against the Black community.

Johns's account of the event also demonstrates the continued violence against Black New Yorkers in the city's theaters, especially as the Black community expanded the geographical boundaries of Black Harlem. No doubt responding to the fact that Black Harlemites demanded equal treatment at a theater that largely served the Black community, the Loew's Victoria had changed its segregated seating policy. But as they did in Robert Thomas's case, white New Yorkers responded with aggression. Thus, this skirmish reveals the literal and violent tensions that sometimes erupted in the city's theaters.

Keenly aware of this, Johns poignantly tied the white "savagery" in this Harlem theater to the Armwood lynching that had occurred exactly a month before he published his article. On October 18, 1933, George Armwood of Princess Anne, Maryland, was pulled from a prison cell and lynched, dragged across town from the back of a truck, and set on fire. Armwood had been accused of sexually assaulting an elderly white woman, and despite claims of his "feeble-mindedness," he was brutally murdered by the white residents of Princess Anne.[71] By finding connections between these two cases, of theater discrimination and lynching, Johns explains that white supremacy in all its forms are intimately related. It stretches from mob law to demeaning representations and "uncouth actions" inside a darkened theater, exposing the many ways that, according to Johns, the "white race is degenerating."[72]

Despite this, Johns's class and, potentially, his "stranger within our gates" status made it difficult for him to reckon with the use of theaters as potential liberatory spaces for Black New Yorkers.[73] In November 1932, he wrote a scathing article on Black reception in Harlem's theaters, lamenting that those responsible for setting up entertainment for Black consumers struggled with "why they [the audience] will laugh at what are obviously the wrong things." He aggressively discounted the argument that it boiled down to emotion. Instead, he insisted that these Harlemites "are in a low mental state of mind . . . and are incapable of deep feeling—they are merely seeking pleasure and see humor in everything." Testing this theory, he watched a film at one all-white theater on Broadway, where he was the only Black patron, and then at three Harlem theaters. He learned that at every single Harlem theater, the audience "missed half the laughs and guffawed and squealed at all the sad bits."[74] Rather than consider the ways that Harlemites were potentially resisting the Hollywood narrative and engaging in reconstructive spectatorship, Johns bemoaned their supposedly embarrassing behavior.[75]

So worried was Johns about Harlem's theaters and theatergoers, "whose behavior in public places leaves much to be desired," that he wrote two more articles criticizing them.[76] First, he attacked ushers. According to him, they "have the wrong slant on their job; they are much too big for them and treat all except their immediate friends with an air of indifference that is just downright impertinence."[77] Angry that these ushers flirted with women in their seats or ignored people who needed help, Johns pushed managers to take their ushers downtown to learn their trade at, presumably, white theaters. While the managers of those theaters on Harlem's main thoroughfares could "relate a dozen tales a day of the trouble they have with their Negro patrons," those "on 125th and 116th Streets who have an all-white staff of ushers," he insisted, "will tell you that the Negro part of their audiences give no trouble."[78] Johns boiled this down to a fear and discomfort around white people that was dropped in Harlem when surrounded by other Black people. Regardless of Johns's inability to recognize it, this behavior, such as laughing at the seemingly wrong time or having fun with friends on the job, reveals the multiplicity of ways that Harlem's theaters offered potential spaces of respite from the harsh city.

An example of the "expectations and pressures blacks created for each other" in public, particularly in movie theaters, Johns's denunciation of the audience and Harlem's theaters holds echoes of Walton's own complaints years earlier.[79] In 1909, Walton expressed concern over a downtown theater's decision to exclude all Black patrons because of the misbehavior of two Black men (whose supposed flirtations with white women angered two white male guests). At the same time that he criticized the managers, Walton also insisted "each Negro wakes up to the importance of his conduct at all times and in all places, and becomes imbued with the idea that the acts of each and every one of us tend to determine and mark out the well-being and the enjoyment of rightful privileges for us all."[80] The two articles, written over two decades apart, suggest a sustained policing of Black people in the city's theaters, both within and outside of the Black community, and indicate that this self-policing was still deemed a necessity. This was especially so because Blackness remained on display, both on the screen and throughout the city, in ways that limited Black New Yorkers' ability to be their full selves without judgment from the white community (or even from cultural critics within the Black community) and assumptions that certain behaviors would confirm stereotypes.

Yet, even as Johns was critical of Harlem's theaters and the public displays within them, he did recognize that Black theaters had the potential to offer particular opportunities for the community. Though he continued to express what he deemed serious concerns over audience behavior, the run-down nature of Harlem's theaters, or the crude shows put on during vaudeville performances in the neighborhood, he eventually took on the role as manager of the Renaissance Theatre. Johns most likely did this in an attempt to remedy many of these problems, revealing his dedication to Black film culture in the city. Though only there for less than a year, between May and September 1933, Johns was applauded for his work, which included installing a new air conditioner (the first theater in Harlem to have one) and "repainting and redecorating" the main lobby. Under Johns, the theater was cited as "living up to its name with a new birth."[81]

In his first of just a few articles published in 1935, Johns reflected on the past year of Black actors and actresses in film. "What of the future?" he asked.

Figure 5.3 Renaissance Theatre. *(Courtesy Municipal Archives, City of New York)*

"So what? So nothing!" he responded. "I woefully realize that we are no further ahead than the same time a year ago." He was disappointed that Broadway failed to keep a steady offering of Black productions and that popular Black films were few and far between. Johns, like Walton, generally offered a disheartening view on cinema, its surrounding institutions, and its potentiality as a tool of liberation. He was of the mindset that "drama's the thing" and advocated for Black-owned theaters for the sake of control and autonomy.[82] Yet his provocative rhetoric communicated a strong will to defend Blackness against the dehumanizing nature of Hollywood. He recognized the potential of mass resistance to discrimination and disrespect and called for Black Americans to spend their money deliberately in order to enact change. Though he may have been instigative or downright inflammatory at times, his commentary lays bare the complexity of the city's Black press in the early twentieth century, especially as it relates to cinema.

The concomitant rise in film's popularity in the early twentieth century and the persistent use of stereotypes and segregated seating in New York's theaters was not lost on the city's Black moviegoers. In response, cultural critics endeavored to create an atmosphere of protest in and around theater spaces. As Harlem's motion picture operators turned to picket signs to demand fair pay, journalists employed their trade to insist on equitable treatment in theaters and on the screen. Men like Lester Walton and Vere E. Johns reported regularly on discrimination within the film industry, using their columns to inform Harlemites of ongoing court battles against a particular theater or warning against patronizing theaters that showed disparaging films. Outside of their commentary on specific films, Walton's and Johns's writings also reveal the continuously complicated nature of Harlem's theaters as spaces for resisting or even avoiding racism.

Ultimately, the journalists discussed in this chapter took on that 1909 call to action, using their words as a means to educate, inspire, and fight back. The Black press, and especially the *Age*, undoubtedly played a major role in these fights. The paper was an important space where opinions were published but also where stories were told for those without a voice. The issues discussed here demonstrate Black New Yorkers' multifaceted interactions with and negotiations of some of the racist practices of moviegoing. The range of rhetorical analyses and strategies formed in the first three decades of cinema's popularity, including journalistic responses to racism in theaters, laid the groundwork for how Black New Yorkers continued to experience Black film culture in the city throughout the twentieth century.

Epilogue

By the early years of the Great Depression, some journalists had begun to wax poetic about the history of film in Harlem and "its stamp on the present." In 1929, Romeo Dougherty of the *Amsterdam News* "recall[ed] the days when five cents admitted one to a motion picture show and the time when many stars of yesterday and today first hit Harlem." Tracing this long history, he felt, required opening with Maria C. Downs, the Cuban entrepreneur who founded the Lincoln. "When Harlem began to grow into what is now a community of over two hundred thousand Negroes," he explained, "she started a little motion picture place of the kind that was being built all over the country."[1] While placing the Lincoln in the nexus of national developments, he also gave weight to its local significance as the very first motion picture theater in the city to cater to Black audiences. Perhaps this is why, a year later, another journalist wrote an extensive eulogy for the theater.

Bemoaning the news that the Lincoln was being turned into a church, Don Romilio was disappointed that "the announcement did not give the slightest hint of the part played by this little house in the life of what the intelligentsia refers to as Mr. Van Vechten's Harlem." "The Lincoln Theatre," he argued, "served as the foundation," which was then "followed by all the other houses catering exclusively to Negroes in this section of the city."[2] Romilio insisted that it was the Lincoln that set the standard for other nearby theaters in terms of performance caliber, charity in times of need, and managers willing to listen to journalists' critiques.

Occurring on the "street that pleasure left behind," the Lincoln's transformation left many in the neighborhood feeling nostalgic, but other changes were taking place too.[3] Beyond the closing of community fixtures like the Lincoln and eventually the Lafayette, small theaters were being bought out and put under consolidated ownership. Leo Brecher and Frank Schiffman continued to buy theaters in Harlem into the 1930s, securing a near monopoly over them. Others were added to a Loew's or RKO circuit. The Black community, expanding as it was beyond the geographical confines of 125th Street by the Great Depression, also found themselves increasingly more welcome at theaters on 116th Street. Though they did not always actively cater to Black audiences, the Regun and Jewel Theatres now counted Black moviegoers in their seats and occasionally chose to advertise in the Black press.

In this atmosphere of shifting ownership, management, and audience, community events remained a big part of how the neighborhood's theaters operated, especially those in central Harlem and even some that stretched into Brooklyn. During World War II, the Regent, for example, helped sponsor an event led by the Women's Auxiliary of the 369th Regiment.[4] Using the theater as a base, they raised funds and secured gifts for the soldiers, which included bundles of personal toiletries, candy, and cigarettes. That same year, in 1942, the RKO Brevoort in Brooklyn held a draft day where 150 people enrolled for active duty with the local draft board. The event was momentous, with over three hundred people in attendance, smiling proudly and waving the American flag in front of the theater.

The theater space itself also continued to affect Black New Yorkers. The intellectual and activist James Baldwin remembers quite well his experiences in Harlem's motion picture theaters. Reflecting on his childhood, he wrote "My first conscious calculation as to how to go about defeating the world's intentions for me and mine began that Saturday afternoon at what we called *the movies*."[5] His recollections of various films and his intellectual trajectory continuously align, as he processed what he saw on the screen in places like the Lincoln, the Franklin, and the Odeon (the very same place where the young migrant Dora Ross, mentioned in Chapter 2, met her procurer years earlier). It was in these and other Harlem theaters that this eminent literary figure and civil rights luminary, at the young age of seven, began to consider the ways movies can at once reflect and teach race. He made important connections between himself and the Black community by watching films such as *A Tale of Two Cities* (1935) and *They Won't Forget* (1937), stories of poverty and the questionable nature of the southern justice system, respectively. As he grew up and maintained a regular movie theater presence, Baldwin grap-

Figure E.1 Crowd outside RKO Regent for the opening of "The Pride of the Yankees," ca. 1942. *(Photo by Austin Hansen Prints, Image provided by Photographs and Prints Division, Schomburg Center for Research in Black Culture, The New York Public Library)*

pled with the significance of race relations as they are reproduced in film, taking cues from his fellow audience members.

By the time he went to see Stanley Kramer's *The Defiant Ones* (1958), Baldwin was well versed in the fact that movies, particularly their sharp divisions between the lived realities of Black and white, "were simply a reflection" of the world around him.[6] The film portrays the story of two escaped convicts, chained to each other, who need to get along to avoid capture. In the film's final moments, the Black prisoner, Noah (Sidney Poitier), who has just jumped a train toward freedom, changes his mind in order to stay behind with the dying white prisoner, now his friend. Baldwin explains that as Poitier gave up his own freedom, the Harlem audience "was outraged, and yelled, *Get back on the train, you fool!*"[7] This audience, through its shouts, revealed its anger not only with the film's ending but also with the film's imaginary conception of race relations in America. As Baldwin notes, Poitier "jumps off the train in order to reassure white people, to make them know that they are not hated," but, he qualifies, "the reassurance is false."[8] The audience members no doubt shaped his conceptualization of the film, interacting with the screen as they were, unashamed and willing to embody their rage and frustration at the images unfurling before them.

By 1958, when Baldwin saw the film, most likely at the Loew's Victoria or 116th Street Theatre, the city had undergone impressive changes toward racial equity. The post–World War II years saw a widespread no-nonsense attitude toward racism among Black Americans. After the "Double V" campaign, a battle for victory at home and abroad against authoritarianism and racial violence, Black Americans saw little room for continued racial discrimination in their lives. Consequently, Black New Yorkers pushed relentlessly to end segregation and discrimination in all its continued vestiges in the city. The end to seating segregation at theaters was wrapped up in struggles for access to public swimming pools, restaurants, and hotels.[9] Even the fact that the audience members screamed at the screen during *The Defiant Ones*, clearly unconcerned with management or others around them, signaled important shifts in the area. Just three decades earlier, Robert Thomas had literally fought his way into those seats; now, Harlem's Black audiences were comfortable enough in them to talk back to a film's racial ineptitude.

The film culture that Black New Yorkers forged during the first three decades of the twentieth century informed how they continued to interact with the medium and its surrounding institutions. To be sure, Baldwin's testimony to the life-altering experiences provided by the movies and theater space is both a response to the absences mentioned in Chapter 1 and a result of all the efforts outlined in *Reel Freedom*. Before the Great Depression, Black New Yorkers interacted with film culture in various ways to make it undeniably their own. They patronized theaters in Midtown and, in the face of segregation, publicly denounced discrimination. Those oriented with a flair for business and race pride managed and owned theaters purposefully placed in the densely populated pockets of Black New York. These theaters often subsequently became centers of the community, where meetings and church services could be attended; lovers and criminals butted heads or clasped hands; and race films were viewed with enthusiasm and, occasionally, derision. Some theaters, like the Lafayette, were the subject of both praise and scorn within the Black press, which spearheaded a plethora of struggles against inequality in the city's theaters. Ultimately, Black New Yorkers used film culture to demand equality, challenge racism, and create space for themselves in a city and industry that consistently attempted to deny them these opportunities.

Notes

INTRODUCTION

1. Walter White to Fred Moore, October 20, 1924, "Theatre Segregation and Civil Rights Legislation in New York State," Papers of the National Association for the Advancement of Colored People, Library of Congress (hereafter Papers of the NAACP). White sent these letters to the *New York Amsterdam News, New York Age, Chicago Defender, Harlem Home News, New York News*, and *Tattler*.

2. While the *Age* and *Amsterdam News* refer to Thomas as Richard, the magistrate documents name him as Robert. Docket 8357, April 27, 1926, Magistrates' Court Docket Books, 10th District—Manhattan, New York City Municipal Archives, reel 45.

3. "Attempted Discrimination at Loew's 125th St. Theatre Leads to Riot Call," *New York Age*, May 1, 1926.

4. "Thomas Appeals Eviction Case," *New York Amsterdam News*, May 5, 1926.

5. "It Happened in Harlem," *New York Age*, May 8, 1926.

6. "Carteret, N.J., White Burn $3,000 Church of Colored Congregation, and Assault and Banish Colored Residents," *New York Age*, May 1, 1926.

7. Ibid. See also "Killing of Defenseless Momentarily Expected," *New York Amsterdam News*, April 28, 1926; "Carteret Race Riot Laid to Wage Clash," *New York Times*, May 3, 1926; "Street Brawl Causes Riot in N. Jersey," *Chicago Defender*, May 8, 1926.

8. "It Happened in Harlem."

9. Elton Fax, in Jeff Kisseloff, *You Must Remember This: An Oral History of Manhattan from the 1890s to World War II* (San Diego: Harcourt Brace Jovanovich, 1989), 265.

10. Docket 8357.

11. Shannon King, *Whose Harlem Is This, Anyway? Community Politics and Grassroots Activism during the new Negro Era* (New York: New York University Press, 2015), 34.

12. Robert C. Allen, "Motion Picture Exhibition in Manhattan, 1906–1912: Beyond the Nickelodeon," *Cinema Journal* 18, no. 2 (1979): 2–15; Ben Singer, "Manhattan Nick-

elodeons: New Data on Audiences and Exhibitors," *Cinema Journal* 34, no. 3 (1995): 5–35; Allen, "Manhattan Myopia; Or, Oh! Iowa!" *Cinema Journal* 35, no. 3 (1996): 75–103.

13. David Nasaw, *Going Out: The Rise and Fall of Public Amusements* (Cambridge, MA: Harvard University Press, 1993), 172.

14. Scholarship that does similar work includes Douglas Gomery, *Shared Pleasures: A History of Movie Presentation in the United States* (Madison: University of Wisconsin Press, 1992), 155–163; Karen Sotiropoulos, *Staging Race: Black Performers at the Turn of the Century* (Cambridge, MA: Harvard University Press, 2008), 228; Agata Frymus, "Black Moviegoing in Harlem: The Case of the Alhambra Theatre, 1905–1931," *Journal of Cinema and Media Studies* 62, no. 1 (2023): 80–101; David Morton and Agata Frymus, "'A United Stand and a Concerted Effort': Black Cinema-going in Harlem and Jacksonville during the Silent Era," in *The Palgrave Handbook of Comparative New Cinema Histories*, ed. Treveri Gennari et al. (Cham: Springer International, 2024), 53–71; Pardis Dabashi, "'There Is No Gallery': Race and the Politics of Space at the Capital Theatre, New York," *Early Popular Visual Culture* 21, no. 2 (2023): 208–222.

15. Alison Griffiths and James Latham, "Film and Ethnic Identity in Harlem, 1896–1915," in *American Movie Audiences: From the Turn of the Century to the Early Sound Era*, ed. Richard Maltby and Melvyn Stokes (London: Bloomsbury, 1999), 46–63.

16. Paula Massood, *Black City Cinema: African American Urban Experiences in Film* (Philadelphia: Temple University Press, 2003), 19.

17. Richard Koszarski, *Hollywood on the Hudson: Film and Television in New York from Griffith to Sarnoff* (New Brunswick, NJ: Rutgers University Press, 2008).

18. Agata Frymus, "Mapping Black Moviegoing in Harlem, New York City, 1909–1914," in *New Perspectives on Early Cinema History: Concepts, Approaches, Audiences*, ed. Mario Slugan and Daniël Biltereyst (London: Bloomsbury, 2022), 193–212; Frymus, "White Screens, Black Fandom: Silent Film and African American Spectatorship in Harlem," *Early Popular Visual Culture* 21, no. 2 (2023): 248–265.

19. Jacqueline Stewart, *Migrating to the Movies: Cinema and Black Urban Modernity* (Berkeley: University of California Press, 2005); Davarian Baldwin, *Chicago's New Negroes: Modernity, the Great Migration, and Black Urban Life* (Chapel Hill: University of North Carolina Press, 2007); Cara Caddoo, *Envisioning Freedom: Cinema and the Building of Modern Black Life* (Cambridge, MA: Harvard University Press, 2014); Anna Everett, *Returning the Gaze: A Genealogy of Black Film Criticism, 1909–1949* (Durham, NC: Duke University Press, 2001). A very small sampling of Regester's extensive work includes "Oscar Micheaux on the Cutting Edge: Films Rejected by the New York State Motion Picture Commission," *Studies in Popular Culture* 17, no. 2 (1995): 61–72; "From the Buzzard's Roost: Black Movie-Going in Durham and Other North Carolina Cities during the Early Period of American Cinema," *Film History* 17, no. 1 (2005): 113–124; "The African-American Press and Race Movies, 1909–1929," in *Oscar Micheaux and His Circle: African American Filmmaking and Race Cinema of the Silent Era*, ed. Pearl Bowser, Jane Gaines, and Charles Musser (Bloomington: Indiana University Press, 2001), 34–49.

20. Stewart, *Migrating*, 12–15.

21. Nathaniel Brennan, "The Great White Way and the Way of All Flesh: Metropolitan Film Culture and the Business of Film Exhibition in Times Square, 1929–1941," *Film History: An International Journal* 27, no. 2 (2015), 2.

22. Kathryn Fuller, *At the Picture Show: Small-Town Audiences and the Creation of Fan Culture* (Washington: Smithsonian Institution Press, 1996), x; Robert C. Allen, "Decentering Historical Audience Studies: A Modest Proposal," in *Hollywood in the Neighborhood: Historical Case Studies of Local Moviegoing*, ed. Kathryn Fuller-Seeley (Berkeley: University of California Press, 2008), 21.

23. Stewart, *Migrating*, 14.

24. Gregory A. Waller, "Another Audience: Black Moviegoing, 1907–16," *Cinema Journal* 31, no. 2 (1992): 5. Both Jacqueline Stewart and Davarian Baldwin utilize a similar method that informs this manuscript. See Baldwin, *Chicago's New Negroes*; Baldwin, "The Great Migration and the Rise of an Urban 'Race Film' Culture," in *Early Race Filmmaking in America*, ed. Barbara Tepa Lupack (New York: Routledge, 2016), 163–182.

25. Allyson Nadia Field, *Uplift Cinema: The Emergence of African American Film and the Possibility of Black Modernity* (Durham, NC: Duke University Press, 2015), 25.

26. David Levering Lewis, *When Harlem Was in Vogue* (Oxford: Oxford University Press, 1981), 48.

27. Baldwin, *Chicago's New Negroes*, 234.

28. Bruce A. Glasrud and Cary D. Wintz, eds., *The Harlem Renaissance in the American West: The New Negro's Western Experience* (New York: Routledge, 2012); Davarian Baldwin and Minkah Makalani, *Escape from New York: The New Negro Renaissance beyond Harlem* (Minneapolis: University of Minnesota Press, 2013). See also Jeffrey O. G. Ogbar, ed., *The Harlem Renaissance Revisited: Politics, Arts, and Letters* (Baltimore: Johns Hopkins University Press, 2010). Earlier literature also expanded the limited definition of the Harlem Renaissance along the lines of gender and location. See Cheryl A. Wall, *Women of the Harlem Renaissance* (Bloomington: Indiana University Press, 1995); Gloria T. Hull, *Color, Sex, and Poetry: Three Women Writers of the Harlem Renaissance* (Bloomington: Indiana University Press, 1987).

29. Some of the few scholars to provide explicit, deep treatments of the relationship of Black film culture and Black film to the New Negro movement are Baldwin, *Chicago's New Negroes*; Erin D. Chapman, "The New Negro and the New South," *A Companion to the Harlem Renaissance*, ed. Cherene Sherrard-Johnson (West Sussex: Wiley Blackwell, 2015), 65–80.

30. James Weldon Johnson, "Harlem: The Cultural Capital," in *The New Negro: An Interpretation*, ed. Alain Locke (New York: Albert and Charles Boni, 1925).

31. Victoria W. Wolcott, *Race, Riots, and Roller Coasters: The Struggle over Segregated Recreation in America* (Philadelphia: University of Pennsylvania Press, 2012), 3.

32. Frymus, "Case of the Alhambra," 101.

33. Angel David Nieves, "Introduction: Cultural Landscape of Resistance and Self-Definition of the Race: Interdisciplinary Approaches to a Socio-spatial Race History," in *"We Shall Independent Be": African American Placemaking and the Struggle to Claim Space in the United States*, ed. Angel David Nieves and Leslie M. Alexander (Boulder: University of Colorado, 2008), 2.

34. Though focused on Philadelphia, J. T. Roane's *Dark Agoras: Insurgent Black Social Life and the Politics of Place* offers a compelling exploration of Black working-class migrant life and placemaking efforts. According to Roane, placemaking sometimes occurred at the edges of what was deemed permissible or even possible, yet "represented resources and knowledges for navigating catastrophe and displacement with meaningful

insight about how to imagine and creative means to collective futures in the face of enclosure." Roane, *Dark Agoras* (New York: New York University Press, 2023), 68.

35. Ruth Wilson Gilmore, "Fatal Couplings of Power and Difference: Notes on Racism and Geography," *Professional Geographer* 54, no. 1 (2002): 16.

36. Quoted from the title of *Escape from New York: The New Negro Renaissance beyond Harlem*; Nieves, "Introduction," is a critical source for considering these linkages throughout the history of Black New York.

37. Saidiya Hartman, *Wayward Lives, Beautiful Experiments: Intimate Histories of Social Upheaval* (New York: W. W. Norton, 2019), 248.

38. Ernest P. Coulter, qtd. in Ellie Alma Walls, "The Delinquent Negro Girl in New York: Her Need of Institutional Care" (Master's thesis, Columbia University, 1912), 12.

39. Cheryl D. Hicks, *Talk with You Like a Woman: African American Women, Justice, and Reform in New York, 1890–1935* (Chapel Hill: University of North Carolina Press, 2010), 3.

40. Paula C. Austin, *Coming of Age in Jim Crow DC: Navigating the Politics of Everyday Life* (New York, 2019), 11.

41. J. Douglas Smith, "Patrolling the Boundaries of Race: Motion Picture Censorship and Jim Crow in Virginia, 1922–1932," *Historical Journal of Film, Radio, and Television* 21, no. 3 (2001): 273.

42. Ellen C. Scott, *Cinema Civil Rights: Regulation, Repression, and Race in the Classical Hollywood Era* (New Brunswick, NJ: Rutgers University Press, 2015), 2–3.

43. "G." to the editors of *Moving Picture World*, "An Operators' League, and Why?" *Moving Picture World*, March 9, 1907.

44. Sotiropoulos, *Staging Race*, 74.

45. Gunnar Myrdal, *An American Dilemma: The Negro Problem and Modern Democracy* (New York: Harper and Brothers, 1944), 908.

CHAPTER 1

1. "Edison's Vitascope Cheered," *New York Times*, April 24, 1896.

2. "Edison's Latest Triumph," *New York Times*, April 14, 1896.

3. Michael Lobel, *John Sloan: Drawing on Illustration* (New Haven, CT: Yale University Press, 2014), 2; Rebecca Zurier, *Picturing the City: Urban Vision and the Ashcan School* (Berkeley: University of California Press, 2006), 2.

4. Zurier, *Picturing the City*, 65.

5. There is another reading of this painting that privileges tension. While most descriptions of this work suggest that the white woman in the middle of the frame is staring at the viewer, it also could be argued that she is caught in the act of glancing backward at the Black woman in the audience.

6. Michael Lobel has shown that Sloan's initial sketch for *Movies, Five Cents* was different from the final painting. For example, the viewer was initially a member of the audience, not, as with the final piece, someone viewing the theater space and audience. It is unclear to me whether or not the Black woman was a later addition to the piece as well or whether this is more of an imagined audience than a real one. This seems not to matter, as Sloan is widely recognized as a realist who viscerally portrayed the realities of urban living at a pivotal moment in history. Lobel, *John Sloan*, 113–114.

7. As Allyson Nadia Field suggests in defense of speculative methods, "Instead of working with archival abundance we are faced with degrees of archival silence; what survives is often fragmentary at best and deliberately elided or effaced at worst. If these challenges are basic to historical work, they are endemic to the study of Black cinema, for example." Field, "Editor's Introduction: Sites of Speculative Encounter," *Feminist Media Histories* 8, no. 2 (Spring 2022): 3.

8. Mike Wallace, *Greater Gotham: A History of New York City from 1898 to 1919* (Oxford: Oxford University Press, 2017), 418.

9. "Negro Problems to Be Discussed," *New York Times,* May 4, 1896; "The Colored Race in Cities," *New York Times,* July 12, 1896; David Levering Lewis, *W.E.B. Du Bois: Biography of a Race, 1868–1919* (New York: Henry Holt, 1993), 218.

10. W. E. B. Du Bois, "The Black North," *New York Times*, November 17, 1901.

11. Austin, *Coming of Age in Jim Crow DC,* 44.

12. Robert C. Allen, *Vaudeville and Film, 1895–1915: A Study in Media Interaction* (New York: Arno, 1980), 226–230.

13. Ibid., 230.

14. Ibid., 245.

15. Allen, "Motion Picture Exhibition in Manhattan"; Singer, "Manhattan Nickelodeons"; Allen, "Manhattan Myopia."

16. Sotiropoulos, *Staging Race,* 228; Nasaw, *Going Out,* 171–172.

17. A case study of the Capitol Theatre, which was built without a balcony, challenges this. Dabashi, "There Is No Gallery."

18. Griffiths and Latham, "Film and Ethnic Identity in Harlem, 1896–1915"; Frymus, "Case of the Alhambra."

19. James Weldon Johnson, *Black Manhattan* (New York: Arno, 1968), 127.

20. E. S. Martin, "This Busy World," *Harper's Weekly*, September 1, 1900.

21. Jno. Gilmer Speed, "The Negro in New York: A Study of the Social and Industrial Condition of the Colored People in the Metropolis," *Harper's Weekly*, December 22, 1900.

22. "Race Riots in New York," *New York Age,* July 13, 1905.

23. Robin D. G. Kelley, *Thelonious Monk: The Life and Times of an American Original* (New York: Free Press, 2009), 18–19.

24. King, *Whose Harlem*, 154.

25. Mary McLeod Bethune, "The Problems of the City Dweller," *Opportunity* (February 1925): 54.

26. Ibid., 55.

27. Henry J. McGuinn, "Recreation," in *Negro Problems in Cities: A Study Made under the Direction of T.J. Woofter, Jr.* (Garden City, NY: Double Day, Doran, 1928), 261–262.

28. Jessie Fauset, *Plum Bun: A Novel Without a Moral* (New York: Frederick A. Stokes Company, 1929), qtd. in Nolan Gear, "*Spectatrices:* Moviegoing and Women's Writing, 1925–1945" (Ph.D. diss., Columbia University, 2021), 94.

29. Ibid., 96.

30. "Prof. Moses M. Mimms," *New York Age*, October 10, 1907.

31. "Prof. Mimms' Opening: Largest Dance Ever Held in New York a Monster Success," *New York Age*, October 24, 1907.

32. The Harlem River Park was built atop the Harlem African Burial Ground. Many of Black New Yorkers' communal celebrations, therefore, took place on the very same

ground where the first Black people in the state were laid to rest. See Anthony Carrion, "Harlem African Burial Ground Task Force Vision and Mission Statements," *New York City Economic Development Corporation*, 2016, available at https://edc.nyc/sites/default/files/2019-09/final_habg_presentation_boards_english.pdf; Andrea E. Frohne, "Reclaiming Space: The African Burial Ground in New York City," in Nieves and Alexander, *"We Shall Independent Be,"* 489–510.

33. Caddoo, *Envisioning Freedom*, 16.

34. R. R. Wright Jr., "The Migration of Negroes to the North," *Annals of the American Academy of Political and Social Science* 27 (May 1906): 99; Caddoo, *Envisioning Freedom*, 96.

35. "St. Mark's Lyceum Closes," *New York Age*, July 2, 1908.

36. "Unique Churches of Methodism—VIII: Saint Mark's New York City, a Living Church of and for the Negro," *Christian Advocate*, January 7, 1915.

37. "St. Paul's Baptist Church," *New York Age*, October 29, 1908.

38. Prof. Mimms advertisement, *New York Age*, September 24, 1908; Caddoo, *Envisioning Freedom*, 9.

39. "The Passion Play," *New York Age*, December 29, 1910.

40. "The Moving Picture Theatre," *New York Age*, December 15, 1910.

41. Ibid.

42. W. E. B. Du Bois, "On the Problem of Amusement," *Southern Workman* 26 (1897): 181.

43. Ibid., 183.

44. Everett, *Returning*, 154–159. Early film exhibition in DC and other cities was somewhat similar to the situation in New York City in terms of churches serving as some of the earliest potential venues. See, Marya Annette McQuirter, "Claiming the City: African Americans, Urbanization, and Leisure in Washington, D.C., 1902–1957" (Ph.D. diss., University of Michigan, 2000), 83.

45. Everett, *Returning*, 154.

46. "Hold Services in Playhouse," *New York Age*, March 3, 1910.

47. This relationship is, arguably, quite the opposite of what was displayed in other areas throughout the country as "the networks of black churches that once popularized moving pictures were now used to mount the campaign against them." Caddoo posits that in some cities, by the emergence of film's classical period, theaters and Black churches "grew apart." Caddoo, *Envisioning Freedom*, 112–113.

48. "Flushing, N.Y.," *New York Age*, January 28, 1915; *New York Age*, September 28, 1918.

49. *New York Age*, December 10, 1921.

50. *New York Age*, March 22, 1919. After a decades-long battle for the establishment of a Black regiment in the state, the Fifteenth Regiment was first authorized in 1913, as part of the New York National Guard. During World War I, in 1918, members of the Fifteenth were renumbered into the 369th Infantry Regiment while fighting in France. For many years after the war, members of the original Fifteenth Regiment (and some within the local Black press) refused to call themselves the 369th because the latter designated a draftee status, when in truth they were all originally volunteers. See Jeffrey T. Sammons and John H. Morrow Jr., *Harlem's Rattlers and the Great War: The Undaunted 369th Regiment and the African American Quest for Equality* (Lawrence: University Press of Kansas, 2014), chaps. 2, 7. The most recognized film on the 15th/369th

Regiment from this period is *From Harlem to the Rhine*, which was generally well received at the Lafayette Theatre in 1920. Yet film footage of the regiment had been circulating in the city even before then during lectures and special presentations in churches. Perhaps further research will elucidate a potential connection between the earlier footage and the later film.

51. "To Reach the Churchless," *New York Age*, February 28, 1925.

52. "Church Federation to Hold Meetings," *New York Amsterdam News*, March 10, 1926.

53. "To Reach the Churchless."

54. "Moving Picture Theatre."

55. "Rush Memorial Church," *New York Age*, May 10, 1930.

56. There is some debate over whether the Crescent or the Lincoln was the first theater for Black audiences in Harlem, especially given the geographical proximity of the two and the potentially identical opening year. While the Crescent is deemed the first by Lester Walton and scholar Bernard Peterson Jr., Henry T. Sampson claims the Lincoln opened in 1908. The Lincoln added "the first colored theatre in Harlem" to its advertisements in Black weeklies in 1928, and, given that the Crescent opened in the middle of December 1909, it is somewhat more likely that the Lincoln opened first. The *Amsterdam News* also notes, "The Lincoln Theatre served as the foundation for everything we have in theatrical entertainment in Harlem today. The building of the Crescent Theatre lower down on 135th Street was prompted by the success of Mrs. Downs at the Lincoln." "The Passing of a Landmark," *New York Amsterdam News*, August 13, 1930.

57. *Pittsburgh Courier*, August 6, 1921, qtd. in Sister Mary Francesca Thompson, "The Lafayette Players, 1915–1932" (Ph.D. diss., University of Michigan, 1972), 15.

58. Theophilus Lewis, *The Messenger*, June 1924, qtd. in John Gilbert Monroe, "A Record of Black Theatre in New York City, 1920–1929" (Ph.D. diss., University of Texas at Austin, 1980), 43–44.

59. "Mrs. Downs' Lincoln and Martinson and Nibur's Crescent Were Pioneers," *New York Amsterdam News*, March 9, 1927.

60. "Crescent Theatre Has Big Opening," *New York Age*, December 23, 1909.

61. "Kelly and Catlin Amuse," *New York Age*, December 1, 1910; "Change of Policy at the Crescent," *New York Age*, April 6, 1911.

62. Henry T. Sampson, *Blacks in Blackface: A Sourcebook on Early Black Musical Shows* (Metuchen, NJ: Scarecrow, 1980), 119; Lester Walton, "Crescent Theatre Sold," *New York Age*, August 24, 1911.

63. Walton, "Crescent Theatre Sold."

64. "Theatrical Jottings," *New York Age*, January 20, 1910.

65. Field, *Uplift Cinema*, 91.

66. "At the Theatres," *New York Age*, July 13, 1916.

67. Lucien White, "The Colored American (Winning His Suit)," *New York Age*, July 20, 1916.

68. "Crescent Theatre," *New York Age*, March 13, 1913.

69. "Pictures at Crescent," *New York Age*, March 19, 1914; Caddoo, *Envisioning Freedom*, 102.

70. Richard Newman, "The Lincoln Theatre," *American Visions* 6, no. 1 (1991), 31–32.

71. Naomi Washington, in Kisseloff, *You Must Remember This*, 306.

72. "Lincoln Installs Broadway Musical Program," *New York Age*, January 22, 1927.

73. "Lincoln to Give Screen Tests," *New York Age*, October 20, 1928. See also Judith Weisenfeld, *Hollywood Be Thy Name: African American Religion in Film* (Berkeley: University of California Press, 2007), 23.

74. See, Field, *Uplift Cinema*, 19–21.

75. "Conduct Automobile Schools in New York," *New York Age*, February 3, 1913.

76. Gilbert Osofsky, *Harlem: The Making of a Ghetto; Negro New York, 1890–1930* (1966; repr., Chicago: Elephant Paperbacks, 1996), 33.

77. Kevin Gaines, *Uplifting the Race: Black Leadership, Politics, and Culture in the Twentieth Century* (Chapel Hill: University of North Carolina Press, 1996), 14.

78. Gregory Waller, *Main Street Amusements: Movies and Commercial Entertainment in a Southern City, 1896–1930* (Washington, DC: Smithsonian Institution Press, 1995), 173. See also Stewart, *Migrating*, 156, 185.

79. Caddoo, *Envisioning Freedom*, 87.

80. "The 59th Street Theatre," *New York Age*, May 1, 1913.

81. Not to be confused with the Palace Theatre that opened in 1913 on Forty-Seventh Street and Broadway, which eventually featured Black vaudeville stars like Bert Williams.

82. "Plays Santa Claus," *New York Age*, December 4, 1913; "Wins Buick Automobile," *New York Age*, July 10, 1913.

83. "59th Street Theatre."

84. Ibid.

85. Jennifer Fronc, "The Horns of the Dilemma: Race Mixing and the Enforcement of Jim Crow in New York City," *Journal of Urban History* 33, no. 1 (2006): 3, 21.

86. "Fifty-Ninth St. Theatre," *New York Age*, May 8, 1913.

87. Lester Walton, "Manager Made Mistake," *New York Age*, June 26, 1913.

88. "59th St. Theatre," *New York Age*, January 29, 1914; "Fire at 59th St. Theatre," *New York Age*, January 22, 1914. The theater's last advertisement in the *Age* was on April 16, 1914.

89. Monroe, "Record of Black Theatre," 14.

90. Lester Walton, "The Crescent as a Stepping Stone," *New York Age*, November 7, 1912.

91. Ibid.

92. "Drawing Color Line Is Resented," *New York Age*, November 14, 1912.

93. "The Lafayette Theatre Passes into New Hands," *New York Age*, May 7, 1914.

94. "Harriet Tubman Monument Benefit," *New York Age*, September 3, 1914.

95. Osofsky, *Harlem*, 109.

96. "Elks Night at Lafayette Theatre," *New York Age*, November 29, 1919.

97. "Present Week's Offering Will Be Held Over for Week Commencing Mar. 16," *New York Amsterdam News*, March 11, 1925.

98. Wallace Thurman, *Negro Life in New York's Harlem: A Lively Picture of a Popular and Interesting Section* (Girard, KS: Haldeman-Julius, 1927), 37.

99. Wallace Thurman, *The Blacker the Berry: A Novel of Negro Life* (New York: Macaulay, 1929), 200.

100. Ibid.

101. Ibid.

102. Stewart, *Migrating*, 181.

103. King, *Whose Harlem*, 28.

104. "New Theatre for Harlem," *New York Age*, November 30, 1911.

105. King, *Whose Harlem*, 15.

106. Walton, "Crescent Theatre Sold."

107. Ibid.

108. "Tuskegeean Theatre," *New York Age*, February 15, 1912; "Hogan Theatre," *New York Age*, February 15, 1912.

109. "Walker-Hogan-Cole Theatre," *New York Age*, March 7, 1912.

110. Walton, "The Crescent as a Stepping Stone."

111. Despite insisting from the very beginning that all money given to the Johnson Amusement Company was in good hands, the corporation went bankrupt shortly after breaking ground. The last advertisement for the company asking for investments was printed on August 12, 1912. See also Sampson, *Blacks in Blackface*, 121.

112. McQuirter, "Claiming the City," 96.

113. Renaissance Theatre advertisement, *New York Age*, January 29, 1921.

114. "'Renaissance' Opens," *New York Age*, January 22, 1921.

115. Thurman, *Negro Life in New York's Harlem*, 25.

116. Renaissance Theatre advertisement, *New York Age*, January 29, 1921.

117. "New Jersey," *New York Age*, September 11, 1926.

118. Romeo Dougherty, "My Observations: An Opportunity for the Alhambra Theatre," *New York Amsterdam News*, September 1, 1934.

119. Renaissance Theatre advertisement, *New York Age*, January 29, 1921.

120. "'Renaissance' Opens."

121. "'Peter Pan' Is Shown to 1000 Children Free at Renaissance Theatre," *New York Age*, January 2, 1926.

122. Sammons and Morrow argue that members of the Fifteenth Regiment preferred to call themselves the "Old 15th" or the "Rattlers." "Never," they insist, "the 369th or some of the other sensationalist names (such as Hell Fighters) that others would later apply to them." Sammons and Morrow, *Harlem's Rattlers*, 196–197, 207.

123. "Deny Renaissance Buildings Are Properties of Hebrews," *New York Age*, February 24, 1923.

124. "Renaissance Inaugurates All-Talking Pictures with 'In Old Arizona,'" *New York Age*, March 9, 1929; "Renaissance Theatre Has Perfect Audition for Talking Pictures," *New York Age*, April 20, 1929. Yet even as the Black press and the Renaissance positioned these renovations as essential for maximum audience entertainment, local musicians were critical of these adjustments, fearing that they would put musicians out of the job. One editorial blamed the Renaissance for accelerating this trend specifically in Harlem, revealing the differences between early cinema and sound film in the neighborhood, when Black musicians were less needed in the theater space than before.

125. Vere E. Johns, "Loss of Renaissance a Blow to Race Business," *New York Age*, May 7, 1932.

126. Romeo Dougherty, "My Observations: A Tragic Occurrence in Our Onward March," *New York Amsterdam News*, April 27, 1932.

127. "Renaissance's Director Out," *New York Amsterdam News*, November 15, 1933.

128. Leo Brecher also owned theaters in Midtown and the Bronx.

129. King, *Whose Harlem*, 28.

130. Carla L. Peterson, "Contesting Space in Antebellum New York: Black Community, City Neighborhoods, and the Draft Riots of 1863," in Nieves and Alexander, *"We Shall Independent Be,"* 48.

CHAPTER 2

1. Thurman, *Negro Life in New York's Harlem*, 1.
2. Ibid., 6.
3. Ibid., 8–9.
4. Inmate 3748, History Blank, May 30, 1924, Bedford Hills Correctional Facility, W0010–77B Inmate Case Files, ca. 1915–1930, Records of the Department of Correctional Services, New York State Archives, State Education Department (hereafter BHCF). I have provided pseudonyms for inmates but kept their case numbers.
5. Ibid.
6. Henry James Forman, *Our Movie Made Children* (New York, 1933), 25.
7. Gary Rhodes, *The Perils of Moviegoing in America: 1896–1950* (London: Bloomsbury, 2011), xiv.
8. King, *Whose Harlem*, 139. Davarian Baldwin makes a similar claim about theaters when he notes, "The theater, like the rent party and sports stadium, also became a showcase for audiences as well as a place of public privacy for stolen moments." Baldwin, *Chicago's New Negroes*, 107.
9. Hazel V. Carby, "Policing the Black Woman's Body in an Urban Context," *Critical Inquiry* 18 (1992): 739.
10. LaKisha Michelle Simmons, *Crescent City Girls: The Lives of Young Black Women in Segregated New Orleans* (Chapel Hill: University of North Carolina Press, 2015), 5. See also Stewart, *Migrating*, 138. On respectability, see Evelyn Brooks Higginbotham, *Righteous Discontent: The Women's Movement in the Black Baptist Church, 1880–1920* (Cambridge, MA: Harvard University Press, 1993); Victoria W. Wolcott, *Remaking Respectability: African American Women in Interwar Detroit* (Chapel Hill, NC: University of North Carolina Press, 2001).
11. Hicks, *Talk with You Like a Woman*, 3.
12. My understanding of how Black girls and women chose to interact with cinema as a form of agency is informed by multiple scholars: Kathy Peiss, *Cheap Amusements: Working Women and Leisure in Turn-of-the-Century New York* (Philadelphia: Temple University Press, 1986); Peiss, "'Charity Girls' and City Pleasures: Historical Notes on Working-Class Sexuality, 1880–1920," in *Passion and Power: Sexuality in History*, ed. Kathy Peiss and Christina Simmons (Philadelphia: Temple University Press, 1989), 57–69; Tera W. Hunter, *To 'Joy My Freedom: Southern Black Women's Lives and Labors after the Civil War* (Cambridge, MA: Harvard University Press, 1997), 146–186; Baldwin, *Chicago's New Negroes*, 103–109; Hicks, *Talk with You Like a Woman*, 211–219; Hartman, *Wayward Lives*. See also Sonia Brand-Fisher, "Proto-cinephilia: Retheorizing Working Class Women's Moviegoing Pre-1920," *Early Popular Visual Culture* 19, no. 4 (2021): 301–323.
13. For a detailed analysis of the range of bodily dangers within theaters throughout the country, see Rhodes, *Perils of Moviegoing in America*.
14. Kim Gallon, *Pleasure in the News: African American Readership and Sexuality in the Black Press* (Urbana: University of Illinois Press, 2020), 40–43.

15. "Ushers Beat Man in Theatre Row," *New York Amsterdam News*, October 5, 1927.

16. "Fight Starts Panic in Harlem Theatre," *New York Times*, May 31, 1932.

17. "Fight at Theatre Causes Near Riot," *New York Amsterdam News*, July 5, 1933.

18. "Theatre Fans Horrified by Fatal Fight," *New York Amsterdam News*, October 2, 1937.

19. Ibid.

20. WAS, "Theatre Reviews: Haven," *Times Herald*, August 28, 1935; Bennie Butler, "Harlem Goes Wild as Crooning Notes Herald New 'Find,'" *Pittsburg Courier*, February 18, 1933.

21. "Arrest 2 in Plot to Rob N.Y. Theater," *Chicago Defender*, May 1, 1926.

22. Robin D. G. Kelley, *Race Rebels: Culture, Politics, and the Black Working Class* (New York: Free Press, 1994), 8–10.

23. United States Department of Labor, "Retail Prices of Food in 51 Cities on Specified Dates," *Monthly Labor Review* 16 (March 1923): 29.

24. "Harlem Police Reserve Kills Suspected Thief and Is Shot by Police," *New York Age*, February 27, 1926.

25. Shelley Stamp, *Movie-Struck Girls: Women and Motion Picture Culture after the Nickelodeon* (Princeton, NJ: Princeton University Press, 2000), 47–49.

26. "Captain Mulrooney Tells Police to Be on Lookout for Masher around Theatres," *New York Age*, April 25, 1925.

27. "Juvenile Vice Rampant," *New York Amsterdam News*, February 10, 1926.

28. Ibid.

29. LaShawn Harris, *Sex Workers, Psychics, and Numbers Runners: Black Women in New York City's Underground Economy* (Urbana: University of Illinois Press, 2016), 52; On Black women's bodies and the racial uplift project, see Douglas Flowe, *Uncontrollable Blackness: African American Men and Criminality in Jim Crow New York* (Chapel Hill: University of North Carolina Press, 2020), 133; Hartman, *Wayward Lives*, 81–122.

30. Erin Chapman, *Prove It on Me: New Negroes, Sex, and Popular Culture* (Oxford: Oxford University Press, 2012), 14, 77; Hicks, *Talk with You Like a Woman*, 107.

31. "Little Girl with a Key," *New York Age*, February 13, 1926. For more on the intraracial tensions regarding children's use of the streets for play, see Jessica Klanderud, *Struggle for the Street: Social Networks and the Struggle for Civil Rights* (Chapel Hill: University of North Carolina Press, 2023), chap. 2.

32. In Ralph Ellison's short story "King of the Bingo Game," the main character takes part in a bingo game held at a movie theater.

33. Cornelius Willemse, *Beyond the Green Lights* (Garden City, NJ: A. A. Knopf, 1931), 71.

34. Ibid.; Kali N. Gross, *Colored Amazons: Crime, Violence, and Black Women in the City of Brotherly Love, 1880–1910* (Durham, NC: Duke University Press, 2006), 72.

35. Harris, *Sex Workers, Psychics, and Numbers Runners*, 142–143.

36. Ibid., 143.

37. Langston Hughes, in *The Collected Works of Langston Hughes*, vol. 13, *Autobiography: The Big Sea*, ed. Joseph McLaren (Columbia: University of Missouri Press, 2002), 183.

38. Wallace Thurman, "Cordelia the Crude," *Fire!! A Quarterly Devoted to the Younger Negro Artists* (November 1926): 5–6.

39. Ibid.

40. Thurman, *Blacker the Berry*, 142.

41. Ibid., 143.

42. James McQuade, "Chicago Letter," *Film Index*, October 15, 1910.

43. McQuade, "Chicago Letter," *Film Index*, October 29, 1910.

44. "The Lap of Luxury," *Pictures and Picturegoers*, April 10, 1915.

45. Victoria Earle Matthews, "Some of the Problems Confronting Southern Women in the North" (address, Hampton Negro Conference, July 21, 1898).

46. Paul Laurence Dunbar, "The Negroes of the Tenderloin," *New York Sun*, September 4, 1897.

47. Hicks, *Talk with You Like a Woman*, 95–103; Steve Kramer, "Uplifting Our 'Downtrodden Sisterhood': Victoria Earle Matthews and New York City's White Rose Mission, 1897–1907," *Journal of African American History* 91, no. 3 (2006): 243–266.

48. Frances Kellor, "The Criminal Negro," *The Arena* (March 1901): 310.

49. Jane Edna Hunter, *Nickel and a Prayer* (Nashville: Eli Kani, 1940), 83.

50. Lee Grieveson, *Policing Cinema: Movies and Censorship in Early-Twentieth-Century America* (Berkeley: University of California Press, 2004), 15–18. For a discussion of the tensions between film exhibitors appealing directly to (white) women and the uneasy incorporation of (white) women into cinema's audiences, see Stamp, *Movie-Struck Girls*, esp. chap. 2.

51. Naomi Washington, in Kisseloff, *You Must Remember This*, 274.

52. Hicks, *Talk with You Like a Woman*, 106.

53. See Hartman, *Wayward Lives*; Carby, "Policing the Black Woman's Body."

54. Inmate 3711, History Blank, August 2, 1924, BHCF.

55. Ibid.; Inmate 3708, History Blank, July 19, 1924, BHCF; Inmate 2496, Information Concerning Patient, August 13, 1917, BHCF; Inmate 3703, History Blank, July 18, 1924, BHCF.

56. Inmate 3718, History Blank, August 12, 1924, BHCF.

57. William H. Jones, *Recreation and Amusement among Negroes in Washington, D.C.* (Washington, DC: Howard University Press, 1927), 180.

58. Inmate 2503, Staff Meeting, September 29, 1917, BHCF.

59. Chapman, *Prove It on Me*, 77.

60. Hartman, *Wayward Lives*, 108.

61. Inmate 3365, History Blank, n.d., BHCF.

62. Inmate 2493, Statement of Girl, July 12, 1917, BHCF.

63. Cheryl Greenburg, *"Or Does It Explode?": Black Harlem in the Great Depression* (Oxford: Oxford University Press, 1997), 24.

64. Inmate 2493, Statement of Girl.

65. Record from Isaac T. Hopper Home, February 17, 1930, February 24, 1930, Box 108: Case Files, "We–Williams, C," Women's Prison Association of New York records, Manuscripts and Archives Division, New York Public Library (hereafter WPA).

66. Hunter, *To 'Joy My Freedom*, 179.

67. Simmons, *Crescent City Girls*, chaps. 1–2.

68. Brian Purnell and Jeanne Theoharis, introduction to *The Strange Careers of Jim Crow North: Segregation and Struggles outside of the South*, ed. Brian Purnell and Jeanne Theoharis, with Komozi Woodard (New York: New York University Press 2019), 26.

69. Elizabeth Clanton, interview by Leon Fink, October 24, 1975, recording, New York City Immigrant Labor History Project Oral History Collection, Tamiment Library

and Robert F. Wagner Archive, New York University (hereafter NYCILHP), available at http://digitaltamiment.hosting.nyu.edu/s/nyciloh/item/94.

70. Mabele Mitchell, interview by Steven Holmes, March 26, 1973, recording, NYCILHP, available at http://digitaltamiment.hosting.nyu.edu/s/nyciloh/item/495.

71. Osofsky, *Harlem*, 123; James Weldon Johnson, *Black Manhattan* (New York: Arno, 1968), 146–147.

72. "Raid in Front of Lafayette," *New York Amsterdam News*, September 1, 1926.

73. "Gangsters Kill Harlem Woman," *New York Age*, 1932.

74. "Judge Knox, in Federal Court, Grants Injunctions That Close Twenty Hootch Joints in Harlem," *New York Age*, March 15, 1924.

75. Jones, *Recreation and Amusement*, 111, 112.

76. Thurman, *Negro Life in New York's Harlem*, 35, 36.

77. Record from Isaac T. Hopper Home, August 11, 1932, Box 108: Case Files, "We–Williams, C," WPA.

78. Record from Isaac T. Hopper Home, May 25, 1939, Box 69: Case Files, "But–Cav," WPA.

79. Deborah Gray White, *Ar'n't I a Woman? Female Slaves in the Plantation South* (New York: W. W. Norton, 1985), 124. See also Lauren Rabinovitz, *For the Love of Pleasure: Women, Movies, and Culture in Turn-of-the-Century Chicago* (New Brunswick, NJ: Rutgers University Press, 1998), 12.

80. Record from Isaac T. Hopper Home, January 27, 1935, Box 80: Case Files, "Gos–Hai," WPA.

81. Record from Isaac T. Hopper Home, January 28, 1935, Box 80: Case Files, "Gos–Hai," WPA.

82. Darlene Clark Hine, "Rape and the Inner Lives of Black Women in the Middle West," *Signs* 14 (1989): 915; Danielle L. McGuire, *At the Dark End of the Street: Black Women, Rape, and Resistance—a New History of the Civil Rights Movement from Rosa Parks to the Rise of Black Power* (New York: Alfred A. Knopf, 2010), xviii. My interpretation of Georgia's openness with WPA workers about her sexual assault is also informed by Hicks, *Talk with You Like a Woman*, 208–209.

83. Record from Isaac T. Hopper Home, January 28, 1935, Box 80: Case Files, "Gos–Hai," WPA.

84. Record from Isaac T. Hopper Home, January 23, 1935, Box 80: Case Files, "Gos–Hai," WPA.

85. Record from Isaac T. Hopper Home, January 29, 1935, Box 80: Case Files, "Gos–Hai," WPA; Record from Isaac T. Hopper Home, January 21, 1935, Box 80: Case Files, "Gos–Hai," WPA.

86. Record from Isaac T. Hopper Home, January 21, 1935, Box 80: Case Files, "Gos–Hai," WPA.

87. My understanding of the importance of Black women's public testimonials is drawn from Gwendolyn D. Pough, *Check It While I Wreck It: Black Womanhood, Hip-Hop Culture, and the Public Sphere* (Lebanon, NH: Northeastern University Press, 2004), esp. chap. 2; Danielle L. McGuire, "Joan Little and the Triumph of Testimony," in *Freedom Rights: New Perspectives on the Civil Rights Movement*, ed. John Dittmer and Danielle L. McGuire (Lexington: University Press of Kentucky, 2011), 191–221.

88. Record from Isaac T. Hopper Home, January 29, 1935, Box 80: Case Files, "Gos–Hai," WPA.

89. Record from Isaac T. Hopper Home, January 28, 1935, Box 80: Case Files, "Gos–Hai," WPA.

90. Record from Isaac T. Hopper Home, January 21, 1935, Box 80: Case Files, "Gos–Hai," WPA.

91. Jane Addams, *The Spirit of the Youth and the City Streets* (1909; repr., Champaign: University of Illinois Press, 1972), 76.

92. Simmons, *Crescent City Girls*, 175.

93. Stewart, *Migrating*, 100, 94. See also Jacqueline Bobo, *Black Women as Cultural Readers* (New York: Columbia University Press, 1995), esp. introduction and chap. 1; Frymus, "White Screens, Black Fandom," 248–265.

94. Chapman, *Prove It on Me*, 83.

95. Record from Isaac T. Hopper Home, February 25, 1935, Box 80: Case Files, "Gos–Hai," WPA.

96. Record from Isaac T. Hopper Home, February 4, 1935, Box 80: Case Files, "Gos–Hai," WPA.

97. Record from Isaac T. Hopper Home, January 29, 1935, Box 80: Case Files, "Gos–Hai," WPA.

98. Record from Isaac T. Hopper Home, January 21, 1935, Box 80: Case Files, "Gos–Hai," WPA.

99. Inmate 2505, Statement of Girl, August 10, 1917, BHCF.

100. Mary White Ovington, "Fresh Air Work among Colored Children in New York City," *Charities and the Commons*, October 13, 1906, Box 3, Folder 17, Mary White Ovington Collection, Papers, 1854–1948, Walter P. Reuther Library, Wayne State University.

101. Inmate 2505, Information concerning the Patient, August 10, 1917, BHCF.

102. Inmate 2505, Statement of Girl.

103. Inmate 2505, Mental Examination, September 18, 1917, BHCF.

104. Inmate 2480, Statement of Girl, June 23, 1917; Verified History, June 23, 1917, BHCF.

105. Inmate 2480, Verified History.

106. Elizabeth Alice Clement, *Love for Sale: Courting, Treating, and Prostitution in New York City, 1900–1945* (Chapel Hill: University of North Carolina Press, 2006), 45. See also Peiss, "'Charity Girls' and City Pleasures," 60–61; Peiss, *Cheap Amusements*, 107–113.

107. Richard Maltby, "The Social Evil, the Moral Order and the Melodramatic Imagination, 1890–1915," in *Melodrama: Stage, Picture, Screen*, ed. Jacky Bratton, Jim Cook, and Christine Gledhill (London: British Film Institute, 1994), 218.

108. Inmate 2505, Information concerning the Patient. Clement argues that in the 1930s, working-class women began to accept more tangible things in exchange for sex, but Charlotte's experiences predate this. She was living with a man who paid her rent in 1917. Clement, *Love for Sale*, 214–217.

109. Inmate 2480, Information concerning the Patient, June 23, 1917, BHCF.

110. Inmate 3748, untitled document, March 24, 1926.

CHAPTER 3

1. Oscar Micheaux, "The Negro and the Photo-Play," *Half-Century Magazine*, May 1919.

2. Everett, *Returning*, 133.

3. Oscar Micheaux, "Producer Can Succeed Only with Our Aid," *Pittsburgh Courier*, December 13, 1924.

4. Jane Gaines, *Fire and Desire: Mixed-Race Movies in the Silent Cinema* (Chicago: University of Chicago Press, 2000), 231.

5. Charlene Regester, "Oscar Micheaux on the Cutting Edge: Films Rejected by the New York State Motion Picture Commission," *Studies in Popular Culture* 17, no. 2 (1995): 62.

6. "Picture Shows All Put Out of Business," *New York Times*, December 25, 1908.

7. Grieveson, *Policing Cinema*, 22.

8. The board was initially named the New York Board of Censorship of Moving Pictures, but when it realized that it could influence national decisions on appropriate themes in film, its name was changed to the National Board of Review of Motion Pictures. The name change also reflected members' desires to distance themselves from what they considered the negative stigma of censorship.

9. Andrea Friedman, *Prurient Interests: Gender, Democracy, and Obscenity in New York City, 1909–1945* (New York: Columbia University Press, 2000), 30–31.

10. Ibid., 26.

11. Grieveson, *Policing Cinema*, 188; Jennifer Fronc, "Local Public Opinion: The National Board of Review of Motion Pictures and the Fight against Film Censorship in Virginia, 1916–1922," *Journal of American Studies* 47, no. 3 (2013): 741.

12. General Laws of the State of New York, Chapter 715 § 1 (West 1921).

13. Grieveson, *Policing Cinema*, 18.

14. Fronc, "Horns of the Dilemma," 4.

15. Dan Streible, "Race and Reception of Jack Johnson Fight Films," in *The Birth of Whiteness: Race and the Emergence of U.S. Cinema*, ed. Daniel Bernardi (New Brunswick, NJ: Rutgers University Press, 1996), 178.

16. David Krasner, *A Beautiful Pageant: African American Theatre, Drama, and Performance in the Harlem Renaissance* (New York: Palgrave Macmillan, 2002), 54.

17. Streible, "Race and Reception," 170. See also Susan Courtney, *Hollywood Fantasies of Miscegenation: Spectacular Narratives of Gender and Race, 1903–1967* (Princeton, NJ: Princeton University Press, 2005), 54–57.

18. "Ban Being Placed on Fight Pictures," *Show World*, July 9, 1910.

19. "Fight-Picture Ban Is Now Widespread," *New York Times*, July 7, 1910.

20. Lester Walton, "Johnson Is Now Undisputed Champion," *New York Age*, July 7, 1910.

21. Ibid.

22. Reverdy C. Ransom, "No Race Champion," *New York Times*, June 6, 1910.

23. "Fight-Picture Ban Is Now Widespread."

24. "Women See Fight Pictures," *Film Index*, August 13, 1910. See also: "Among the Exhibitors," *Film Index*, July 30, 1910; "Among the Exhibitors," *Film Index*, September 24, 1910.

25. Grieveson, *Policing Cinema*, 122.

26. Ibid., 124.

27. Daniel J. Leab, *From Sambo to Superspade: The Black Experience in Motion Pictures* (Boston: Houghton Mifflin, 1975), 27.

28. This quotation is taken from a subtitle card from *The Birth of a Nation*.

29. Lary May, *Screening Out the Past: The Birth of Mass Culture and the Motion Picture Industry* (Chicago: University of Chicago Press, 1983), 81.

30. James Weldon Johnson, "Uncle Tom's Cabin and The Clansman," *New York Age*, March 4, 1915.

31. Elaine Frantz Parsons, "Revisiting *The Birth of a Nation* at 100 Years," *Journal of the Gilded Age and Progressive Era* 14, no. 4 (2015): 596. Susan Courtney notes that the film's focus on various forms of miscegenation "generate[s] much of the film's most famous editing and mise-en-scéne," effectively linking the film's narrative with its form. Courtney, *Hollywood Fantasies*, 63.

32. Johnson, "Uncle Tom's Cabin and The Clansman."

33. Ibid.

34. James Weldon Johnson, "Perverted History," *New York Age*, April 22, 1915.

35. Johnson, "Uncle Tom's Cabin and the Clansman."

36. Fred Moore, "Still Showing Vicious Picture," *New York Age*, March 11, 1915 (emphasis mine).

37. Mary Carbine, "'The Finest Outside the Loop': Motion Picture Exhibition in Chicago's Black Metropolis, 1905–1928," *Camera Obscura* 23, no. 2 (1990): 9–41; Stewart, *Migrating*, 105–106; Manthia Diawara, "Black Spectatorship: Problems of Identification and Resistance," in *Black American Cinema*, ed. Manthia Diawara (New York: Routledge, 1993); bell hooks, "The Oppositional Gaze: Black Female Spectators," in Diawara, *Black American Cinema*.

38. For a detailed account of local protests in Boston and Philadelphia against *Birth* and linkages to class and police brutality, see Cara Caddoo, "*The Birth of a Nation*, Police Brutality, and Black Protest," *Journal of the Gilded Age and Progressive Era* 14, no. 4 (2015): 608–611. For an overview of how Black film critics responded to *Birth*, see Everett, *Returning*, chap. 2.

39. Davarian Baldwin, "'I Will Build a Black Empire': *The Birth of a Nation* and the Specter of the New Negro," *Journal of the Gilded Age and the Progressive Era* 14, no. 4 (2015): 600.

40. Thomas Cripps, "The Reaction of the Negro to the Motion Picture *Birth of a Nation*," *Historian* 25, no. 3 (1963): 351.

41. Ibid.; "Fighting Race Calumny," *The Crisis*, May 1915, 40.

42. "Vicious Picture Film Condemned by Censors," *New York Age*, April 3, 1915.

43. "Fighting Race Calumny," 41.

44. "Promise to Tone Down Two Scenes of Vicious Photo Play," *New York Age*, April 1, 1915.

45. Ibid.

46. "Fighting Race Calumny," 42.

47. Nancy Rosenblum, "In Defense of Moving Pictures: The People's Institute, the National Board of Censorship and the Problem of Leisure in Urban America," *American Studies* 33, no. 2 (1992), 57. See also Jennifer Fronc, *Monitoring the Movies: The Fight over Film Censorship in Early Twentieth-Century Urban America* (Austin: University of Texas Press, 2017), 59–60.

48. Friedman, *Prurient Interests*, 57. See also May, *Screening Out the Past*, 54–55; Grieveson, *Policing Cinema*, 101.

49. Friedman, *Prurient Interests*, 34.

50. Rosenblum, "In Defense of Moving Pictures," 57. Micheaux did, for example, successfully submit *Within Our Gates* (1919) to the National Board without any issue. It is unclear, though, if Micheaux ever exhibited it anywhere in the city.

51. Gaines, *Fire and Desire*, 235.

52. Richard Norman to Bruce, September 2, 1922, Series 1: Correspondence, Box 1, Folder "September–October, 1922," Richard E. Norman and Race Filmmaking Collection, 1912–1997, Black Film Center/Archive, Indiana University, Bloomington (hereafter RNRFC).

53. Patrick McGilligan, *Oscar Micheaux: The Great and Only: The Life of America's First Black Director* (New York: Harper Perennial, 2008), 150–151.

54. "Micheaux to Produce in New York," *Billboard*, June 18, 1921.

55. Pearl Bowser and Louise Spence, *Writing Himself into History: Oscar Micheaux, His Silent Films, and His Audiences* (New Brunswick, NJ: Rutgers University Press, 2000), 43–44; Cary D. Wintz, "The Lafayette Theatre: Crucible of African American Dramatic Arts," in Lupack, *Early Race Filmmaking*, 157, 159–161.

56. Claude McKay, *Home to Harlem* (New York: Harper and Brothers, 1928), 15.

57. Micheaux would later add an "-e" to his surname.

58. Larry Tye, *Rising from the Rails: Pullman Porters and the Making of the Black Middle Class* (New York: Henry Holt, 2004), 28.

59. Oscar Micheaux, "Where the Negro Fails," *Chicago Defender*, March 19, 1910.

60. Oscar Micheaux, *The Conquest*, 145, in Bowser and Spence, *Writing Himself into History*, 19.

61. Bowser and Spence, *Writing Himself into History*, 19–21; Field, *Uplift Cinema*, x–xiv.

62. McGilligan, *Oscar Micheaux*, 112.

63. Oscar Micheaux to Lincoln Motion Picture Company, May 3, 1918, qtd. in McGilligan, *Oscar Micheaux*, 113–114.

64. General Laws of the State of New York, Chapter 715 § 1 (West 1921).

65. May, *Screening Out the Past*, 55. For the role of women in censorship efforts, see Alison M. Parker, "Mothering the Movies: Women Reformers and Popular Culture," in *Movie Censorship and American Culture*, ed. Francis G. Couvares (Washington, DC: Smithsonian Institution Press, 1996), 73–96; Fronc, "Local Public Opinion."

66. New York State Motion Picture Commission (hereafter NYSMPC) to Micheaux Film Corp., May 20, 1922, A1418: License Application Case Files, Motion Picture Scripts Collection, New York State Archives (hereafter Case Files).

67. Charlene Regester, "Black Films, White Censors: Oscar Micheaux Confronts Censorship in New York, Virginia, and Chicago," in Couvares, *Movie Censorship and American Culture*, 171.

68. John William Leonard, *Woman's Who's Who of America: A Biographical Dictionary of Contemporary Women of the United States and Canada* (New York: American Commonwealth, 1914), 150–151; Susan Goodier, *No Votes for Women: The New York State Anti-suffrage Movement* (Urbana: University of Illinois Press, 2013), 89.

69. *Official Report of the Proceedings of the Seventeenth Republican National Convention* (New York: Tenny, 1920), 60.

70. For example, the Republican Party, at least on their national platform in 1920, called on Congress to put forth antilynching legislation. Still, the platform was also for restrictions on immigration and immigrants' free speech. Ibid., 104–105.

71. Parker, "Mothering the Movies," 78.

72. Ibid., 89–90.

73. NYSMPC to Oscar Micheaux, January 16, 1924, Case Files.

74. "Derogatory Titles," n.d., Folder: Titles: Derogatory (censorship), A1428–77: Censorship Files, 1927–1945, Motion Picture Scripts Collection, New York State Archives (hereafter Censorship Files).

75. Regester, "Black Films, White Censors," 173.

76. Though the 1924 version of *Birthright* is nonextant, I have used the censorship files from the 1938 sound version to reconstruct this scene, which follows the silent original very closely, according to the archival documents and newspaper reviews. For reference, see NYSMPC to Oscar Micheaux, January 16, 1924; NYSMPC to Micheaux Pictures Corp., June 4, 1938, Case Files.

77. For more on wartime and postwar racial violence, see Alfred L. Brophy, *Reconstructing the Dreamland; The Tulsa Race Riot of 1921, Race, Reparations, and Reconciliation* (Oxford: Oxford University Press, 2002); James Grossman, "A Chance to Make Good, 1900–1929," in *To Make Our World Anew: The History of African Americans from 1880*, ed. Robin D. G. Kelley and Earl Lewis (Oxford: Oxford University Press, 2000), 120–123.

78. NYSMPC to Oscar Micheaux, September 20, 1924, Case Files.

79. Micheaux Film Corporation, Oscar Micheaux to NYSMPC, September 27, 1924, Case Files.

80. Ibid.

81. Ibid.

82. It is worth noting that Mrs. Hosmer was the censor who reversed the initial decision against *Son of Satan* and was also the sole reviewer of *The Crimson Skull*.

83. Richard Norman to Bruce, March 27, 1922, Series: Correspondence, Box 1, Folder: "March, 1922," RNRFC.

84. For more on Micheaux and the larger uplift project in the early twentieth century, see Field, *Uplift Cinema*, preface.

85. Micheaux, "Producer Can Succeed."

86. Bowser and Spence, *Writing Himself into History*, 184; Leab, *From Sambo to Superspade*, 81.

87. Baldwin, *Chicago's New Negroes*, 142.

88. Micheaux, "Producer Can Succeed."

89. Ibid.

90. This critique was frequent in Micheaux's films, making an appearance in *The Homesteader, Within Our Gates*, and *Body and Soul*.

91. Oscar Micheaux to NYSMPC, November 11, 1925, Case Files.

92. Charles Musser, "To Redream the Dreams of White Playwrights," *Yale Journal of Criticism* 12, no. 2 (1999): 344–345.

93. Gerald R. Butters Jr., "Capitalizing on Race: White Producers of All-Black Cinema," in Lupack, *Early Race Filmmaking*, 114.

94. "Royal," *Afro-American*, January 22, 1927, qtd. in Bowser, Gaines, and Musser, *Oscar Micheaux and His Circle*, 261.

95. Grieveson, *Policing Cinema*, 204.

96. For more on the significance of numbers running in New York City, see Irma Watkins-Owens, *Blood Relations: Caribbean Immigrants and the Harlem Community, 1900–1930* (Bloomington: Indiana University Press, 1996); Shane White et al., *Playing*

the Numbers: Gambling in Harlem between the Wars (Cambridge, MA: Harvard University Press, 2010); Harris, *Sex Workers, Psychics, and Numbers Runners*, 2016.

97. Charlene Regester, "Oscar Micheaux the Entrepreneur: Financing the House behind the Cedars," *Journal of Film and Video* 49, no. 1–2 (1997): 17. Micheaux may have done this in other states as well and throughout his long career. A note in *Film Bulletin* suggests that he was fined $110.00 for shipping an uncensored print to the Forrest Theater in Philadelphia. Jaywalker, "Short Subjects: From Philly," *Independent Exhibitors Film Bulletin* 4, no. 13 (July 2, 1938), 18. See also Smith, "Patrolling the Boundaries of Race," 279.

98. *The Devil's Disciple* (1925), *The Conjure Woman* (1926), *The House behind the Cedars* (1924–1925), *The Girl from Chicago* (1932), *Wages of Sin* (1929), *When Men Betray* (1929), and *Temptation* (1936) were all also advertised or written about in New York City's Black press but were never brought before the Motion Picture Commission for review.

99. Oscar Micheaux to NYSMPC, December 12, 1927, Case Files.

100. Levy Dep., 6, January 3, 1928, Case Files.

101. Oscar Micheaux to NYSMPC, December 3, 1927, Case Files.

102. "Renaissance Theatre," *New York Age*, April 2, 1930.

103. Dermody Dep., 2, April 12, 1930, Case Files. Micheaux was actually showing *Daughter of the Congo* under the license he had received for *The Millionaire*.

104. Dermody Dep., 6, April 12, 1930, Case Files.

105. Dermody Dep., 7, April 12, 1930, Case Files.

106. "Crime: Slavery," n.d., Folder: Titles: Derogatory (censorship), Censorship Files.

107. For more on how Micheaux manipulated the press surrounding this case, see Charlene Regester, "Headline to Headlights: Oscar Micheaux's Exploitation of the Rhinelander Case," *Western Journal of Black Studies* 22, no. 3 (1998): 195–204.

108. Theophilus Lewis, "The Harlem Sketchbook," *New York Amsterdam News*, April 16, 1930.

109. John Harding, "Motion Picture Is Withdrawn after Protest in New York," *New York Age*, May 28, 1938.

110. Lou Layne, "Moon over Harlem," *New York Age*, May 25, 1935.

111. Richard Norman to Albert Fish, June 8, 1925, Series: Correspondence, Box 1, Folder: "June–December, 1925," RNRFC.

112. WCC, "Micheaux's Latest Seems to Be His Best," *New York Amsterdam News*, April 27, 1935.

113. LL, "Lem Hawkins' Confession at Apollo Prevents Bill from Being World Beater," *New York Age*, May 18, 1935.

114. Ebenezer Ray, "A Paragrapher's Dottings: Wanted: A Good Story," *New York Age*, August 12, 1939.

115. McGilligan, *Oscar Micheaux*, 272. On a separate occasion in the mid-1920s, Micheaux's films were also briefly banned from the Lenox Theatre in Harlem. See Richard Norman to Oscar Micheaux, August 9, 1926, RNRFC.

116. Dan Burley, "History of Negro Films Described What Fans Want Again Stressed," *New York Age*, September 30, 1939.

117. Bank Statement, March 30, 1951, Box 6, Folder 11: Financial Bank Records, 1951, Oscar Micheaux Papers, 1871–1951, Schomburg Center for Research in Black Culture, Manuscripts, Archives and Rare Books Division, New York Public Library.

118. Koszarski, *Hollywood on the Hudson*, 255–256, 376–377.

CHAPTER 4

1. "Projection Booth in Renaissance Theatre Crashes into Orchestra Killing One, Injuring 31," *New York Age*, April 19, 1930.

2. "Inspectors Probing Renaissance Crash," *New York Amsterdam News*, April 16, 1930.

3. "Projection Booth in Renaissance Theatre Crashes."

4. Ibid.

5. "Inspectors Probing."

6. "Prisoner of the Booth," *Exhibitor's Trade Review*, April 22, 1922, 1465.

7. "Colored Motion Picture Tenders Issue Statement," *New York Amsterdam News*, September 29, 1926.

8. Everett, *Returning*, 108.

9. King, *Whose Harlem*, 62.

10. The *Amsterdam News*' participation in these protests may well have been a result, if only slightly, of an earlier choice to capitulate to a local theater. In 1916, Hubert Harrison wrote a somewhat negative review of the Lincoln Theatre's theatrical offerings in the paper. When the theater revoked all of its advertising, the *Amsterdam News*, according to Harrison, went begging for its return. When the advertising was finally restored, the *Amsterdam News* did not publish any more negative reviews of the theater. Perhaps, the paper was trying to recover some of its reputation in 1925, especially in the midst of the New Negro movement. Jeffrey B. Perry, *Hubert Harrison: The Voice of Harlem Radicalism, 1883–1918* (New York: Columbia University Press, 2009), 264–266.

11. Richard Koszarski, *Evening's Entertainment: The Age of the Silent Picture, 1915–1928* (Berkeley: University of California Press, 1990), 159.

12. Louis M. Townsend, "Problems of a Projectionist," *Transactions of S.M.P.E.* no. 25 (September 1926): 79–86.

13. John F. Rider, "The Projectionist Must Learn Sound to Survive, Rider Says," *Motion Picture News*, May 3, 1930, 49.

14. H. Rubin, "Some Problems in the Projection of Sound Movies," *Transactions of S.M.P.E.* 12, no. 35 (1928): 867.

15. L. Gardette, "Conducting the Nickelodeon Program," *The Nickelodeon*, March 1909, 79–80.

16. "Boyertown, Pa.," *Moving Picture World*, January 18, 1908.

17. "Danger of Careless Film Operators: Fire, Panic, Death of an Operator, in Safeguarded Film Theater, due to Lack of Care and Competence," *Safety Engineering* 26 (1913): 125–126.

18. Some scholars argue that these incidents can be read as resistance to industrial interference in the laborers' workplace. Roberta E. Pearson and William Uricchio, "Coming to Terms with New York City's Moving Picture Operators, 1906–1913," *Moving Image: The Journal of the Association of Moving Image Archivists* 2 (2002): 78.

19. Eileen Bowser, *The Transformation of Cinema, 1907–1915* (Berkeley: University of California Press, 1990), 38.

20. Steve Wurtzler, "Standardizing Professionalism and Showmanship: The Performance of Motion Picture Projectionists during the Early Sync-Sound Era," in *Keyframes: Popular Cinema and Cultural Studies*, ed. Matthew Tinkcom and Amy Villarejo (London: Routledge, 2001), 365.

21. F. H. Richardson, "Operators," *Moving Picture World*, May 1908.

22. F. H. Richardson, "The Wages of Operators," *Moving Picture World*, September 1909.

23. Application for License to Operate Moving Picture Apparatus and Connections, Department of Water Supply, Gas, and Electricity, A1429–77 Subject Files, 1923–1965, Motion Picture Scripts Collection, New York State Archives; F. H. Richardson, "Projection Department," *Moving Picture World*, March 2, 1918.

24. The City of New York, Department of Water Supply, Gas, and Electricity, *Annual Report*, 1908, 1912, 1922. New York City. By 1912, the department received ten times the number of applications, with their yearly total coming to 2,373, over half of which were those trying to renew their licenses. Ten years later in 1922 after the exams became more stringent, that number was just a bit higher at 2,494, of which 1,991 were renewals.

25. Starting in 1911, the union was actually responsible for pushing the city to put apprenticeships into place. "Local 35 Holds Big Meeting," *Film Index*, April 1, 1911. See also Mary White Ovington, "The Negro in the Trade Unions in New York," *Annals of the American Academy of Political and Social Science* 27, no. 3 (1906): 553; Marc Karson and Ronald Radosh, "The American Federation of Labor and the Negro Workers, 1894–1949," in *The Negro and the American Labor Movement*, ed. Julius Jacobson (Garden City, NY: Doubleday, 1968), 158.

26. "Succumbs," *New York Amsterdam News*, December 4, 1937.

27. Pearson and Uricchio, "Coming to Terms," 82.

28. "Important to Operators of Greater New York," *Motion Picture News*, December 2, 1916, 3518.

29. Donald Crafton, *The Talkies: American Cinema's Transition to Sound, 1926–1931* (Berkeley: University of California Press, 1997), 218.

30. "Prisoner of the Booth II," *Exhibitor's Trade Review*, May 6, 1922, 1621.

31. Ibid.

32. Karson and Radosh, "The American Federation of Labor and the Negro Workers," 155–187; Eric Arnesen, "Following the Color Line of Labor: Black Workers and the Labor Movement before 1930," *Radical History Review* 55 (1993): 71–77.

33. William E. Clark, "White Stage Hands Attack Colored Employees in Harlem," *New York Age*, March 18, 1922.

34. Independent Black labor organizations were not uncommon, and, though this was not the case for UACMPO members, some Black workers actually preferred them as a means of gaining autonomy and avoiding abusive white workers. See Arnesen, "Following the Color Line of Labor," 61–62.

35. Caddoo, *Envisioning Freedom*, 32–33. Caddoo has pointed out that some of the first Black exhibitors were women, such as Mmes. Bunn, Conley, and Hawkins. By necessity, these pioneering female exhibitors doubled as operators.

36. The minimum age to apply for an operator's license in New York City was twenty-one, so it is likely that Brown was an apprentice of one of the other men.

37. "Biographical Sketch of FRANK R. CROSSWAITH," Negro Labor News Service, ca. 1936, Frank R. Crosswaith Papers, 1917–1965, Schomburg Center for Research in Black Culture Manuscripts, Archives and Rare Books Division, New York Public Library (hereafter FCP). For more on Black radicalism in Harlem, see Minkah Makalani, *In the Cause of Freedom: Radical Black Internationalism from Harlem to London, 1917–1939* (Chapel Hill: University of North Carolina Press, 2011); Makalani, "Black Women's

Intellectual Labor and the Social Spaces of Black Radical Thought in Harlem," in *Race Capital? Harlem as Setting and Symbol*, ed. Andrew M. Fearnley and Daniel Matlin (New York: Columbia University Press, 2019), 141–164.

38. "Copy of Article Submitted by . . . of the YWCA," n.d., FCP.

39. Ibid.

40. "Three Theatres Catering Almost Exclusively to Colored Patronage Will Give Operators a Chance," *New York Amsterdam News*, July 1, 1925.

41. Ibid.

42. "War between Brecher and Operators," *New York Amsterdam News*, September 15, 1926.

43. "Prisoner of the Booth," *Exhibitor's Trade Review*, April 22, 1922.

44. "Motion Picture Operators State Their Side of Case," *New York Amsterdam News*, March 24, 1926.

45. Ibid.

46. Ibid.

47. King, *Whose Harlem*, 83. See also Bruce Nelson, *Divided We Stand: American Workers and the Struggle for Black Equality* (Princeton, NJ: Princeton University Press, 2002); Marcy Sacks, *Before Harlem: The Black Experience in New York City before World War I* (Philadelphia: University of Pennsylvania Press, 2006), 124–130; Nelson Lichtenstein, *State of the Union: A Century of American Labor* (Princeton, NJ: Princeton University Press, 2002); Charles Lionel Franklin, *The Negro Labor Unionists: Problems and Conditions among Negroes in the Labor Unions in Manhattan with Special Reference to the NRA and Post-NRA Situations* (New York: Columbia University Press, 1936).

48. Ira Reid, *Negro Membership in American Labor Unions* (New York: National Urban League, 1930), 97.

49. Ibid.

50. Ibid., 98.

51. On the *New York Age*, see Arnesen, "Following the Color Line of Labor," 74–75.

52. "About Things Theatrical," *New York Amsterdam News*, April 21, 1926.

53. Ibid.

54. "About Things Theatrical," *New York Amsterdam News*, June 23, 1926; "Give Our Motion Picture Operators a Chance," *New York Amsterdam News*, July 28, 1926.

55. "Motion Picture Men Get Raise," *New York Age*, July 24, 1926.

56. "Lafayette Owner Issues Statement of His Stand in Present Harlem Fight," *New York Amsterdam News*, September 22, 1926.

57. "Operators' Union Demands Same Salary for Motion Picture Machine Tenders There as Given Elsewhere," *New York Amsterdam News*, September 15, 1926.

58. "A Motion Picture Operator Says a Few Words," *New York Amsterdam News*, September 15, 1926.

59. "War between Brecher and Operators."

60. "Motion Picture Operator Says a Few Words."

61. Ibid.

62. "Lafayette Owner Issues Statement"; "Leo Brecher Tells of Efforts of Union to Get Negro Operators out of the Lafayette," *New York Age*, October 2, 1926.

63. "Lafayette Owner Issues Statement."

64. "Colored Motion Picture Tenders Issue Statement."

65. Ibid.
66. Ibid.
67. "Prisoner of the Booth."
68. Ibid.
69. "Colored Motion Picture Tenders Issue Statement."
70. "Lafayette Owner Issues Statement."
71. Ibid.
72. Frank Schiffman, "Letter from Mr. Schiffman," *New York Amsterdam News*, November 17, 1926.
73. Ibid.
74. "War between Brecher and Operators."
75. "Colored Motion Picture Tenders Issue Statement."
76. "The Battle Rages," *New York Amsterdam News*, October 6, 1926.
77. "Motion Picture License Bureau and Union Officials Alleged to Be in Conspiracy to Bar Negro Operators," *New York Age*, October 9, 1926.
78. Hubert Harrison, "As Harrison Sees It," *New York Amsterdam News*, October 6, 1926.
79. Ibid.
80. "Prof. Williams, Who Took Stump for Negro Operators, Submits Findings," *New York Amsterdam News*, November 10, 1926.
81. Ibid.
82. "Negro Union Motion Picture Operators Again at Lafayette at Union Wages," *New York Amsterdam News*, June 8, 1927.
83. Ibid.
84. "Our Motion Picture Operators," *New York Amsterdam News*, June 29, 1927.
85. Crafton, *Talkies*, 8–18.
86. Steve Wurtzler, *Electric Sounds: Technological Change and the Rise of Corporate Mass Media* (New York: Columbia University Press, 2007), 155.
87. F. H. Richardson, "The Importance of Good Projection to the Producer," *Transactions of S.M.P.E.* 12, no. 34 (1928), 355.
88. Ibid.
89. F. H. Richardson, "The Effect of Sound Synchronization upon Projection," *Transactions of S.M.P.E.* 12, no. 25 (1928): 874.
90. Warren Nolan, "Talking Pictures and the Public," *Transactions of the S.M.P.E.* 13, no. 37 (1929): 133.
91. William F. Canavan, "Motion Picture Projection," *Projection Engineering* 1, no. 4 (1929): 31, cited in Wurtzler, *Electric Sounds*, 154.
92. Wurtzler, *Electric Sounds*, 157. Wurtzler's overall argument is that, during the transition to sound, projectionists became "performers" of sound and thus enjoyed a "new power." But as Wurtzler himself points out, and I detail in the preceding two sections, industry experts and projectionists themselves had been advocating for their significance to the success of the film industry since the early 1900s.
93. "Negro Motion Picture Operators Declare War on Two Local Theatres," *New York Amsterdam News*, September 3, 1930.
94. "Union Officials Explain Reason for Picketing Theatres," *New York Age*, September 20, 1930.

95. W. B. Simms, "The Operators' Side," *New York Amsterdam News*, September 24, 1930.

96. "A Message to Harlem Theatre Patrons," n.d., FCP.

97. Ibid.

98. "Renaissance Theatre Management States Position in Operators' Fight," *New York Amsterdam News*, September 17, 1930.

99. Ibid.

100. "Negro Motion Picture Operators Declare War on Two Local Theatres"; "Negro Operators Secure Orient," *New York Amsterdam News*, February 26, 1930.

101. "Renaissance Theatre Management States Position in Operators' Fight."

102. In 1925, the Black-owned Sarco Realty Company went out of business, most likely resulting in the property falling into white hands. At that time, the various businesses housed in the large Renaissance building, including the Renaissance Theatre, remained under Black management. "Despondent Renaissance Official Ends Own Life," *New York Amsterdam News*, April 27, 1932.

103. "Theatre Chain and Union End Battles," *New York Amsterdam News*, October 14, 1931.

104. The Man at the Window, "Looking at Life," *New York Age*, October 22, 1932.

105. "So They're Picking on Flatbush!" *Brooklyn Daily Eagle*, August 24, 1932.

106. "Pickets Again Go on Patrol," *New York Amsterdam News*, February 8, 1933.

107. Roy Wilkins to William Green, October 31, 1934, "AFL. February 10, 1934–November 22, 1934," Papers of the NAACP.

108. "Negro Movie Workers Accuses Union Heads," *New York Times*, June 14, 1935.

109. F. H. Richardson, "Better Projection," *Moving Picture World*, December 26, 1925.

110. "Operators Picket 2 Theatres in Harlem," *New York Amsterdam News*, March 16, 1940.

111. "Operators Win Strike at Local Theatre," *New York Amsterdam News*, March 16, 1935.

112. "Motion Picture Operators Break Union Stranglehold," *New York Amsterdam News*, April 14, 1945. It is unclear when the Empire State Union was absorbed into Local 306, as the former had been trying since the late 1930s, but it most likely occurred after the 1940s.

113. Romeo Dougherty, "My Observations: The Negro Motion Picture Operator Again," *New York Amsterdam News*, February 24, 1932.

114. The Man at the Window, "Looking at Life," ellipses in original.

115. Harold Cruse, *The Crisis of the Negro Intellectual: A Historical Analysis of the Failure of Black Leadership* (New York: William Morrow, 1967), 71–83; King, *Whose Harlem*, 82–92. Harold Cruse argues that the strike was a failure because Harlemites did not align themselves with the operators as they were more interested in watching the Black musical theater and comedy shows that were regularly put on at the Lafayette. Instead of centering any potential failures of the protests, King considers the 1926 strike as an example of the growth of Black unionism in the neighborhood, while adding that Black Harlemites were also particularly loyal to the Lafayette because of its nondiscriminatory seating practices and its offerings, the latter of which he reads as a working-class oppositional consciousness. King's analysis can be extended to assert that Black Harlemites were loyal to the Lafayette for its endeavors to ingratiate itself within the community, which were detailed in Chapter 1.

116. Cruse, *Crisis*, 81.

117. "Colored Motion Picture Tenders Issue Statement."

CHAPTER 5

1. "Discrimination in New York," *New York Age*, January 21, 1909.

2. Sydney H. French, "History of Negro Papers and Periodicals," April 24, 1936, 2, New York Public Library Digital Collections, Schomburg Center for Research in Black Culture, Manuscripts, Archives and Rare Book Division, New York Public Library.

3. Carla L. Peterson, "What Renaissance? A Deep Genealogy of Black Culture in Nineteenth-Century New York City," in Sherrard-Johnson, *Companion to the Harlem Renaissance*, 29.

4. Susan A. Curtis, *Colored Memories: A Biographer's Quest for the Elusive Lester A. Walton* (Columbia: University of Missouri Press, 2008), 266.

5. Sacks, *Before Harlem*, 9.

6. Armistead S. Pride and Clint C. Wilson II, *A History of the Black Press* (Washington, DC: Howard University Press, 1997), 14.

7. Roi Ottley, *New World A-Coming: Inside Black America* (Boston: Houghton Mifflin, 1943), 268.

8. Pride and Wilson, *History of the Black Press*, 122.

9. Emma Lou Thornbrough, "American Negro Newspapers, 1880–1914," *Business History Review* 40, no. 4 (1966): 488; Artee Felicita Young, "Lester Walton: Black Theatre Critics" (Ph.D. diss., University of Michigan, 1980), 44.

10. Fred Carroll, *Race News: Black Journalists and the Fight for Racial Justice in the Twentieth Century* (Urbana: University of Illinois Press, 2017), 19.

11. Sacks, *Before Harlem*, 22–31. Importantly, Sacks also notes the tensions that Black migration from the South wrought within the Black community in New York. The *Age* itself was not always a promoter of migration, insisting instead that Black southerners remain where they were.

12. Eugene E. Gordon, "Outstanding Negro Newspapers: Reiteration and Detail," *Opportunity* (February 1925): 51.

13. Young, "Lester Walton," 44. It is possible that Walton began working at the *Age* before he got an official byline because, in the middle of 1907, more sports and theater articles were added semiregularly to the paper's reportage.

14. Everett, *Returning*, 18.

15. Young, "Lester Walton," 150.

16. Walton's concern for these issues in theaters was not limited to New York. He frequently commented on how African Americans fared in theaters throughout the country. For some examples, see "A Solution Offered," *New York Age*, November 27, 1913; "Theatrical Comment," *New York Age*, March 19, 1914; "Colored Motion Picture Actors Relate Experience in Vicksburg," *New York Age*, August 30, 1921; "Boston Negroes Prevent Showing of Ku Klux Klan Photo Play," *New York Age*, May 21, 1921.

17. Lester Walton, "The Degeneracy of the Moving Picture Theatre," *New York Age*, August 5, 1909.

18. Ibid.

19. Ida B. Wells, *The Red Record: Tabulated Statistics and Alleged Causes of Lynching in the United States, 1895* (Project Gutenberg ebook, 2005).

20. Reverend King, in Wells, *Red Record*.

21. Amy Louise Wood, *Lynching and Spectacle: Witnessing Racial Violence in America, 1890–1940* (Chapel Hill: University of North Carolina Press, 2009), 72–74.

22. Walton, "Degeneracy"; Everett, *Returning*, 20.

23. Walton, "Degeneracy."

24. Wood, *Lynching and Spectacle*, 74.

25. Everett, *Returning*, 21.

26. Wood, *Lynching and Spectacle*, 76. Film studies scholar Alice Maurice argues that the problem of audience believability in synchronized sound films in the 1920s was remedied with the exploitation of Black performers believed to be inherently inclined toward performance. Here, in this nascent use of sound technology paired with images of Smith's murder, a similar practice is at play. In this case, cinema's claims to veracity were based in a widespread tolerance and even celebration of violence against perceived (and imagined) Black criminality and transgressions against the color line. See Alice Maurice, *The Cinema and Its Shadow: Race and Technology in Early Cinema* (Minneapolis: University of Minnesota Press, 2013), esp. chap. 4. Lynching photography was also repurposed by Black activists and journalists in antilynching campaigns. See Wood, *Lynching and Spectacle*, chaps. 7–8.

27. Walton, "Degeneracy."

28. Sabine Haenni, *The Immigrant Scene: Ethnic Amusements in New York, 1880–1920* (Minneapolis: University of Minnesota Press, 2008), 31, 55.

29. Ibid., 31.

30. James S. Metcalfe, qtd. in Lester Walton, "Negroes in New York Theatres," *New York Age*, November 18, 1909.

31. Ibid.

32. Walton, "Negroes in New York Theatres."

33. Ibid. Lizabeth Cohen's articulation of the "Consumer's Republic" after the Second World War is somewhat relevant here. As she notes, even before the war and in the midst of the Great Depression, the importance of the consumer and the role of government in ascertaining certain consumer privileges was increasingly important. Walton's use of "citizen" (and other uses by Black activists in relation to cinema during this period), I would argue, is another early example of a linkage between consumer power and the power of the government, or what she calls the citizen consumer. See Lizabeth Cohen, *A Consumer's Republic: The Politics of Mass Consumption in Postwar America* (New York: Vintage Books, 2003), esp. chap. 1, 41–53.

34. Lester Walton, "Theatre Manager Loses Case," *New York Age*, November 2, 1911 (emphasis mine).

35. Jasmine Nichole Cobb, *Picture Freedom: Remaking Black Visuality in the Early Nineteenth Century* (New York: New York University Press, 2015).

36. Ibid., 5.

37. Henry Louis Gates Jr., "The Trope of a New Negro and the Reconstruction of the Image of the Black," *Representations*, no. 24 (1988): 129–155; Michael Bieze, *Booker T. Washington and the Art of Self-Representation* (New York: Peter Lang, 2008).

38. On Black performers' use of blackface before and during this period, see Sotiropoulos, *Staging Race*; Louis Chude-Sokei, *Bert Williams, Black-on-Black Minstrelsy, and the African Diaspora* (Durham, NC: Duke University Press, 2006).

39. Walton, "Theatre Manager Loses Case."

40. Ibid.

41. Ibid.

42. Lester Walton, "A Notable Decision," *New York Age*, January 25, 1912. In a show of its dismissal of the Levy case, the *New York Times* included a brief summary story of the trial on the very last of its twenty-page edition on January 23, 1913. It offered no commentary whatsoever on the consequences of Levy's conviction.

43. Lester Walton, "The Theatres in Harlem," *New York Age*, January 9, 1913.

44. Ibid.; "Acquire Control of Lafayette Theatre," *New York Age*, February 6, 1913.

45. Film historian Richard Abel has cited the immense difficulty in ascertaining the content of the first two years of American *Pathé Weekly*, which began its run in 1911, because the weekly bulletin citing title and synopsis from this period is very rare. He also notes that generally Pathé's nonfiction films were, when confronted with competition from the American market, considered to specialize in the "exotic" or "primitive." It is worth pointing out that the other subjects in this film included German peasants going to church and President Wilson throwing the first pitch at a baseball game, none of which received negative representation according to Walton. See Richard Abel, *The Red Rooster Scare: Making American Cinema, 1900–1910* (Berkeley: University of California Press, 1999), 229n21, 131–132.

46. Walton, "The Flood Refugees," *New York Age*, June 5, 1913.

47. Ibid.

48. Lester Walton, "The Colored Soldier on the Screen," *New York Age*, August 24, 1918. Walton made note that he was not referencing those films put out by Black independent production companies during this period.

49. Ibid.

50. Ibid.

51. Lester Walton, "Our Colored Heroes in the Movies," *New York Age*, November 30, 1918.

52. "War Talk Starts Riot in Harlem," *New York Times*, July 20, 1919.

53. "Commencing in Next Week's Issue," *New York Age*, January 25, 1919. For more on Walton's participation in the war effort, see Curtis, *Colored Memories*, 261–263.

54. Curtis, *Colored Memories*, 267.

55. Editor, "Vere E. Johns," *Amsterdam News*, October 30, 1929.

56. Vere E. Johns, "In the Name of Art," *New York Age*, March 18, 1933.

57. Ibid. See also Vere E. Johns, "In the Name of Art," *New York Age*, March 25, 1933.

58. Johns, "In the Name of Art," *New York Age*, April 29, 1933.

59. Ibid.

60. Vere E. Johns, "Through My Spectacles," *New York Age*, March 3, 1934. This was not an irregular proscription against racism for Johns. He advocated for similar demonstrations against Harlem department stores that refused to hire Black employees that same year.

61. Johns, "In the Name of Art," April 29, 1933.

62. Will Rogers, *The Good Gulf Show*, January 21, 1934, qtd. in Amy M. Ware, "Will Rogers's Radio: Race and Technology in the Cherokee Nation," *American Indian Quarterly* 33, no. 1 (2009): 76.

63. Vere E. Johns, "In the Name of Art," *New York Age*, February 3, 1934.

64. According to Johns, Mix had sent a telegram to Governor Rolph of California supporting the latter's declaration to ignore the lynching of two murderers, Thomas

Harold Thurmond and John M. Holmes. Though the victims were both white, Johns was clearly opposed to the barbarism of lynching, which was usually meted out against Black men, women, and, sometimes, children and resulted in the breakdown of law and order.

65. Johns, "In the Name of Art," February 3, 1934.

66. For more on the NAACP's campaign against Rogers and Rogers's complex relationship with Blackness, see Ware, "Will Rogers's Radio," 76–83.

67. Romeo Dougherty, "My Observations," *Amsterdam News*, February 21, 1934.

68. Johns, "Through My Spectacles," March 3, 1934; This was not the end of the Johns-Dougherty feud on this particular matter as Johns would write two weeks later that Dougherty was attempting to steal his thunder for the win against Rogers in Harlem. Johns, ever the instigator, claimed Dougherty had been "naughty and it is time for Daddy Vere to do a little spanking." The bounds of their disputes clearly had few limits. Vere E. Johns, "In the Name of Art," *New York Age*, March 17, 1934.

69. Johns, "Through My Spectacles," March 3, 1934.

70. Vere E. Johns, "In the Name of Art," *New York Age*, November 18, 1933.

71. "Another Tribute to Southern 'Culture,'" *New York Age*, October 28, 1933.

72. Vere E. Johns, "Through My Spectacles," *New York Age*, October 28, 1933.

73. Romeo Dougherty of the *Amsterdam News* gave Johns this descriptor. See Doughtery, "An Impartial Opinion," *New York Amsterdam News*, December 11, 1929.

74. Vere E. Johns, "In the Name of Art," *New York Age*, November 5, 1932.

75. Stewart, *Migrating*, chap. 3.

76. Vere E. Johns, "In the Name of Art," *New York Age*, December 3, 1932.

77. Vere E. Johns, "In the Name of Art," *New York Age*, November 26, 1932.

78. Johns, "In the Name of Art," December 3, 1932.

79. Jacqueline Stewart, "Negroes Laughing at Themselves? Black Spectatorship and the Performance of Urban Modernity," *Critical Inquiry* 29 (Summer 2003): 662.

80. Lester Walton, "Music and the Stage," *New York Age*, August 26, 1909.

81. "Cooling System Being Installed at Renaissance Theatre," *New York Age*, June 17, 1933.

82. Vere E. Johns, "In the Name of Art," *New York Age*, January 5, 1935.

EPILOGUE

1. Romeo Dougherty, "Past Performances," *New York Amsterdam News*, December 18, 1929. Future research might find ways to connect Downs's early work at the Lincoln (or the building of the Crescent) with other developments in theaters throughout the country. For example, see Chad Newsom, "Josephine Stiles and Her House of Feature Films: Innovations of a Black Theater Proprietor," *Film History: An International Journal* 35, no. 1 (2023): 21–60.

2. Dan Romilio, "The Passing of Another Landmark," *New York Amsterdam News*, August 13, 1930.

3. Theophilus Lewis, "The Street Pleasure Left Behind," *New York Amsterdam News*, January 15, 1930.

4. This women's auxiliary unit had been in place since 1917, when a number of Black women in the city rallied to support the Fifteenth Regiment working to reach full recruitment numbers. See Sammons and Morrow, *Harlem's Rattlers*, 124–125.

5. James Baldwin, "The Devil Finds Work," in *James Baldwin: Collected Essays*, ed. Toni Morrison (Washington, DC: Library of Congress, 1998), 483 (emphasis Baldwin's).

6. Ibid., 491.

7. Ibid., 525.

8. Ibid., 528.

9. See Martha Biondi, *To Stand and Fight: The Struggle for Civil Rights in Postwar New York City* (Cambridge, MA: Harvard University Press, 2003), chap. 4. For more general desegregation efforts in recreational sites during the post–World War II period, see Wolcott, *Race, Riots, and Rollercoasters.*

Bibliography

ARCHIVES AND SPECIAL COLLECTIONS

Black Film Center/Archive, Indiana University, Bloomington
Richard E. Norman and Race Filmmaking Collection, 1912–1997 (digitized)

Manuscript and Archives Division, New York Public Library, New York
National Board of Review of Motion Pictures records
Women's Prison Association of New York records

Manuscript Division, Library of Congress, Washington, DC
National Association for the Advancement of Colored People Papers (digitized)

Manuscripts, Archives, and Rare Books Division, Schomburg Center for Research in Black Culture, New York
Frank Crosswaith Papers, 1917–1965
Oscar Micheaux Papers, 1871–1951
Writers' Program, New York City: Negroes of New York Collection (digitized)

Municipal Archives, City of New York
Magistrates' Court Docket Books

New York State Archives, State Education Department
Bedford Hills Correctional Facility, Records of the Department of Correctional Services
Motion Picture Scripts Collection

The Tamiment Library and Robert F. Wagner Archive, New York University
New York City Immigrant Labor History Project Oral History Collection (digitized)

Walter P. Reuther Library, Wayne State University
Mary White Ovington Collection, Papers, 1854–1948

NEWSPAPERS AND MAGAZINES

Billboard
Brooklyn Daily Eagle
Chicago Defender
Christian Advocate
The Crisis
Exhibitor's Trade Review
Film Index
Fire!! A Quarterly Devoted to the Younger Negro Artists
Half-Century Magazine
Harper's Weekly
Motion Picture Daily
Motion Picture News
Moving Picture World
New York Age
New York Amsterdam News
New York Sun
New York Times
The Nickelodeon
Pictures and Picturegoers
Pittsburgh Courier
Safety Engineering
Show World
Transactions of S.M.P.E.

PRIMARY SOURCES

Addams, Jane. *The Spirit of the Youth and the City Streets*. 1909. Reprint, Champaign, IL: University of Illinois Press, 1972.

Bethune, Mary McLeod. "The Problems of the City Dweller." *Opportunity* 3 (February 1925): 54–55.

The City of New York, Department of Water Supply, Gas, and Electricity. *Annual Report*. 1908, 1912, 1922.

Du Bois, W. E. B. "On the Problem of Amusement." *Southern Workman* 26 (1897): 181–184.

Dunbar, Paul Laurence. *The Sport of Gods*. New York: Dodd, Mead, 1902.

Forman, Henry James. *Our Movie Made Children*. New York: Macmillan Company, 1933.

Franklin, Charles Lionel. *The Negro Labor Unionists: Problems and Conditions among Negroes in the Labor Unions in Manhattan with Special Reference to the NRA and Post-NRA Situations*. New York: Columbia University Press, 1936.

Hunter, Jane Edna. *Nickel and a Prayer*. Nashville: Eli Kani, 1940.

Johnson, James Weldon. *Black Manhattan*. New York: Arno, 1968.

Jones, William H. *Recreation and Amusement among Negroes in Washington, D.C.* Washington, DC: Howard University Press, 1927.

Kellor, Frances. "The Criminal Negro." *Arena* (1901).

Kisseloff, Jeff. *You Must Remember This: An Oral History of Manhattan from the 1890s to World War II.* San Diego: Harcourt Brace Jovanovich, 1989.

Leonard, John William. *Woman's Who's Who of America: A Biographical Dictionary of Contemporary Women of the United States and Canada.* New York: American Commonwealth, 1914.

Locke, Alain, ed. *The New Negro: An Interpretation.* New York: Albert and Charles Boni, 1925.

Matthews, Victoria Earle. "Some of the Problems Confronting Southern Women in the North." Address given at the Hampton Negro Conference, July 21, 1898.

Myrdal, Gunnar. *An American Dilemma: The Negro Problem and Modern Democracy.* New York: Harper and Brothers Publishers, 1944.

Negro Problems in Cities: A Study Made under the Direction of T.J. Woofter, Jr. Garden City, NY: Double Day, Doran, 1928.

Official Report of the Proceedings of the Seventeenth Republican National Convention. New York: Tenny, 1920.

Ottley, Roi. *New World A-Coming: Inside Black America.* Boston: Houghton Mifflin, 1943.

Ovington, Mary White. "The Negro in the Trade Unions in New York." *Annals of the American Academy of Political and Social Science* 27, no. 3 (1906): 551–558.

Reid, Ira. *Negro Membership in American Labor Unions.* New York: National Urban League, 1930.

Thurman, Wallace. *The Blacker the Berry: A Novel of Negro Life.* New York: Macaulay, 1929.

———. *Negro Life in New York's Harlem: A Lively Picture of a Popular and Interesting Section.* Girard, KS: Haldeman-Julius, 1927.

United States Department of Labor. "Retail Prices of Food in 51 Cities on Specified Dates." *Monthly Labor Review* 16 (March 1923): 51–91.

Walls, Ellie Alma. "The Delinquent Negro Girl in New York: Her Need of Institutional Care." Master's thesis, Columbia University, 1912.

Wells, Ida B. *The Red Record: Tabulated Statistics and Alleged Causes of Lynching in the United States, 1895.*

Willemse, Cornelius. *Beyond the Green Lights.* Garden City, NJ: A. A. Knopf, 1931.

Wright, R. R., Jr. "The Migration of Negroes to the North." *Annals of the American Academy of Political and Social Science* 27 (May 1906): 97–116.

BOOKS AND ARTICLES

Allen, Robert C. "Manhattan Myopia; Or, Oh! Iowa!" *Cinema Journal* 35, no. 3 (1996): 75–103.

———. "Motion Picture Exhibition in Manhattan, 1906–1912: Beyond the Nickelodeon." *Cinema Journal* 18, no. 2 (1979): 2–15.

———. *Vaudeville and Film, 1895–1915: A Study in Media Interaction.* New York: Arno, 1980.

Arnesen, Eric. "Following the Color Line of Labor: Black Workers and the Labor Movement before 1930." *Radical History Review* 55 (1993): 53–87.

Austin, Paula C. *Coming of Age in Jim Crow DC: Navigating the Politics of Everyday Life.* New York: New York University Press, 2019.

Baldwin, Davarian. *Chicago's New Negroes: Modernity, the Great Migration, and Black Urban Life.* Chapel Hill: University of North Carolina Press, 2007.

———. "'I Will Build a Black Empire': *The Birth of a Nation* and the Specter of the New Negro." *Journal of the Gilded Age and the Progressive Era* 14, no. 4 (2015): 599–603.

Baldwin, Davarian, and Minkah Makalani, eds. *Escape from New York: The New Negro Renaissance beyond Harlem.* Minneapolis: University of Minnesota Press, 2013.

Bernardi, Daniel, ed. *The Birth of Whiteness: Race and the Emergence of U.S. Cinema.* New Brunswick, NJ: Rutgers University Press, 1996.

Biondi, Martha. *To Stand and Fight: The Struggle for Civil Rights in Postwar New York City.* Cambridge, MA: Harvard University Press, 2003.

Bobo, Jacqueline. *Black Women as Cultural Readers.* New York: Columbia University Press, 1995.

Bowser, Eileen. *The Transformation of Cinema, 1907–1915.* Berkeley: University of California Press, 1990.

Bowser, Pearl, Jane Gaines, and Charles Musser, eds. *Oscar Micheaux and His Circle: African American Filmmaking and Race Cinema of the Silent Era.* Bloomington: Indiana University Press, 2001.

Bowser, Pearl, and Louise Spence. *Writing Himself into History: Oscar Micheaux, His Silent Films, and His Audiences.* New Brunswick, NJ: Rutgers University Press, 2000.

Brand-Fisher, Sonia. "Proto-cinephilia: Retheorizing Working Class Women's Moviegoing Pre-1920." *Early Popular Visual Culture* 19, no. 4 (2021): 301–323.

Bratton, Jacky, Jim Cook, and Christine Gledhill, eds. *Melodrama: Stage, Picture, Screen.* London: British Film Institute, 1994.

Brennan, Nathaniel. "The Great White Way and the Way of All Flesh: Metropolitan Film Culture and the Business of Film Exhibition in Times Square, 1929–1941." *Film History: An International Journal* 27, no. 2 (2015): 1–32.

Brophy, Alfred L. *Reconstructing the Dreamland: The Tulsa Race Riot of 1921, Race, Reparations, and Reconciliation.* Oxford: Oxford University Press, 2002.

Caddoo, Cara. "*The Birth of a Nation*, Police Brutality, and Black Protest." *Journal of the Gilded Age and Progressive Era* 14, no. 4 (2015): 608–611.

———. *Envisioning Freedom: Cinema and the Building of Modern Black Life.* Cambridge, MA: Harvard University Press, 2014.

Carbine, Mary. "'The Finest Outside the Loop': Motion Picture Exhibition in Chicago's Black Metropolis, 1905–1928." *Camera Obscura* 23, no. 2 (1990): 9–41.

Carby, Hazel V. "Policing the Black Woman's Body in an Urban Context." *Critical Inquiry* 18 (1992): 738–755.

Carroll, Fred. *Race News: Black Journalists and the Fight for Racial Justice in the Twentieth Century.* Urbana, IL: University of Illinois Press, 2017.

Chapman, Erin. *Prove It on Me: New Negroes, Sex, and Popular Culture.* Oxford: Oxford University Press, 2012.

Chatelain, Marcia. *South Side Girls: Growing Up in the Great Migration.* Durham, NC: Duke University Press, 2015.

Clement, Elizabeth Alice. *Love for Sale: Courting, Treating, and Prostitution in New York City, 1900–1945.* Chapel Hill: University of North Carolina Press, 2006.

Cobb, Jasmine Nichole. *Picture Freedom: Remaking Black Visuality in the Early Nineteenth Century*. New York: New York University Press, 2015.

Cohen, Lizabeth. *A Consumer's Republic: The Politics of Mass Consumption in Postwar America*. New York: Vintage Books, 2003.

Couvares, Francis G., ed. *Movie Censorship and American Culture*. Washington, DC: Smithsonian Institution Press, 1996.

Crafton, Donald. *The Talkies: American Cinema's Transition to Sound, 1926–1931*. Berkeley: University of California Press, 1997.

Cripps, Thomas. "The Reaction of the Negro to the Motion Picture *Birth of a Nation*." *Historian* 25, no. 3 (1963): 344–362.

Cruse, Harold. *The Crisis of the Negro Intellectual: A Historical Analysis of the Failure of Black Leadership*. New York: William Morrow, 1967.

Curtis, Susan A. *Colored Memories: A Biographer's Quest for the Elusive Lester A. Walton*. Columbia: University of Missouri Press, 2008.

Dabashi, Pardis. "'There Is No Gallery': Race and the Politics of Space at the Capital Theatre, New York." *Early Popular Visual Culture* 21, no. 2 (2023): 208–222.

Diawara, Manthia, ed. *Black American Cinema*. New York: Routledge, 1993.

Dittmer, John, and Danielle L. McGuire. *Freedom Rights: New Perspectives on the Civil Rights Movement*. Lexington: University Press of Kentucky, 2011.

Everett, Anna. *Returning the Gaze: A Genealogy of Black Film Criticism, 1909–1949*. Durham, NC: Duke University Press, 2001.

Field, Allyson Nadia. *Uplift Cinema: The Emergence of African American Film and the Possibility of Black Modernity*. Durham, NC: Duke University Press, 2015.

Flowe, Douglas. *Uncontrollable Blackness: African American Men and Criminality in Jim Crow New York*. Chapel Hill: University of North Carolina Press, 2020.

Friedman, Andrea. *Prurient Interests: Gender, Democracy, and Obscenity in New York City, 1909–1945*. New York: Columbia University Press, 2000.

Fronc, Jennifer. "The Horns of the Dilemma: Race Mixing and the Enforcement of Jim Crow in New York City." *Journal of Urban History* 33, no. 1 (2006): 3–25.

———. "Local Public Opinion: The National Board of Review of Motion Pictures and the Fight against Film Censorship in Virginia, 1916–1922." *Journal of American Studies* 47, no. 3 (2013): 719–742.

———. *Monitoring the Movies: The Fight over Film Censorship in Early Twentieth-Century Urban America*. Austin: University of Texas Press, 2017.

Frymus, Agata. "Black Moviegoing in Harlem: The Case of the Alhambra Theatre, 1905–1931." *Journal of Cinema and Media Studies* 62, no. 1 (2023): 80–101.

———. "White Screens, Black Fandom: Silent Film and African American Spectatorship in Harlem." *Early Popular Visual Culture* 21, no. 2 (2023): 248–265.

Fuller, Kathryn. *At the Picture Show: Small-Town Audiences and the Creation of Fan Culture*. Washington, DC: Smithsonian Institution Press, 1996.

Fuller-Seeley, Kathryn, ed. *Hollywood in the Neighborhood: Historical Case Studies of Local Moviegoing*. Berkeley: University of California Press, 2008.

Gaines, Jane. *Fire and Desire: Mixed-Race Movies in the Silent Cinema*. Chicago: University of Chicago Press, 2000.

Gaines, Kevin. *Uplifting the Race: Black Leadership, Politics, and Culture in the Twentieth Century*. Chapel Hill: University of North Carolina Press, 1996.

Gallon, Kim. *Pleasure in the News: African American Readership and Sexuality in the Black Press*. Urbana: University of Illinois Press, 2020.

Gates, Henry Louis, Jr. "The Trope of a New Negro and the Reconstruction of the Image of the Black." *Representations*, no. 24 (1988): 129–155.

Gear, Nolan. "*Spectatrices*: Moviegoing and Women's Writing, 1925–1945." Ph.D. diss., Columbia University, 2021.

Gilmore, Ruth Wilson. "Fatal Couplings of Power and Difference: Notes on Racism and Geography." *Professional Geographer* 54, no. 1 (2002): 15–24.

Glasrud, Bruce A., and Cary D. Wintz, eds. *The Harlem Renaissance in the American West: The New Negro's Western Experience*. New York: Routledge, 2012.

Gomery, Douglas. *Shared Pleasures: A History of Movie Presentation in the United States*. Madison: University of Wisconsin Press, 1992.

Goodier, Susan. *No Votes for Women: The New York State Anti-suffrage Movement*. Urbana: University of Illinois Press, 2013.

Greenburg, Cheryl. *"Or Does It Explode?": Black Harlem in the Great Depression*. Oxford: Oxford University Press, 1997.

Grieveson, Lee. *Policing Cinema: Movies and Censorship in Early-Twentieth-Century America*. Berkeley: University of California Press, 2004.

Gross, Kali N. *Colored Amazons: Crime, Violence, and Black Women in the City of Brotherly Love, 1880–1910*. Durham, NC: Duke University Press, 2006.

Haenni, Sabine. *The Immigrant Scene: Ethnic Amusements in New York, 1880–1920*. Minneapolis: University of Minnesota Press, 2008.

Harris, LaShawn. *Sex Workers, Psychics, and Numbers Runners: Black Women in New York City's Underground Economy*. Urbana: University of Illinois Press, 2016.

Hartman, Saidiya. *Wayward Lives, Beautiful Experiments: Intimate Histories of Social Upheaval*. New York: W. W. Norton, 2019.

Hicks, Cheryl D. *Talk with You Like a Woman: African American Women, Justice, and Reform in New York, 1890–1935*. Chapel Hill: University of North Carolina Press, 2010.

Higginbotham, Evelyn Brooks. *Righteous Discontent: The Women's Movement in the Black Baptist Church, 1880–1920*. Cambridge, MA: Harvard University Press, 1993.

Hine, Darlene Clark. "Rape and the Inner Lives of Black Women in the Middle West." *Signs* 14 (1989): 912–920.

Huggins, Nathan Irvin. *Harlem Renaissance*. Oxford: Oxford University Press, 1971.

Hull, Gloria T. *Color, Sex, and Poetry: Three Women Writers of the Harlem Renaissance*. Bloomington: Indiana University Press, 1987.

Hunter, Tera W. *To 'Joy My Freedom: Southern Black Women's Lives and Labors after the Civil War*. Cambridge, MA: Harvard University Press, 1997.

Jacobson, Julius, ed. *The Negro and the American Labor Movement*. Garden City, NY: Doubleday, 1968.

Kelley, Robin D. G. *Race Rebels: Culture, Politics, and the Black Working Class*. New York: Free Press, 1994.

———. *Thelonious Monk: The Life and Times of an American Original*. New York: Free Press, 2009.

Kelley, Robin D. G., and Earl Lewis, eds. *To Make Our World Anew: The History of African Americans from 1880*. Oxford: Oxford University Press, 2000.

King, Shannon. *Whose Harlem Is This, Anyway? Community Politics and Grassroots Activism during the New Negro Era*. New York: New York University Press, 2015.

Klanderud, Jessica. *Struggle for the Street: Social Networks and the Struggle for Civil Rights.* Chapel Hill: University of North Carolina Press, 2023.

Koszarski, Richard. *Evening's Entertainment: The Age of the Silent Picture, 1915–1928.* Berkeley: University of California Press, 1990.

———. *Hollywood on the Hudson: Film and Television in New York from Griffith to Sarnoff.* New Brunswick, NJ: Rutgers University Press, 2008.

Kramer, Steve. "Uplifting Our 'Downtrodden Sisterhood': Victoria Earle Matthews and New York City's White Rose Mission, 1897–1907." *Journal of African American History* 91, no. 3 (2006): 243–266.

Krasner, David. *A Beautiful Pageant: African American Theatre, Drama, and Performance in the Harlem Renaissance.* New York: Palgrave Macmillan, 2002.

Leab, Daniel J. *From Sambo to Superspade: The Black Experience in Motion Pictures.* Boston: Houghton Mifflin, 1975.

Lewis, David Levering. *W.E.B. Du Bois: Biography of a Race, 1868–1919.* New York: Henry Holt, 1993.

———. *When Harlem Was in Vogue.* Oxford: Oxford University Press, 1981.

Lichtenstein, Nelson. *State of the Union: A Century of American Labor.* Princeton, NJ: Princeton University Press, 2002.

Lobel, Michael. *John Sloan: Drawing on Illustration.* New Haven, CT: Yale University Press, 2014.

Lupack, Barbara Tepa, ed. *Early Race Filmmaking in America.* New York: Routledge, 2016.

Maltby, Richard, and Melvyn Stokes, eds. *American Movie Audiences: From the Turn of the Century to the Early Sound Era.* London: Bloomsbury, 1999.

Massood, Paula. *Black City Cinema: African American Urban Experiences in Film.* Philadelphia: Temple University Press, 2003.

———. *Making a Promised Land: Harlem in 20th-Century Photography and Film.* New Brunswick, NJ: Rutgers University Press, 2013.

May, Lary. *Screening Out the Past: The Birth of Mass Culture and the Motion Picture Industry.* Chicago: University of Chicago Press, 1983.

McGilligan, Patrick. *Oscar Micheaux: The Great and Only; The Life of America's First Black Director.* New York: Harper Perennial, 2008.

McGuire, Danielle L. *At the Dark End of the Street: Black Women, Rape, and Resistance— a New History of the Civil Rights Movement from Rosa Parks to the Rise of Black Power.* New York: Alfred A. Knopf, 2010.

McKay, Claude. *Home to Harlem.* New York: Harper and Brothers, 1928.

McLaren, Joseph, ed. *The Collected Works of Langston Hughes.* Vol. 13, *Autobiography: The Big Sea.* Columbia: University of Missouri Press, 2002.

McQuirter, Marya Annette. "Claiming the City: African Americans, Urbanization, and Leisure in Washington, D.C., 1902–1957." Ph.D. diss., University of Michigan, 2000.

Monroe, John Gilbert. "A Record of Black Theatre in New York City, 1920–1929." Ph.D. diss., University of Texas at Austin, 1980.

Morrison, Toni, ed. *James Baldwin: Collected Essays.* Washington, DC: Library of Congress, 1998.

Musser, Charles. *The Emergence of Cinema: The American Screen to 1907.* Berkeley: University of California Press, 1990.

———. "To Redream the Dreams of White Playwrights." *Yale Journal of Criticism* 12, no. 2 (1999): 321–356.

Nasaw, David. *Going Out: The Rise and Fall of Public Amusements.* Cambridge, MA: Harvard University Press, 1993.

Nelson, Bruce. *Divided We Stand: American Workers and the Struggle for Black Equality.* Princeton, NJ: Princeton University Press, 2002.

Newman, Richard. "The Lincoln Theatre." *American Visions* 6, no. 1 (1991): 29–32.

Newsom, Chad. "Josephine Stiles and Her House of Feature Films: Innovations of a Black Theater Proprietor." *Film History: An International Journal* 35, no. 1 (2023): 21–60.

Nieves, Angel David, and Leslie M. Alexander, eds. *"We Shall Independent Be": African American Placemaking and the Struggle to Claim Space in the United States.* Boulder: University of Colorado, 2008.

Ogbar, Jeffrey O. G., ed. *The Harlem Renaissance Revisited: Politics, Arts, and Letters.* Baltimore: Johns Hopkins University Press, 2010.

Osofsky, Gilbert. *Harlem: The Making of a Ghetto; Negro New York, 1890–1930.* 1966. Reprint, Chicago: Elephant Paperbacks, 1996.

Parsons, Elaine Frantz. "Revisiting *The Birth of a Nation* at 100 Years." *Journal of the Gilded Age and Progressive Era* 14, no. 4 (2015): 596–598.

Pearson, Roberta E., and William Uricchio. "Coming to Terms with New York City's Moving Picture Operators, 1906–1913." *Moving Image: The Journal of the Association of Moving Image Archivists* 2 (2002): 74–93.

Peiss, Kathy. *Cheap Amusements: Working Women and Leisure in Turn-of-the-Century New York.* Philadelphia: Temple University Press, 1986.

Peiss, Kathy, and Christina Simmons, eds. *Passion and Power: Sexuality in History.* Philadelphia: Temple University Press, 1989.

Perry, Jeffrey B., ed. *A Hubert Harrison Reader.* Middletown, CT: Wesleyan University Press, 2001.

Peterson, Bernard L. *The African American Theatre Directory, 1816–1960: A Comprehensive Guide to Early Black Theatre Organizations, Companies, Theatres, and Performing Groups.* Westport, CT: Greenwood, 1997.

Pizzitola, Louis. *Hearst over Hollywood: Power, Passion, and Propaganda in the Movies.* New York: Columbia University Press, 2002.

Pough, Gwendolyn D. *Check It While I Wreck It: Black Womanhood, Hip-Hop Culture, and the Public Sphere.* Lebanon, NH: Northeastern University Press, 2004.

Pride, Armistead S., and Clint C. Wilson II. *A History of the Black Press.* Washington, DC: Howard University Press, 1997.

Purnell, Brian, and Jeanne Theoharis, eds. *The Strange Careers of the Jim Crow North: Segregation and Struggles outside of the South.* With Komozi Woodard. New York: New York University Press, 2019.

Rabinovitz, Lauren. *For the Love of Pleasure: Women, Movies, and Culture in Turn-of-the-Century Chicago.* New Brunswick, NJ: Rutgers University Press, 1998.

Regester, Charlene. "From the Buzzard's Roost: Black Movie-Going in Durham and Other North Carolina Cities during the Early Period of American Cinema." *Film History* 17, no. 1 (2005): 113–124.

———. "Headline to Headlights: Oscar Micheaux's Exploitation of the Rhinelander Case." *Western Journal of Black Studies* 22, no. 3 (1998): 195–204.

———. "Oscar Micheaux on the Cutting Edge: Films Rejected by the New York State Motion Picture Commission." *Studies in Popular Culture* 17, no. 2 (1995): 61–72.

———. "Oscar Micheaux the Entrepreneur: Financing the House behind the Cedars." *Journal of Film and Video* 49, no. 1–2 (1997): 17–27.

Rhodes, Gary. *The Perils of Moviegoing in America, 1896–1950*. London: Bloomsbury, 2011.

Roane, J. T. *Dark Agoras: Insurgent Black Social Life and the Politics of Place*. New York: New York University Press, 2023.

Rosenblum, Nancy. "In Defense of Moving Pictures: The People's Institute, the National Board of Censorship and the Problem of Leisure in Urban America." *American Studies* 33, no. 2 (1992): 41–60.

Sacks, Marcy. *Before Harlem: The Black Experience in New York City before World War I*. Philadelphia: University of Pennsylvania Press, 2006.

Sammons, Jeffrey T., and John H. Morrow Jr. *Harlem's Rattlers and the Great War: The Undaunted 369th Regiment and the African American Quest for Equality*. Lawrence: University Press of Kansas, 2014.

Sampson, Henry T. *Blacks in Black and White: A Source Book on Black Films*. Metuchen, NJ: Scarecrow, 1995.

———. *Blacks in Blackface: A Sourcebook on Early Black Musical Shows*. Metuchen, NJ: Scarecrow, 1980.

Scott, Ellen C. *Cinema Civil Rights: Regulation, Repression, and Race in the Classical Hollywood Era*. New Brunswick, NJ: Rutgers University Press, 2015.

Sherrard-Johnson, Cherene, ed. *A Companion to the Harlem Renaissance*. West Sussex: Wiley Blackwell, 2015.

Simmons, LaKisha Michelle. *Crescent City Girls: The Lives of Young Black Women in Segregated New Orleans*. Chapel Hill: University of North Carolina Press, 2015.

Singer, Ben. "Manhattan Nickelodeons: New Data on Audiences and Exhibitors." *Cinema Journal* 34, no. 3 (1995): 5–35.

Singh, Amritjit, and Daniel M. Scott III, eds. *The Collected Writings of Wallace Thurman: A Harlem Renaissance Reader*. New Brunswick, NJ: Rutgers University Press, 2003.

Smith, J. Douglas. "Patrolling the Boundaries of Race: Motion Picture Censorship and Jim Crow in Virginia, 1922–1932." *Historical Journal of Film, Radio, and Television* 21, no. 3 (2001): 273–289.

Sotiropoulos, Karen. *Staging Race: Black Performers in Turn of the Century America*. Cambridge, MA: Harvard University Press, 2006.

Stamp, Shelley. *Movie-Struck Girls: Women and Motion Picture Culture after the Nickelodeon*. Princeton, NJ: Princeton University Press, 2000.

Stewart, Jacqueline Najuma. *Migrating to the Movies: Cinema and Black Urban Modernity*. Berkeley: University of California Press, 2005.

———. "Negroes Laughing at Themselves? Black Spectatorship and the Performance of Urban Modernity." *Critical Inquiry* 29 (Summer 2003): 650–677.

Thompson, Sister Mary Francesca. "The Lafayette Players, 1915–1932." Ph.D. diss., University of Michigan, 1972.

Thornbrough, Emma Lou. "American Negro Newspapers, 1880–1914." *Business History Review* 40, no. 4 (1966): 467–490.

Tinkcom, Matthew, and Amy Villarejo, eds. *Keyframes: Popular Cinema and Cultural Studies*. London: Routledge, 2001.

Tye, Larry. *Rising from the Rails: Pullman Porters and the Making of the Black Middle Class*. New York: Henry Holt, 2004.

Wall, Cheryl A. *Women of the Harlem Renaissance*. Bloomington: Indiana University Press, 1995.

Wallace, Mike. *Greater Gotham: A History of New York City from 1898 to 1919*. Oxford: Oxford University Press, 2017.

Waller, Gregory A. "Another Audience: Black Moviegoing, 1907–16." *Cinema Journal* 31, no. 2 (1992): 3–25.

———. *Main Street Amusements: Movies and Commercial Entertainment in a Southern City, 1896–1930*. Washington, DC: Smithsonian Press, 1995.

Ware, Amy M. "Will Rogers's Radio: Race and Technology in the Cherokee Nation." *American Indian Quarterly* 33, no. 1 (2009): 62–97.

Watkins-Owens, Irma. *Blood Relations: Caribbean Immigrants and the Harlem Community, 1900–1930*. Bloomington: Indiana University Press, 1996.

Weisenfeld, Judith. *Hollywood Be Thy Name: African American Religion in Film*. Berkeley: University of California Press, 2007.

White, Deborah Gray. *Ar'n't I a Woman? Female Slaves in the Plantation South*. New York: W. W. Norton, 1985.

White, Shane, Stephen Garton, Stephen Robertson, and Graham White. *Playing the Numbers: Gambling in Harlem between the Wars*. Cambridge, MA: Harvard University Press, 2010.

Wintz, Cary D. *Black Culture and the Harlem Renaissance*. Houston: Rice University Press, 1988.

Wolcott, Victoria W. *Remaking Respectability: African American Women in Interwar Detroit*. Chapel Hill: University of North Carolina Press, 2001.

Wood, Amy Louise. *Lynching and Spectacle: Witnessing Racial Violence in America, 1890–1940*. Chapel Hill: University of North Carolina Press, 2009.

Wurtzler, Steve. *Electric Sounds: Technological Change and the Rise of Corporate Mass Media*. New York: Columbia University Press, 2007.

Young, Artee Felicita. "Lester Walton: Black Theatre Critics." Ph.D. diss., University of Michigan, 1980.

Zurier, Rebecca. *Picturing the City: Urban Vision and the Ashcan School*. Berkeley: University of California Press, 2006.

Index

Alyssa Lopez is Assistant Professor of History at Providence College.

Also in the series *Urban Life, Landscape, and Policy*: